The Mitchell Beazley pocket guide to

Garden Plants

Hugh Johnson
and Paul Miles

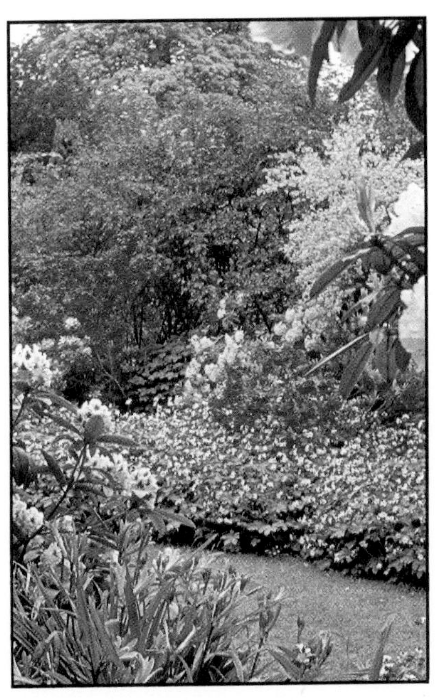

Mitchell Beazley

Nomenclature

The common names of garden plants vary widely and are often misleading, but the scientific (Latin) name is determined by strict international rules. Every plant has a double name, the first is the genus name, the second the species (specific) name. Thus the Peacock or Tiger flower always has the Latin name *Tigridia pavonia*. Each genus contains one or more species and several related genera are grouped into a family. A species may be divided into subspecies showing small variations and have a third name, as in *Dryas octopetala minor*, a miniature form of Mountain avens. Where plants are hybrids derived from the cross breeding of two different species, names are preceded by a multiplication sign, as in the Michaelmas daisy *Aster* × *frikartii*, a hybrid of *Aster amellus* and *Aster thomsonii*. Named cultivars (cultivated varieties) of genera or species are given an additional name within quotation marks: the Lily of the valley *Convallaria majalis* 'Fortin's Giant' is a large-flowered form. Because plant names may be changed, alternatives likely to appear in books and catalogues are denoted in brackets. The bluebell *Hyacinthoides (= Endymion)* is an example.

Contents

Editor Ruth Binney **Executive Editor** Susannah Read
Designer Derek St Romaine **Picture Research** Brigitte Arora
Executive Art Editor Douglas Wilson **Production** Julian Deeming

Edited and designed by
Mitchell Beazley Publishers
87–89 Shaftesbury Avenue London W1V 7AD

Reprinted 1982, 1984

ISBN 0 85533 289 1
Typeset by Tradespools Ltd, Frome
Colour reproduction by Gilchrist Brothers Ltd, Leeds
Printed in Hong Kong by
Mandarin Offset International (H.K.) Ltd.

Picture credits Apart from the photographs detailed below, all the material, including the cover picture, was supplied by The Harry Smith Horticultural Photographic Collection, to whom we are indebted for their help. A–Z Collection: 111tc, 12lb, 135b, 154tc, 157t; Bernard Alfieri: 110t; Heather Angel: 71t/c, 72c, 74t, 154t, 155c; Pat Brindley: 7b, 8t/b, 9c/b, 10c, 11b, 12c, 14c/b, 15c/b, 16tc/bc/b, 17b, 25bc, 35bc, 53c, 55c, 59t, 61c, 78c, 81b, 106t, 110tc/bc, 122b, 125c, 158t, 159c; Valerie Finnis: 46t/b, 49tc/b, 57b, 60b, 62b, 100t, 103b, 127c, 137t; Fryers Nurseries Ltd: 111b; Brian Furner: 74b, 158b; The Iris Hardwick Library: 10t, 113t, 142c, 146tc, 150tc, 159t; Paul Miles: 12t, 30b, 35tc, 45tc, 66b, 75t/tc, 82t, 83c, 85b, 86c, 107tc, 112t, 113bc, 127b, 134b, 139c, 152b; The Royal National Rose Society: 106b, 108bc, 111t; G.S. Thomas: 111c; Michael Warren: 14t; ***Artwork*** by Colin Salmon.
Key t, top; tc, top centre; c, centre; bc, bottom centre; b, bottom

Introduction

No gardener needs telling that trying to fit the glorious richness and variety of garden plants into a truly pocketable book is a foolhardy undertaking. But how marvellous if it comes off. What a boon to be able to unpocket a mere diary-size encyclopedia and look up, there and then, whether the tempting container at the nursery or the towering specimen in a famous show place is a possibility for your own garden.

This book tries, by a combination of clear and graphic illustrations and a double-distilled text, to offer all the essential information about nearly 2,000 garden plants in a portable form. Distillation has its own virtues. The authors can vouch for the fact that, like the prospect of being hanged, it concentrates the mind wonderfully. All the dross, all the flannel, is blue-pencilled away. What is left, like a fine distilled spirit, is pure, strong and (we hope) particularly tasty.

The most popular garden plants have been bred, selected and bred again until their varieties in cultivation (cultivars) are, as sand on the sea shore, without number. To list endless slightly different varieties of the same plant, however beautiful, would be tedious and, more important, would force us to leave out a great number of species that have not had the benefit of so many breeders' attentions. Where the choice has been between another variety and a different species we have come down, therefore, on the side of the species. This means that there are a good number of uncommon plants in this book. We feel very strongly that this is important. As it is, far too many gardeners grow precisely the same, unnecessarily limited, range of plants. If no one seeks out and grows the unusual it will become rare, and from rarity the next step is extinction. Every gardener can help in the conservation of the magnificent variety of plant life by looking around for something different to grow. This is an excellent place to start.

How to use this book

We have divided the world of garden plants into the conventional categories based on their management in the garden. There are many genera that have members with permanent hard wood (shrubs), members that die down to below ground every winter but come up again in spring (herbaceous perennials) and yet others with a one year life span (annuals). Where such names crop up in different sections of the book, symbols, each containing a letter (A for annuals, P for herbaceous perennials etc) refer you at a glance to the appropriate section. In addition, page numbers in the index are suffixed with the same letter.

The information given for each entry in the book is as comprehensive as space allows. As well as a thumbnail sketch it includes the hardiness of the plant, its average height and spread, its most usual months of flowering, its native land and, in most cases, the most convenient method of propagation. Symbols tell you about its preference for sun, soil and water, its ease of cultivation, if it has won the Award of Garden Merit, the supreme accolade of the Royal Horticultural Society, and supply cross references to other sections of the book. Although any plant that has passed our rigorous scrutiny to win a place here automatically carries our recommendation (provisos and warnings about rampant growth are noted where appropriate) the accolade of an asterisk has been added to plants that we particularly like and would urge you to grow. The symbols, plus the abbreviations essential for compression, are explained over the page, followed by a map of hardiness zones, notes on propagation and a glossary of the botanical terms we have used.

Symbols

Plant needs

- Shade
- 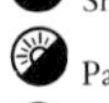 Partial shade
- Sun
- Acid soil
- Alkaline soil
- Well-drained soil
- Heavy soil
- Much water

Plant type

-  Evergreen
- Coniferous
- Aquatic
- Grows in bogs or at water's edge

General

- Easy to grow
- Difficult to grow
- RHS Award of Garden Merit

Cross references

-  A Annuals and biennials
- P Herbaceous perennials
- R Alpines and rock garden plants
- W Bog, waterside and pond plants
- H Herbs
- B Bulbs, corms and tubers
- C Climbers
- S Shrubs

*Authors' personal recommendation

Abbreviations

AGM	Award of Garden Merit (RHS)
alt	alternate
Apr	April
AM	Award of Merit (RHS)
ann	annual
Arct	tolerates "Arctic" conditions
aut	autumn
bi	biennial
bicol	bicolour
br	branch
c.	about
col	colour
con-spic	conspicuous
cv	cultivar
decid	deciduous
diam	diameter
div	division
esp	especially
F	tolerates average frost
fl(d)	flower(ed)
Fl	flowering months
fol	foliage
fr	fruit
frag	fragrant
ft	feet
gdn	garden
gp	group
hr(y)	hair(y)
hrlss	hairless
Ht	height
hyb	hybrid
in	inch(es)
inc	include
incon-spic	inconspicuous
indiv	individual
LF	susceptible to late frost
lf(y)	leaf(y)
lflt	leaflet
lvd	leaved
lvs	leaves
mod	moderately
NF	tolerates no frost
opp	opposite
per	perennial
PF	tolerates prolonged frost
pop	popular
pr(d)	pair(ed)
prop	propagate
ptl	petal
rec	recommended
resp	respectively
RHS	Royal Horticultural Society
rt	root
sev	several
SF	tolerates short frost
sim	similar
smr	summer
sol	solitary
Spd	spread
sp(p)	species (plural)
spl	sepal
spr	spring
stk(d)	stalk(ed)
succ	succulent
unstkd	unstalked
uprt	upright
v	very
var	variety
varieg	variegated
veg	vegetative
vig	vigorous
wtr	winter
Z	zone of hardiness
♂	male
♀	female
1–12	months of the year Jan–Dec

Plant origins

Amer	America
Aust	Australia
C	Central
Cal	California
E	East(ern)
Eur	Europe
GB	Great Britain
Hem	Hemisphere
Him	Himalayas
Is	Islands
Mar	Maritime
Med	Mediterranean
Mts	Mountains
N	North(ern)
NE	Northeast(ern)
NW	Northwest(ern)
NZ	New Zealand
S	South(ern)
SE	Southeast(ern)
SW	Southwest(ern)
Temp	Temperate
Trop	Tropical
USA	United States
USSR	Russia
W	West(ern)

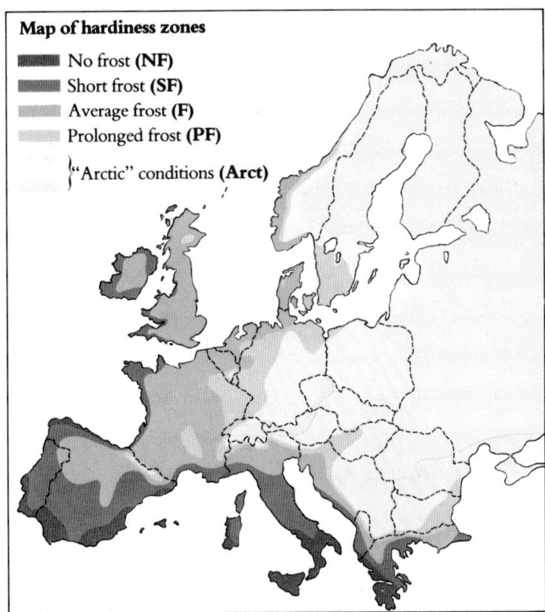

Except for annuals each plant description ends with a guide to the amount of frost it will tolerate, based on the zones (**Z**) on this map:
No frost (NF) zone: no frost at any time
Short frost (SF) zone: overnight frost for no more than 1–2 nights, temperature falling to about −5°C
Frost (F) zone: frost occurring regularly on 3–5 successive nights or over a 24-hour period, temperature falling to about −8°C
Prolonged frost (PF) zone: upwards of a week of frost, sub-zero temperatures persisting 24 hours, possibly several days. Temperature down to −10°C
"Arctic" (Arct) zone: deeper frost may persist for weeks (yellow area) or months (blue area). Minimum temperature to −15°C (yellow area) or down to −50°C (blue area)
Plants susceptible to damage by late frost in early spring growth have the additional letters **LF**
Even on a much larger scale map it would be impossible to indicate with perfect accuracy where any one plant will grow. The adventurous gardener will find that plants are remarkably adaptable, and within each garden there are sheltered corners. If all else fails you can always try a highly desirable plant in a pot, taking it indoors in winter.

Plant propagation

As a rule of thumb, species are propagated from seed, named cultivars by vegetative means. The main exceptions are shrubs, many of which are best increased vegetatively, and bulbs, corms etc which have built-in organs of vegetative reproduction. Common vegetative methods are:
Cuttings stems, roots or leaves removed from the parent plant and treated so as to produce their own roots. Take softwood cuttings from perennials and shrubs in the growing season, hardwood shrub cuttings in autumn.
Division the splitting of a plant into 2 or more parts. Best done in spring. Also describes the separation of groups of bulbs, corms etc.
Layers growing plant stems pegged on to the ground or covered in earth away from, but still attached to, the parent plant. The stems are cut only when roots have formed. Used for plants slow to root as cuttings.
Pipings young stems of pinks or carnations pulled from the main stem at a joint and induced to form roots in sandy compost. Take pipings in summer.
Scales thin flaps, often modified leaves, separated from the parent plant at their base and induced to form roots.

Glossary

Aerial describes above-ground roots common on stems of climbers
Alternate (alt) leaves growing singly at intervals on alternate sides of a stem
Anther pollen-producing part of a flower (often knob-like) borne on a stalk called a filament. The top part of a stamen (see below)
Aroid member of the Arum family having a leafy cloak, the spathe, surrounding a club-like, fleshy flower head, the spadix
Axil angle between a stem and a leaf or bract
Axillary growing in an axil
Basal nearest the ground; basal leaves are often a different shape from those higher up the stem
Bicolour a flower of two distinct, often contrasting, colours
Biennial plant living 2 years, flowering in second year
Bract leaf or petal-like structure at the base of a flower
Bulb swollen underground bud used for propagation and storage
Bulblet, bulbil small bulb; may be in leaf axil or among flowers
Clone group of plants formed from one parent without sex and thus having the same genetic make up, e.g., plant propagated by cuttings
Compound in several parts, as a leaf made up of leaflets
Corm swollen underground stem, an organ of propagation and storage
Cross mating of 2 plants of different species or genera
Cultivar (cv) short for "cultivated variety". A plant chosen for garden qualities that are only faithfully reproduced by vegetative propagation. Does not come true from seed
Double, fully double, semi-double flowers with more than the normal number of petals. A semi-double has fewer petals than a double or fully double flower but more than a single
Floret small individual flower making up the head of a daisy or similar flower; may be disc-like or strap-shaped
Glaucous blue-grey in colour, with a powdery or waxy covering (bloom)
Half-hardy between tender and hardy
Hardy plant capable of completing its life span without any protection in an area of marked seasons
Hybrid (hyb) plant resulting from a cross of 2 different species, true-breeding cultivars or genera. First generation hybrids are called F_1
Leaflet (lflt) several leaflets make a compound leaf
Offset young plant arising at the base of the parent e.g. Houseleek
Opposite (opp) describes leaves placed exactly opposite each other in pairs
Panicle branched flower cluster with groups of stalked flowers e.g. Lilac
Pinnate describes a leaf divided into leaflets placed opposite each other
Raceme long unbranched head of short-stalked flowers, e.g. Foxglove
Reflexed bent back
Reversion change of a plant back to its original form, e.g. a shoot of a variegated plant returning to all-green leaves
Rhizome swollen underground stem; organ of propagation and storage
Runner long prostrate shoot rooting to form a new plant at its tip or elsewhere along its length; an organ of vegetative propagation
Sepals (spls) outer ring of flower parts outside the petals. Often green but may be showy and petal-like as in *Clematis*
Serrated with a toothed edge like a saw
Single flower with the normal number of petals—not double
Spathe, spadix see aroid
Spike long unbranched head of stalkless flowers, e.g. Hollyhock
Spur in flowers, a hollow projection from the back of a petal or sepal e.g. Columbine
Stamen male flower part made up of a pollen-producing anther on a stalk or filament. Often showy and/or protruding, e.g. Bottle brush
Stigma female flower part on to which pollen is deposited. May be knob-like or feathery, usually sticky
Stolon shoot above or below ground producing a new plant at its tip
Sucker shoot growing from roots apart from the main stem or stems; may be taken off and used for vegetative propagation
Tender describes a plant likely to be damaged by frost; needs protection
Terminal at the end or top of a plant or plant part
Tuber swollen underground stem or root used for propagation and storage
Type plant typical of its species; not a hybrid or cultivar
Variety (var) for garden purposes, the equivalent of a cultivar
Variegated (varieg) with leaves marked in white, yellow or other colours
Vegetative (veg) propagation reproduction without sex (see p5). Organs of vegetative propagation include bulbs, corms, rhizomes and stolons

Annuals and biennials

Annuals are conventionally divided into "hardy" sorts that can be sown early in the open garden and will survive spring cold and "half-hardy" ones which must be sown indoors and transplanted or sown outdoors only after the last frosts. Biennials are plants that are sown in summer to survive the winter with or without protection and flower the next year.

Ageratum

Ageratum

A. conyzoides: C Amer. One parent of pop *A.* hybs. Lvs softly hry; fls fluffy heads 2 in wide, pale to rich blue. Try 'Blue Mink' lavender; 'Blue Bunch' mid blue; 'Fairy Pink' salmon. *Ht, Spd:* 9 in; *Fl:* 7–10

Althaea

Hollyhock

A. rosea: Orient. Per best grown as bi (rust disease spoils older plants). Lvs rounded, matt, soft green. Fls many cols, shuttlecock-shaped, 4 in wide on 8 ft stems. Double-flowered cvs inc 'Marjorette' 2 ft; 'Summer Carnival' 6 ft in white, salmon, pink or crimson. *Spd:* 2 ft; *Fl:* 6–7; *Z:* PF

A. rosea

Amaranthus

Amaranthus

A. caudatus Love-lies-bleeding: Tropics. Fls 18 in crimson tassels. Lvs large, stems succ. *A.c. viridis* pale green fls. *Ht:* 3 ft; *Spd:* 18 in; *Fl:* 7–10

A. tricolor Joseph's coat: Tropics. Lvs pink and crimson, marked green, bronze and yellow. 'Molten Fire' coppery crimson. *Ht:* 3 ft; *Spd:* 18 in; *Fl:* 7–9

A. caudatus

Anagallis

Pimpernel

A. arvensis 'Caerulea': Eur (sp). Slight, spreading. Fls rich blue, $\frac{1}{2}$ in wide, 5 ptls; lvs in whorls or pairs. *Ht:* 2 in; *Spd:* 6 in; *Fl:* 7–10

Antirrhinum

Snapdragon

A. majus*: Eur. Pers treated as anns. Lvs dark green, narrow. A huge choice from old singles to excellent rust-resistant hybs. F_1 hyb Rocket series single in tall spikes of pink, white, bronze, yellow, red, purple; also Butterfly, Coronette and double sorts. *Ht:* 3 ft; *Spd:* 18 in; *Fl:* 7–10; *Z:* SF

A. majus 'Scarlet and Gold'

Arctotis

African daisy

A. grandis*: S Africa. Per often treated as ann. Fls white, marguerite-like. Lvs grey-green, toothed. Hybs have bigger fls in warm crimsons, bronzes and yellows. Other large-fld hybs in wider col range, contrasting col bands at ptl bases. *Ht:* to 3 ft; *Spd:* 1 ft; *Fl:* 7–9

Atriplex

Orache

A. hortensis rubra Red mountain spinach, Purple orache: Eur. Fls dull but lvs and stems handsome deep crimson, edible. Highly decorative, useful for cutting. Self seeds but often ruined by birds. *Ht:* 4 ft; *Spd:* 3 ft

Brassica

Brassica

B. oleracea acephala Ornamental kale or cabbage: gdn origin. Pale green or white frilly lvs edged and/or suffused purple, red or pink. V decorative but more col than flavour. *Ht:* 15 in; *Spd:* 1 ft; *Z:* SF

Calceolaria

Calceolaria

C. hybrid

C. hybs: C, S Amer. Fls to 2½ in, massed heads of typical pouting pouches from orange, yellow, red to cream, pink, apricot, mauve. Lvs roughly notched and veined. *C. rugosa* 'Sunshine' 10 in, fls clear yellow. *Ht, Spd:* to 2 ft; *Fl:* 6–10

Calendula

Marigold

C. officinalis hybrid

C. officinalis* Common or pot marigold: S Eur. One of the oldest gdn fls. Lvs pale green, spatula-shaped. Blooms bright orange, daisy-like to 4 in wide. Many variations inc double-flowered sorts. *Ht:* to 2 ft; *Spd:* 18 in; *Fl:* 6–10

Callistephus

China aster

C. chinensis

C. chinensis: China. Single or double daisy-like fls. Lvs soft, green, toothed. Main strains inc 'Princess', soft cols, yellow centres; 'Duchesse', ptls incurved, white, blue, red, pink; 'Singles' and chrysanthemum-like 'Ostrich Feather' in sim cols; 'Master Sunray' showy selection. Also dwarfs e.g. 'Lilliput' 18 in; 'Victoria' 20 in; Pompon 18 in. *Ht:* 2 ft; *Spd:* 18 in; *Fl:* 7–10

Campanula

Bellflower

C. medium Canterbury bell: Eur. Hry lvs in basal rosette. Fls bell-shaped or with collar in old-fashioned form. 'Calycanthema' with blue, pink or white fls. Singles are tall, pyramidal; fls rose pink, violet blue. Doubles (offered as mixed seed) come *c.* 65% true. *Ht:* 3 ft; *Spd:* 18 in; *Fl:* 5–6

C. pyramidalis* Chimney bellflower: Eur. Tall bi. Fls open bells forming dense pyramid in icy pale blue or crystalline white. *Ht:* 4 ft; *Spd:* 18 in; *Fl:* 7; *Z:* SF

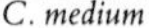

C. medium

Celosia

Celosia

C. cristata Cockscomb: Trop Asia. Common in conservatories but good in gdns. Fls crimson crests to 5 in wide, also mixed cols. *C. thompsonii magnifica* 20 in, bright red or mixed. *Ht:* 2 ft; *Spd:* 1 ft; *Fl:* 7–10

Centaurea

Knapweed

C. cyanus Cornflower: Eur. Stems slim, lvs narrow, fls like miniature crowns 2 in wide, intense cornflower blue. *C.* × 'Blue Diadem' rich double blue. Red, white and carmine also available. *Ht:* 3 ft; *Spd:* 1 ft; *Fl:* 7–9; *Z:* SF

C. moschata Sweet sultan: E Med. Effective frag full-petalled fl heads white, pink, mauve, purple or yellow on long stems. Lvs lyre-shaped, cleft at ends, bright green. *Ht:* to 2 ft; *Spd:* 10 in; *Fl:* 6–10

C. cyanus

Cheiranthus

Wallflower

C. cheiri*: Eur. Per in warm, dry places but normally treated as bi. Sweet scent epitomizes spr. Bushy; lvs narrow, fresh green. Hybs in white and yellows to reds and rust. 'Harpur Crewe' double yellow; 'Tom Thumb' miniatures 8 in tall. *Ht:* 1 ft; *Spd:* 10 in; *Fl:* 4–5; *Z:* F

Chrysanthemum

Chrysanthemum

C. carinatum Tricoloured chrysanthemum: Morocco. Bushy plant; lvs smooth, fleshy, almost feathery. Fls white, yellow inner zone, crimson centre disc. New hybs inc doubles, crimson-ptlld sorts. *Ht:* 2 ft; *Spd:* 15 in; *Fl:* 7–8

C. coronarium Crown daisy: S Eur. Taller, lvs blunter; fls v pale yellow, may be double. *Ht:* 3 ft; *Spd:* 4 ft; *Fl:* 7–9

C. carinatum hybrid

Clarkia

Clarkia

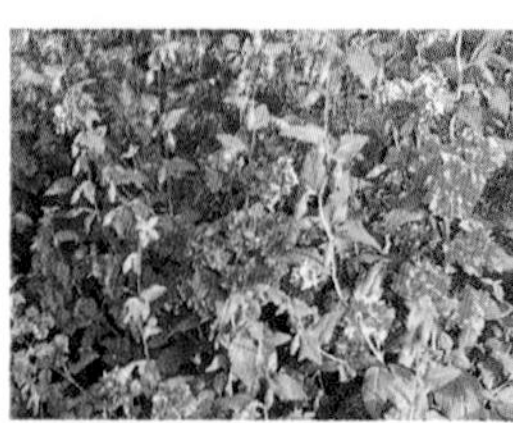

C. *elegans*

C. elegans: Cal. Fls like small ruffled hollyhocks in tapering 8 in spikes. Sp has 4 ptls, most hybs generously double in soft red or pinks, deep purple or white. Fls May–June from autumn sowing. *Ht:* 2 ft; *Spd:* 1 ft; *Fl:* 6–7

C. pulchella: Cal. Elegant; fls single, with 4 clawed ptls, lavender to white, massed in sprays. *Ht:* 15 in; *Spd:* 1 ft; *Fl:* 6–7

Cleome

Spider flower

***C. spinosa**:** W Indies. Strong prickly plant with strange spidery-petalled white or pale pink fls with protruding anthers. 'Helen Campbell' white, other cvs rose or purple. *Ht:* 4 ft; *Spd:* 2 ft; *Fl:* 7–10

Coleus

Coleus

C. blumei: Java. Bushy per grown as ann. Lvs large, oval, coarsely toothed, usually 2 or 3 cols inc purple, orange, brown, yellow, pink, silver, bright green. Pinch out white or purple fls. For hot zones. *Ht:* 3 ft; *Spd:* 18 in

Convolvulus

Convolvulus, Bindweed

C. tricolor Dwarf convolvulus*: SW Eur. Like a little bushy Morning glory of darker col. Fls brilliant blue funnels $1\frac{1}{2}$ in wide with yellowish-white throat and centre. Lvs downy. *Ht:* 15 in; *Spd:* 9 in; *Fl:* 7–9

Coreopsis

Coreopsis, Tickseed

C. *tinctoria* 'Dwarf Dazzler'

C. drummondii: Cal, Texas. Short ann version of border per. Whole plant slightly hry; daisy fls single, yellow, crimson/brown centre zone. *Ht:* 1 ft; *Spd:* 18 in; *Fl:* 6–9

C. tinctoria: N Amer. Hrlss; lvs sparse, fls deep yellow or rich brown. Untidy windblown look. *Ht:* 2 ft; *Spd:* 1 ft; *Fl:* 6–9

Cosmos

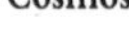

Cosmos

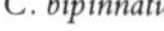

C. *bipinnatus*

C. bipinnatus: Mexico. Graceful; lvs finely cut; fls big, single daisies in rose pink or purple, yellow centre disc. Hybs in reds, pinks, white. *Ht:* 3 ft; *Spd:* 1 ft; *Fl:* 6–9

C. sulphureus: Mexico. Smaller sulphur-yellow sp, parent of sev orange double and semi-double cvs e.g. 'Goldcrest'. *Ht:* 2 ft; *Spd:* 1 ft; *Fl:* 6–9

Delphinium

Larkspur

***D. ajacis**:** S Eur. One parent of gdn-bred ann hybs. 3 main sorts: Hyacinth flowered are earliest; Imperial larkspurs in white, pinks, lilac and blue; Stock flowered (form of *D. consolida**) sim cols, 'Rosamund' v good unfading rose-pink. All have dark green divided lvs. *Ht:* 3 ft; *Spd:* 1 ft; *Fl:* 6–7

D. ajacis

Dianthus

Pink, Carnation

D. barbatus Sweet William*: Eur. Best grown as bi. Jointed stems, fls in flat dome-shaped heads, white, pink, crimson often zoned and with white eye; frag. *Ht:* 2 ft; *Spd:* 1 ft; *Fl:* 6–7; *Z:* Arct

D. chinensis Chinese or Indian pink*: E Asia. Compact single or double fls, fringed ptls, often darker or contrasting centre. *Ht:* 1 ft; *Spd:* 6 in; *Fl:* 6–9; *Z:* Arct

D. chinensis 'Juliette'

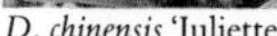

Digitalis

Foxglove

***D. purpurea**:** W. Eur. Bi with rosette of large sage-green basal lvs. Fls tubular, slightly pinched, purplish-pink to white, often spotted. 'Excelsior' hybs have fls all round stem. *Ht:* 4 ft; *Spd:* 18 in; *Fl:* 6–7; *Z:* F

Dimorphotheca

Cape marigold, African daisy

D. calendulacea* Star of the Veldt: S Africa. Dark-centred glistening daisy fls open with the sun. Sp orange-yellow, hybs yellow, white, orange, salmon pink. Lvs narrow. *Ht:* 1 ft; *Spd:* 8 in; *Fl:* 6–9

Echium

Bugloss

E. plantagineum hybs: Med (sp). Recent hybs have coarsely hry narrow dark green lvs and v many papery rich blue fls in dense head. Pink, lavender and white sorts available but inferior. *Ht:* 1 ft; *Spd:* 8 in; *Fl:* 6–10

E. plantagineum 'Blue Bedder'

Erysimum

Erysimum

E. perofskianum: Caucasus. Dwarf, wallflower-like. Lvs dull green; frag fls bright orange and yellow in short spikes. Can be sown in aut to fl in spr. *Ht:* 2 ft; *Spd:* 1 ft; *Fl:* 6–7; *Z:* F

Eschscholzia   

Poppy

E. californica

E. californica* Californian poppy: NW Amer. Brilliant yellow 4-petalled poppies. Lvs fern-like, glaucous. Hybs with *E. crocea* have orange, orange-red, crimson, scarlet, cream or white fls, some with contrasting ptl reverses. Double sorts shorter and lacking in charm. *Ht:* 18 in; *Spd:* 1 ft; *Fl:* 6–7

Euphorbia    

Spurge

E. marginata Snow on the mountain: N Amer. Spurge with white fl heads and white-margined pale green, sometimes completely white, lvs. *Ht:* to 2 ft; *Spd:* 8 in; *Fl:* 9

Glaucium   

Horned poppy

G. flavum

G. corniculatum: Eur. Native of sea shore; lvs glaucous, dissected; fls poppy-like, 2 in wide, crimson, black spot at ptl base. *Ht, Spd:* 1 ft; *Fl:* 6

G. flavum* Yellow horned poppy: Eur. Brilliant yellow fls 3 in wide; lvs as above. Curved seed pod to 1 ft like a horn. May survive several seasons; a thrill to grow. *Ht, Spd:* 2 ft; *Fl:* 6–8

Godetia       

Godetia

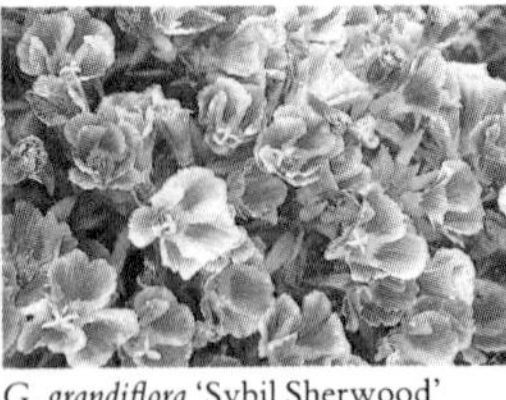
G. grandiflora 'Sybil Sherwood'

G. amoena: W N Amer. Sp has reddish-pink fls, sev to a head on slim stems. Sev brighter hybs. *Ht:* 2 ft; *Spd:* 10 in; *Fl:* 7–8

G. grandiflora: Cal. Single hibiscus-like fls have satin sheen. Many shades from rose-red/white/crimson. Hybs double, anemone- and azalea-flowered. *Ht:* 15 in; *Spd:* 6 in; *Fl:* 6–8

Gypsophila   

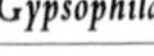

Gypsophila

G. elegans: Asia Minor. Ann version of per Baby's breath. Greeny-grey stems and lvs. Tiny white fls in light clouds. Pale pink, white or carmine sorts available. *Ht, Spd:* to 20 in; *Fl:* 5–9

Helianthus    

Sunflower

H. annuus* Common sunflower: USA. The monster ann to 10 ft+. Huge heavy round fls to 1 ft wide, orange or yellow pts, edible oily seeds. Hybs chestnut, yellow zoned red and brown, or double. *Spd:* 3 ft; *Fl:* 7–9

Helichrysum

Everlasting flower, Straw flower

H. bracteatum: Aust. Uprt, branching; fls double, daisy-like, 2 in wide, bright red, rose-pink, yellow, copper or white. Narrow lvs may have a few hrs. For drying, pick fls as they open. *Ht:* 4 ft; *Spd:* 15 in; *Fl:* 6–9

Helipterum

Everlasting flower

H. humboldtianum: Aust. Fls more open than sim *Helichrysum*, 3 or 4 rows of ptls round golden disc, clean yellow, sev to a head. Lvs, hry when young, clasp stem. *Ht:* 18 in; *Spd:* 6 in; *Fl:* 7–9

H. roseum: Aust. Fol slightly grey-green, freely branching. Fls as above but pink or white. *Ht:* 15 in; *Spd:* 6 in; *Fl:* 7–9

H. roseum

Iberis

Candytuft

I. amara: Eur. Low, bushy; fls white in round trusses 2 in wide. Lvs narrow, pointed tips. Also larger and dwarf forms available. *Ht, Spd:* 1 ft; *Fl:* 6–9

I. umbellata: S Eur. Taller, will grow in partial shade. Sp pink, hybs bright reds and purple to white. Dwarf forms make good edging. *Ht:* 15 in; *Spd:* 6 in; *Fl:* 5–6

I. umbellata hybrids

Impatiens

Balsam

I. balsamina: Asia. Dense, succ, tender; lvs toothed, oval, pointed; fls red, single, wide wings and spur. *L. b. camelliaeflora* double, pink, purple or red, sometimes spotted. Taller *I. biflora* (N Amer) has orange fls spotted purple-brown. *Ht:* 15 in; *Spd:* 1 ft; *Fl:* 7–9

Kochia

Kochia

K. scoparia trichophila Summer cypress, Burning bush: S Eur–Japan. Pale green thin-lvd densely bushy plant the shape of a bearskin helmet. Turns ember-hot purple/red in late smr. Fls inconspic. *Ht:* 3 ft; *Spd:* 2 ft

Lathyrus

Sweet pea

L. odoratus*: Sicily. Sweet peas have suffered many supposed "improvements" over 300 yrs and many have lost their fragrance. Cols white, reds, purples, blue; fls pea-like, 5–7 per stem. Lvs often have tendrils. 'Knee High' self supporting, bushy to 3 ft; 'Grandiflora' (smaller fls!) has sweetest smell. *Ht:* 8 ft (with support); *Spd:* 2 ft; *Fl:* 6–9

L. odoratus 'Topscore'

Lavatera

Mallow

L. trimestris (=rosea)*:* Med. Shrubby; soft round lvs; fls single, open hibiscus-like, 4 in wide, rose-pink. 'Loveliness' deep rose-pink and less tall. *Ht:* 4 ft; *Spd:* 2 ft; *Fl:* 6–10

Linaria

Toadflax

L. maroccana hybs

L. maroccana*:* Morocco. Dainty, uprt. Lvs narrow; ½ in fls like massed miniature snapdragons. Sp purple, hybs from red to white and yellow eg × 'Fairy Bouquet'. *Ht:* 1 ft; *Spd:* 6 in; *Fl:* 6–9

L. reticulata: Portugal. Fls sim but larger, purple, yellow or orange in "snap". *Ht:* 3 ft; *Spd:* 1 ft; *Fl:* 5–7

Linum

Flax

L. grandiflorum rubrum

L. grandiflorum*:* N Africa. Stemmy, branching; lvs narrow, pointed. Fls rose-pink, saucer-shaped, single shiny with deeper central zone. *L. g. rubrum* rich crimson. Also a white-flowered form. *Ht:* 1 ft; *Spd:* 6 in; *Fl:* 6–7

L. usitatissimum Linseed: Eur. Fls as above but clear blue. *Ht:* 15 in; *Spd:* 6 in; *Fl:* 6–7

Lobelia

Lobelia

L. erinus 'Cambridge Blue'

L. erinus: S Africa. Per used as an ann; traditional edging plant. Lvs small, pale or v dark green; fls open tubes with violet-like 3-petalled lower lip, Cambridge or Oxford blue with white or yellow eye. Also carmine, red and white sorts and trailers for planting in hanging baskets or window boxes. *Ht, Spd:* 6 in; *Fl:* 6–10

Lobularia (=Alyssum)

Alyssum

L. maritima*:* Eur. W Asia. Dwarf, bushy. Lvs tiny, fls also tiny, white, on stumpy spikes, honey scent. 'Little Dorrit' white; 'Pink Heather' bluish pink; 'Oriental Night' violet. *Ht:* 8 in; *Spd:* 1 ft; *Fl:* 6–9

Lunaria

Honesty

L. annua (=biennis)*:* Eur. Bi but can fl in 1st yr. Lvs big, rough; fls bright mauve; frs like small opaque tennis rackets, silvery sheen. *L. a. variegata* with cream/green lvs v handsome. *Ht:* 2 ft; *Spd:* 1 ft; *Fl:* 5–7; *Z:* F

Matthiola

Stock

M. bicornis Night-scented stock: Greece. Wayward lilac-fld crucifer. Fls open at night, strongly frag. *Ht:* 15 in; *Spd:* 9 in; *Fl:* 6–10
M. incana and hybs: S Eur. All bi; hybs in 4 gps: Early Flowering (Mar–Apr) bushy; Brompton (May–June) v bright clear cols; Summer Bedding (June–Aug); East Lothian clean cols. *Ht:* 15 in; *Spd:* 1 ft; *Z:* F

M. incana

Molucella

Molucella

M. laevis Shell flower, Bells of Ireland: Syria. Lvs coarse, pale green. Exciting shell-shaped spl structures surrounding small white fls. Good for arranging as spls dry well. *Ht:* 2 ft; *Spd:* 15 in; *Fl:* 8

Myosotis

Forget-me-not

***M. alpestris**:** Eur. Short-lived densely bushy per grown as bi. Myriads of brilliant blue fls with tiny yellow-white eye. Rec cvs 'Royal Blue' 1 ft; 'Ultramarine' 6 in. Also pink or white hybs. *Ht, Spd:* 8 in; *Fl:* 4–6

Nemesia

Nemesia

N. strumosa: S Africa. Brilliantly coloured fls rather like tailless nasturtiums but smaller and clustered in small dome. Fls in rich cols from red through orange and yellow to deep blue, cream and white. Hybs are dwarf strain to 8 in tall. *Ht:* to 2 ft; *Spd:* 6 in; *Fl:* 7–8

N. strumosa hybrid

Nemophila

Nemophila

N. menziesii* Baby blue eyes: Cal. Spreading with hrs; lvs deep lobed. Fls single, 5-petalled, clear, bright sky blue with large white eye. Also a white form. *Ht, Spd:* 8 in; *Fl:* 6–10

Nicotiana

Tobacco plant

***N. alata (=affinis)**:** Brazil. Rather coarse plant but worthy for its scent alone. Fls tubular, deliciously frag in evening. Sp yellowish-white, modern hybs white, pink, reds. 'Lime Green' fashionable cv. *Ht:* to 3 ft; *Spd:* 15 in; *Fl:* 7–9
N. tabacum: Trop Amer. Sim to above but fls smaller, pink, in loose clusters open in daytime. *Ht:* 5 ft; *Spd:* 2 ft; *Fl:* 7–9

N. alata 'Lime Green'

Nigella

Nigella

N. damascena* Love-in-a-mist: Med. Light blue fls in a froth of bright green feathery lvs and bracts. Seed pods green, turning fawn, bladder-like with "horns". Hybs white, pink, yellowish. *Ht, Spd:* 1 ft; *Fl:* 6–9

Papaver

Poppy

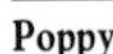

P. nudicaule

P. glaucum* Tulip poppy: Asia. Tulip-shaped buds open to brilliant crimson-scarlet fls. *Ht:* 15 in; *Spd:* 1 ft; *Fl:* 6–10

P. nudicaule* Iceland poppy: Sub-Arctic. Treat as bi. Fragile pink, orange, yellow, red or white fls. *Ht, Spd:* 1 ft; *Fl:* 5–6; *Z:* Arct

P.* × *rhoeas: gdn origin. Bristly hyb; fls have satin sheen. *Ht, Spd:* 2 ft; *Fl:* 6–8

P. somniferum* Opium poppy: Near E. Matt blue-grey lvs; big greyish-purple fls. Also fine pink, red, white and v double forms. *Ht:* 2 ft; *Spd:* 10 in; *Fl:* 6–9

Pelargonium

Pelargonium, Geranium

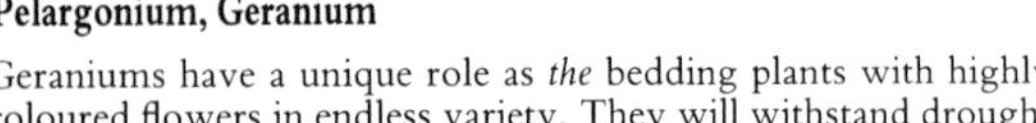

Geraniums have a unique role as *the* bedding plants with highly coloured flowers in endless variety. They will withstand drought (but not freezing) and cuttings root with effortless ease.

P. peltatum 'Lyme Regis'

P. zonale 'Salmon Rings'

P. zonale 'Caroline Schmidt'

P. hybs* Bedding geraniums: gdn origin. Many shades and col combinations inc white, pink, reds, mauve and purple. Fls single, semi-double, double or "rosettes", eg semi-doubles 'Gustav Emich' vermilion; 'Lady Ilchester' pink; 'Vera Dillon' Tyrian purple with touch of red in centre. Prop by cuttings. *Ht:* 2 ft; *Spd:* 15 in; *Fl:* 5–10

P. peltatum* Ivy-leaved geranium: S. Africa. Trailing; waxy roundish lobed lvs may have dark zone. Fls in dome-shaped heads in shades of pink or white. *Ht:* 2 ft; *Spd:* 3 ft; *Fl:* 6–10

P. zonale* Zonal or horseshoe geranium: S Africa. Bedding plants with horseshoe-shaped mark or series of marks in single or concentric bands on lvs in yellow, black or silver. Sev forms of sp have plain green lvs but 5 narrow spoon-shaped ptls, 3 forming broad lip, 2 swept back. Best cvs inc: 'Caroline Schmidt' lvs green/white, fls turkey red, double; 'Golden Oriole' lvs green/copper, fls salmon pink, single; 'Skies of Italy' lvs red/yellow/green/bronze, yellow edge, vermilion fls with central eye. *Ht:* to 6 ft; *Spd:* 1 ft; *Fl:* 5–10

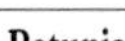

Petunia

Petunia

P. × hybrida★: S Amer. One of the best anns for dry soil and hot sun. Range of superb dwarf to double bedding plants. All have clammy lvs and big funnel-shaped velvety-throated fls with cloying scent in all cols inc striped and frilly-edged (picotee) sorts in white, pink, yellow, pale and navy blue. *Ht, Spd:* 1 ft; *Fl:* 6–10

P. × hybrida 'Satellite'

Phacelia

Phacelia

P. campanularia★: Cal. One of the truest-blue anns—strident as a gentian. Bushy, softly hry with oval lvs. Fls clustered, individually bell-shaped, 1 in wide. *Ht:* 9 in; *Spd:* 6 in; *Fl:* 6–9

Phlox

Phlox

P. drummondii★ Annual phlox: Texas, New Mexico. Bright-eyed bushy plants with large fl heads v like border pers. Rich cols—fls pink, red, scarlet, crimson, mauve, blue or white. *Ht, Spd:* 18 in; *Fl:* 6–9

Reseda

Mignonette

R. odorata: N Africa. Sub-shrubby; can be per in frost-free gdn. Lvs blunt, oval; fls yellowish, open, star-like in loose spike, v strongly frag. Try 'Crimson Giant'; 'Golden Goliath'. *Ht, Spd:* 2 ft; *Fl:* 6–10

Rudbeckia

Coneflower

R. bicolor Annual rudbeckia: S USA. Hybs of sp as restrained as Indian war-paint. Lvs dark green, bristly; fls daisy-like, large central disc or cone, in reddish brown/ yellow bicol, disc purple-brown. Also double, 1-col and dwarf forms. 'Hurst's Marmalade' has fls to 5 in wide. *Ht, Spd:* 15 in; *Fl:* 6–10

R. bicolor 'Hurst's Marmalade'

Salpiglossis

Salpiglossis

S. sinuata★: Chile. Exotically striped and veined hyb; petunia-like, trumpet-shaped sticky fls to 2 in. in gold, rose, red, blue, violet, cream and bicols. Lvs wavy-edged. *Ht:* 2 ft; *Spd:* 1 ft; *Fl:* 7–9

Salvia

Sage

S. splendens★ Scarlet sage: Brazil. Guardsman-scarlet tubular fls in slim spikes on stocky bush. Lvs bright green, dark in hybs. *S. patens* taller with fls of glorious singing blue. *Ht:* 1 ft; *Spd:* 10 in; *Fl:* 7–10

Scabiosa

Scabious, Pincushion flower

S. atropurpurea Sweet scabious: SW Eur. Pale stemmy plant with jaggedly cut lvs. Fls pretty maroon pincushions of stamens among ptls. Also brighter forms from scarlet to powder blue. *Ht:* 3 ft; *Spd:* 1 ft; *Fl:* 7–9

Senecio

Ragwort

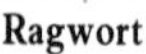

S. (=Cineraria) maritima Cineraria, Sea ragwort: Eur. Grown for its deep-lobed almost white lvs which have silver effect. Fls inconspic. 'Silver Dust' and 'Diamond' fern-like and v pale resp. *Ht, Spd:* 2 ft

Tagetes

Marigold

T. erecta 'Diamond Jubilee'

T. erecta* African marigold: Mexico. Dissected lvs and distinctive smell. Pompons of full-ptld double fls to 5 in wide. Hybs pale to deep yellow or orange. *Ht:* 3 ft; *Spd:* 1 ft; *Fl:* 7–10

T. patula French marigold: Mexico. Hybs in all shades of yellow-orange, plain or bicol, single, double, crested, brocaded. *Ht:* 1 ft; *Spd:* 10 in; *Fl:* 7–10

Tropaeolum

Tropaeolum

T. majus* Nasturtium, Indian cress: Peru. Bushy, trailing, sometimes climbing. Pale, round, tasty lvs. Fls tubular, long-spurred; singles in primary shades or pale green. Doubles decorative, less elegant. Lvs of *T. alaska* hybs marbled and striped cream. *Ht, Spd:* 4 ft; *Fl:* 6–10

Verbena

Verbena

V. × hybrida: gdn origin. Per grown as ann. Small lvs; tiny primula-like fls in circular heads 3 in wide in white, blue, red, often with lighter eye; v frag. Tender *V. rigida* good for bedding. *Ht, Spd:* 1 ft; *Fl:* 7–11

Zea

Maize, Indian corn, Mealies

Z. mays: gdn origin. Ornamental sweet corn, sub-tropical in looks. Long lvs enclose broad shining ears ripening yellow, brown, red or varieg in Aug–Sept. Cvs have varieg or multicoloured fol. *Ht:* 4 ft; *Spd:* 2 ft

Zinnia

Zinnia

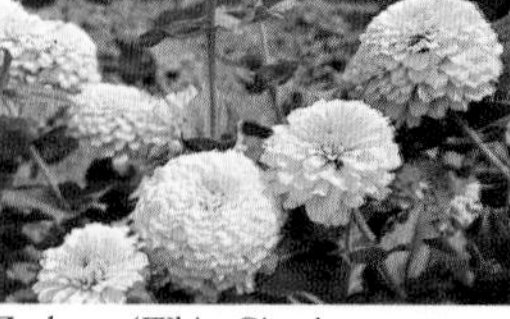

Z. elegans 'White Giant'

Z. elegans Youth and age: Mexico. Sev strains under this name, all uprt with coarse oval pointed lvs. Fls double or single rosettes of closely packed ptls notched at tip in poster-paint cols—pink, red, white, yellow, orange. 'Envy' is superb Chartreuse green. *Ht:* 3 ft; *Spd:* 8 in; *Fl:* 7–9

Herbaceous perennials

Most "border" plants are classed as herbaceous perennials, i.e. permanent plants that die back to ground level in winter. In practice some are evergreen and a few (notably *Helleborus*) actually flower in winter. The demands of herbaceous perennials vary from dust-dry to swampy soil where they merge with bog plants. Most flower best in full sun but those of woodland origin—which are usually early-flowering—need some shade.

Acanthus

Bear's breeches

***A. spinosus**:** S Eur. Statuesque with lustrous deeply divided evergreen hry lvs to 3 ft and stiff 18 in fl spikes of squat white and purple tubes interspersed with spiny bracts. *Ht:* to 4 ft; *Spd:* 30 in; *Fl:* 7–8; *Z:* F

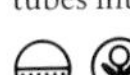

Achillea

Yarrow, Milfoil

Flat, generally yellow or white composite flower heads over rough-textured feathery foliage. Robust and wiry, long lasting and drying well. More useful than glamorous as garden plants.

A. filipendulina: Caucasus. Stout plant with hry greyish-green aromatic lvs. Fls golden yellow in densely packed heads. 'Gold Plate'* one of the best cvs. Prop by div. *Ht:* 4 ft; *Spd:* 18 in; *Fl:* 7–8; *Z:* Arct

***A. 'Moonshine'**:** gdn origin. Shorter cv with silvery-green lvs and bright yellow fls. *Ht:* 2 ft; *Spd:* 18 in; *Fl:* 6–8; *Z:* PF

A. filipendulina 'Gold Plate'

Aconitum

Monkshood

A. napellus: Eur, Asia. Poisonous tuberous-rooted plant with stiff stems bearing dark green deeply divided lvs and spikes of helmet-shaped 1½ in fls from July–Aug; × 'Bicolor' is one of sev good gdn hybs with bright blue and white fls. Other sorts are indigo, e.g. 'Spark's Variety', or white. Prop by div. *Ht:* 3 ft; *Spd:* 8 in; *Z:* Arct

Agapanthus

Blue African lily

Tall swaying stems supporting bunches of blue or white lily-like flowers over smooth leaves. One of the best late summer flowers.

***A. campanulatus**:** S Africa. Smaller in all its parts and hardier than *A. umbellatus* with sky-blue 2 in fls. There are also white and deep blue forms. Prop by div in spring, seedlings variable. *Ht:* 30 in; *Spd:* 18 in; *Fl:* 7–8; *Z:* SF

A. umbellatus (= africanus, orientalis, praecox): S Africa. Strap-shaped glossy deep green lvs 2 ft × 2 in; green unbranched stems and terminal heads of deep blue funnel-shaped 3 in fls. Pop 'Headbourne Hybrids' hardier with violet to pale blue fls. Prop by div. *Ht:* 4 ft; *Spd:* 30 in; *Fl:* 7–9; *Z:* SF

A. campanulatus

Agave  

Century plant

A. americana: Mexico. Sub-tropical succ, spectacular in foliage and fl with thick, fleshy, glaucous, spiny 4 ft lvs. Produces stems to 20 ft with yellowish fls after many yrs then dies. Tender. *Ht:* 4 ft; *Spd:* 9 ft; *Fl:* 8; *Z:* F

Ajuga  

Bugle

A useful low leafy carpeter, creeping with stoloniferous roots; a native of clay soils. In early spring spikes of bluish flowers arise. Admirable cover for short-stemmed spring bulbs.

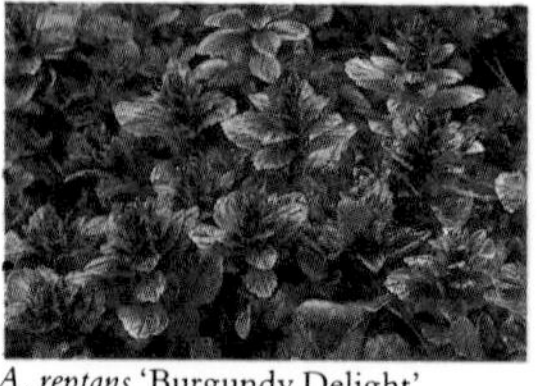

A. reptans 'Burgundy Delight'

A. pyramidalis: Eur. Dark green, rounded lvs and blue-purple fls in pyramidal 6 in spikes. *Ht:* 4 in; *Spd:* 18 in; *Fl:* 5–7; *Z:* Arct

A. reptans: Eur. Fls blue, white or pink. Cvs 'Multicolor', 'Variegata' and 'Burgundy Delight' have darker, variegated and metallic lvs respectively. Prop by div. *Ht:* 3½ in; *Spd:* 15 in; *Fl:* 6–7; *Z:* Arct

Alchemilla    

Lady's mantle

A. mollis

A. mollis*: Asia Minor. Forms dense clumps of rounded, downy, pale greyish-green lvs on long single stalks. Much praised when spangled with dew or raindrops. Branched fl stems bear myriads of yellow-green star-like ¼ in fls. Prop by div or seed. *Ht:* 18 in; *Spd:* 2 ft; *Fl:* 6–8; *Z:* Arct

Aloe    

Aloe

A. aristata: S Africa. A succ, sprawling rosette of alt narrow fleshy-toothed lvs and flared tubular orange fls on branched 1 ft spikes in late June. Fairly hardy in a v dry place. *Ht:* 2 ft; *Spd:* 3 ft; *Z:* SF

Alstroemeria    

Peruvian lily

Little lily-like flowers in generous bunches on tall pliant stems. Needs deep planting, slow to establish, but long-lasting.

A. aurantiaca

A. aurantiaca*: Chile. Smooth-stemmed slightly fleshy-leaved clumps; terminal clusters of open fierce orange 2 in tubes. Also a yellow form. Rts inclined to run, stems need support. Prop by seed. *Ht:* 3 ft; *Spd:* 1 ft+; *Fl:* 6–8; *Z:* PF

A. ligtu*: Chile. Chiefly seen as 'Ligtu Hybrids' ranging in col from bright pink to yellow, orange and salmon pink. Prized as cut fls. Prop by seed, plant from pots. *Ht:* to 4 ft; *Spd:* 18 in; *Fl:* 6–8; *Z:* PF

Anaphalis

Pearl everlasting

A. cinnamomea: Asia. Stems uprt, lvs rich green on top, woolly white beneath. Fls long-lasting branched flat heads of yellow-centred white. Tolerates more moisture than sim spp. *Ht:* 18 in; *Spd:* 2 ft; *Fl:* 8; *Z:* Arct

Anchusa

Anchusa

A. azurea: Caucasus. Top-heavy middle-of-the-border plant with v branched hairy lvs and stems; ⅓ in fls are open funnels in a rare, valuable shade of intense blue. 'Loddon Royalist' (AGM) is one of the best. Short lived; renew by seed or root cuttings. *Ht:* to 4 ft; *Spd:* 2 ft; *Fl:* 5–8; *Z:* Arct

A. azurea 'Loddon Royalist'

Anemone

Anemone, windflower

A. hupehensis* Japanese anemone: China. Among the most useful, graceful and long-lasting late smr fls. *A. hybrida (=japonica)* sim. Lvs rough, vine-like, 2 in fls dusky pink, purplish or white. 'Luise Uhink' (AGM) is semi-double white. *Ht:* to 4 ft; *Spd:* 2 ft; *Fl:* 8–10; *Z:* Arct

Aquilegia

Columbine

A. hybrid strains: gdn origin. Pretty but short-lived plants with tap roots and fern-like, sometimes glaucous lvs. Fls to 3 in across have spurs at the back and come in a wide range of plain and mixed cols. Casual crossing often produces muddy cols; purchase guaranteed seed. 'McKana Hybrids' are large-flowered, yellow and crimson. *Ht:* 3 ft; *Spd:* 1 ft; *Fl:* 5–6; *Z:* Arct

A. 'McKana Hybrids'

Arctotis

Arctotis

A. decurrens: S Africa. Woolly divided evergreen lvs and open single white purplish-centred daisy fls *c.* 2 in wide. Several spp have been crossed with venidiums to produce × *Venidio-arctotis* (p 56), half-hardy perennials and bedding plants. *Ht:* to 30 in; *Spd:* 30 in; *Fl:* 7–8; *Z:* NF

Armeria

Thrift, Sea pink

A. plantaginea Giant thrift: Eur. Large sp with long green lvs and rounded heads of pink fls on stiff stems. 'Bees Ruby' (AGM) has deep reddish-pink fls. *Ht:* 18 in; *Spd:* 1 ft; *Fl:* 6–8; *Z:* Arct

Artemisia

Wormwood

Members of the daisy family on the borderline between perennials and shrubs. All but *A. lactiflora* are grown for their foliage.

A. ludoviciana

A. absinthium: Eur. Woody with finely-dissected shining silvery-grey lvs. 'Lambrook Silver'★ is best selection. Prop by cuttings. *Ht:* 2 ft; *Spd:* 3 ft; *Z:* Arct

A. lactiflora: Asia. Uprt plant with terminal 8 in spikes of creamy white fls on stiff stems of coarse-lobed green lvs. Prop by div. *Ht:* to 5 ft; *Spd:* 2 ft; *Fl:* 7–8; *Z:* Arct

A. ludoviciana: N Amer. Sprawling, white-stemmed with narrow grey-green lvs. 'Silver Queen' is smaller with divided lvs. May run. *Ht:* 3 ft; *Spd:* 2 ft; *Z:* Arct

Aruncus

Goat's beard

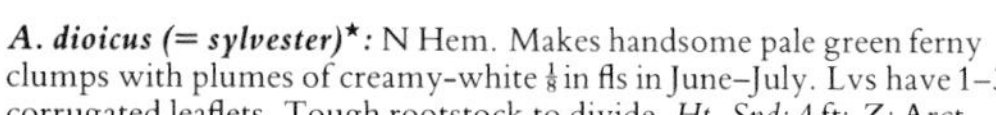

A. dioicus (= sylvester)★: N Hem. Makes handsome pale green ferny clumps with plumes of creamy-white $\frac{1}{8}$ in fls in June–July. Lvs have 1–3 corrugated leaflets. Tough rootstock to divide. *Ht, Spd:* 4 ft; *Z:* Arct

Asclepias

Milkweed

A. tuberosa Butterfly weed, Pleurisy root: N Amer. Tap-rooted plant best in poor soil. Pointed lvs and stems hry. Orange $\frac{1}{4}$ in fls from late June–Aug form bun-shaped heads. Prop by seed. *Ht:* to 30 in; *Spd:* 18 in; *Z:* Arct

Aster

Aster, Michaelmas daisy

Chiefly late and long-flowering and all with blooms on the white-purple side of the spectrum. Varied in size, vigour and proneness to disease but all best propagated vegetatively.

A. novi-belgii

A. novae-angliae

A. amellus: Italy. Useful late-flowering sp with coarse lvs and stems. Fls $1\frac{1}{2}$ in wide, pink, mauve or violet in late July or Oct depending on cv. *Ht:* 14 in; *Spd:* 2 ft; *Z:* Arct

A. × frikartii: gdn origin. Taller and larger in fl than *A. amellus* which is one of its parents. 'Mönch'★ with bright blue fls and pronounced yellow centre disc is best form. *Ht:* 30 in; *Spd:* 18 in; *Fl:* 7–9; *Z:* Arct

A. novae-angliae: N Amer. Tough back-of-the-border sp with rough stems and lvs. 'Harrington's Pink' a familiar favourite, also mauve, crimson and purple-blue sorts. *Ht:* $4\frac{1}{2}$ ft; *Spd:* 2 ft; *Fl:* 8–9; *Z:* Arct

A. novi-belgii: E USA. Shorter than above but a wider selection of white, pink, red, blue and purple-flowered sorts, e.g. 'Winston Churchill' ruby red. *Ht:* to 4 ft; *Spd:* 28 in; *Fl:* 9–10; *Z:* Arct

Astilbe

Handsome long-lasting plume flowers; some straight and single, others multiple or drooping. Happy in boggy ground.

***A. × arendsii**:** gdn origin. Dense lfy clumps and tapering fluffy 1 ft plumes in the white-red col range dying to a handsome dark brown. A race of hybs, e.g. 'Rheinland' rose-pink. Prop by div. *Ht:* to 3 ft; *Spd:* to 2 ft; *Fl:* 7–8; *Z:* PF
***A. chinensis* 'Pumila':** China. One of sev dwarf sorts. Needs dampness and partial shade. Fl spikes mauve. *Ht, Spd:* 1 ft; *Fl:* 7–8; *Z:* PF
***A. taquetii**:** China. Distinct tall sp. Fls rich reddish mauve esp in the selection 'Superba'. *Ht:* to 4 ft; *Spd:* 2 ft; *Fl:* 8; *Z:* PF

A. × *arendsii*

Astrantia

Masterwort

***A. major**:** Eur. Quietly attractive plant with bold divided lvs and wiry green stems. Tiny purplish-white fls arranged in a dome on a saucer of larger ptl-like bracts, sev on a stem. *A. maxima* is light pink and shorter, *A. carniolica* 'Rubra' reddish. Prop by div or seed. *Ht:* 2 ft; *Spd:* 18 in; *Fl:* 7–8; *Z:* PF

A. *major*

Baptisia

Blue or false indigo

***B. australis**:** E USA. Uprt member of the pea family with glaucous leaflets and paler stems. Indigo-blue fls $\frac{3}{4}$ in wide in June followed by decorative seed pods. Prop by seed. *Ht:* to 4 ft; *Spd:* 2 ft; *Z:* Arct

Bergenia

Bergenia

Valuable low evergreen with bold rounded upright or flopping fleshy leaves of shining green. Pink flowers in spikes in spring.

B. cordifolia* (= *Saxifraga megasea*) Pig squeak: Siberia. Toothed rounded lvs turning bronze in winter and 1 in fls in sprays on thick stems. Prop by div. *Ht:* 15 in; *Spd:* 2 ft; *Fl:* 3–4; *Z:* PF
B. crassifolia: Siberia. Has woody rootstock and oval lvs becoming reddish in wtr. Fls of the sp 1 in long, light pink; gdn forms can be pink or rosy red. Prop by div. *Ht:* 2 ft; *Spd:* 18 in; *Fl:* 3–4; *Z:* PF
***B. 'Silberlicht'* (= 'Silver Light')*:** gdn origin. A white-flowered form with spoon-shaped lvs a shade lighter green. Prop by div. *Ht:* 1 ft; *Spd:* 18 in; *Fl:* 4–5; *Z:* PF

B. *cordifolia*

Bromelia

Bromeliad

B. agavifolia: Cayenne. Tender rosette-former with spiny near-stemless lvs. Fls pale red in collar of short lvs. *Ht:* 4 ft; *Spd:* 5 ft+; *Fl:* 3; *Z:* SF

Brunnera

Brunnera

B. macrophylla (= Anchusa myosotidiflora)*: Caucasus-Iran. Big heart-shaped soft green lvs and sprays of ¼ in bright forget-me-not-blue fls. There is a less vig variegated form*. *Ht:* 18 in; *Spd:* 2 ft;*Fl:* 4–6 *Z:* Arct

Campanula

Bellflower

Varying from tall border plants to tiny alpines but all with clear-cut flowers on the grey or purple side of blue (or white).

C. latiloba

C. lactiflora*: Caucasus. Fls palest blue, bell-shaped, 1½ in wide, many per stem. Good cvs inc 'Loddon Anna' pale pink; 'Prichard's Variety' violet blue. Prop by div. *Ht:* 5 ft; *Spd:* 2 ft; *Fl:* 7–9; *Z:* Arct

C. latifolia Great bellflower: Kashmir-Eur. Reliable per. Fls blue, funnel-shaped, 2 in. Rts inclined to run. 'Brantwood' is a deeper col. *C. latiloba* equally good but smaller. *Ht:* 5 ft; *Spd:* 20 in; *Fl:* 7; *Z:* Arct

C. persicifolia Peach-leaved bell-flower: Eur, N Africa, W Asia. Clumps of narrow-lvd rosettes. Hrlss stems to 3 ft, fls large, open, blue. *Spd:* to 3 ft; *Fl:* 7–8; *Z:* Arct

Canna

Canna

C. indica

C. iridiflora: Peru. V tall elegant plant with exciting long pendulous, rose-pink, tube-like 3 in fls and ptls curved back at the mouth. Lvs wide, glaucous, to 2 ft long. Prop by div. Related *C. indica* grown as a bulb. *Ht:* 4 ft; *Spd:* 3 ft; *Fl:* 7–8; *Z:* SF

Catananche

Cupid's dart

C. caerulea

C. caerulea: Med. Forms a clump of short, narrow, hoary lvs. Papery blue fls 1½ in wide are cornflower-like on 2 ft stems. 'Major' is deep lavender blue. 'Perry's White' less tall. Prop cvs by div, spp by seed. *Spd:* 18 in; *Fl:* 6–8; *Z:* SF

Knapweed

Flowers in intricate thistle-like design, easy to grow in sunny, well-drained preferably limy soil.

C. hypoleuca: Iran. Deeply lobed green lvs are whitish on their underside. Fls rose-pink, 2 in wide. Forms dense clumps but inclined to run: 'John Coutts'★ is the best form. Prop by div. *Ht:* 2 ft; *Spd:* 18 in; *Fl:* 6–7; *Z:* Arct

C. macrocephala: Caucasus. Taller and with coarser lvs and hollow stems. Fls to 4 in wide, bright yellow, borne on rounded, scaly heads. Prop by div. *Ht:* to 4 ft; *Spd:* 30 in; *Fl:* 7; *Z:* Arct

C. montana Mountain knapweed: Eur. Rather floppy plant with narrow green lvs and wide cornflower-like heads of fls from late April–June. Blue, but purplish, white and reddish sorts available. Prop by div. *Ht:* 18 in; *Spd:* 2 ft; *Z:* Arct

C. hypoleuca 'John Coutts'

C. macrocephala

Centranthus

Valerian

C. (= Kentranthus) ruber: Eur. Almost woody; glaucous lvs and bold heads of clustered $\frac{1}{4}$ in fls pink in the type but in best forms, 'Albus' and 'Atrococcineus', white and reddish resp. *Ht:* 30 in; *Spd:* 18 in; *Fl:* 6; *Z:* Arct

Cephalaria

Scabious

C. gigantea (= tartarica) Giant or Tartarian scabious: Siberia. Has pale creamy-yellow scabious-like fls on tall stems above basal clumps of dark green lvs. Prop by div in spr. *Ht:* 7 ft; *Spd:* 4 ft; *Fl:* 6–7; *Z:* Arct

C. gigantea

Chelone

Turtle head

C. obliqua Rose turtle head: USA. Dark green plant with shiny lvs in pairs on $2\frac{1}{2}$ ft stems. Fls 1 in, mop-like, turtle-head-shaped, deep rose-pink. Prop by div, seed, soft cuttings. *Spd:* 1 ft; *Fl:* 8–9; *Z:* Arct

C. obliqua

Chrysanthemum

Chrysanthemum

Indispensable daisy flowers in infinite variety from spring to autumn, lacking only in shades of blue.

C. maximum

C. *coccineum* Pyrethrum: Caucasus-Iran. Simple 3 in fls on slim stems over fern-like lvs. Plant named cvs, e.g. 'Kelway's Glorious' crimson; 'Marjorie Robinson' rose-pink. *Ht:* to 30 in; *Spd:* 18 in; *Fl:* 5–6; *Z:* Arct

C. *maximum* Shasta daisy: Pyrenees. Invaluable white full-petalled fls. Needs regular div. Try 'Wirral Supreme' double fls; 'T.E. Killin' semi-double. *Ht:* to 3 ft; *Spd:* 2 ft; *Fl:* 7–8; *Z:* Arct

Cimicifuga

Black snakeroot, Bugbane

Slender, graceful white or whitish flower spikes in late summer over distinctly stylish leaves. Needs moisture but not support.

C. racemosa

***C. racemosa**:** E N Amer. Clumps of deeply cut rounded lvs give rise to tall branching slender stems with 1 ft pokers of white fls. Prop by div or fresh seed. *Ht:* to 8 ft; *Spd:* to 2 ft; *Fl:* 6–8; *Z:* Arct

C. simplex (=foetida intermedia): USSR-Japan. Toothed lvs and branched stems of greenish-yellow ¼ in fls. Prop as above. *Ht:* to 5 ft; *Spd:* 2 ft; *Fl:* 8–10; *Z:* Arct

Cineraria

Cineraria

C. stellata

C. stellata: singles: gdn origin. Hybs derived from *Senecio cruentus*, a Canary Is sp. Useful as pot plants and in gdns in warm countries. Lvs big, light green, fls daisy-like, 3 in wide in round heads and clean cols from red-pink to white and blue. Best from seed and may be treated as biennials. *Ht, Spd:* 18 in; *Fl:* 12–3, 6; *Z:* NF

Clematis

Clematis

C. integrifolia

C. integrifolia: S Eur. Woody sp, needs support. Lvs dark green, oval, pointed, clasping. Fls deep blue, bell-shaped, 1½ in diam. Slow from seed, difficult by div. *Ht:* to 4 ft; *Spd:* 2 ft; *Fl:* 6–8; *Z:* Arct

C. recta: Eur. Free-flowering, frag, straggling bush. Lvs divided, the best sorts are purplish. Fls ¾ in diam, seed heads fluffy. *Ht:* to 4 ft; *Spd:* 3 ft; *Fl:* 6–7; *Z:* Arct

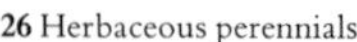

Coreopsis

Coreopsis, Tickseed

C. verticillata 'Grandiflora'

G. grandiflora: S USA. Lfy branching per. Lvs smooth, green, fls bright yellow, daisy-like to 1½ in wide. 'Mayfield Giant' and 'Sunburst' are among the best cvs. *Ht:* 3 ft; *Spd:* 30 in; *Fl:* 6–8; *Z:* PF

C. verticillata*★*: E USA. Neat and bushy; bedecked with yellow stars. 'Grandiflora' is larger and better. *Ht:* 30 in; *Spd:* 20 in; *Fl:* 6–9; *Z:* PF

Cortaderia

Pampas grass

C. selloana (= argentea): Temp S Amer. Giant grass with narrow glaucous lvs and immense silky white fl plumes. 'Sunningdale' is shorter but excellent. Burn off dead lvs in wtr. *Ht:* to 10 ft; *Spd:* 6 ft; *Fl:* 10; *Z:* F

Crambe

Crambe

C. cordifolia

C. cordifolia*★*: Caucasus. Spectacular with huge limp dark green lvs below much-branched stems bearing clouds of tiny frag white fls. Stems whiten when dead and are handsome in wtr. *Ht, Spd:* 6½ ft; *Fl:* 6–7; *Z:* PF

C. maritima Seakale: Eur. Pale grey elaborately lobed lvs; frag white cabbage fls. Often grown for its edible stems. *Ht:* 2 ft; *Spd:* 30 in; *Fl:* 6; *Z:* PF

Dactylorrhiza

Orchid

***D. (= Orchis) elata*★** Algerian orchid: Algeria. An easy garden orchid with long spikes of rich violet-purple fls and plain green lvs. Propagate by dividing tubers. *Ht:* 2 ft; *Spd:* 8 in; *Fl:* 6; *Z:* PF

Delphinium

Delphinium

The true-blue aristocrats of the summer border: magnificent flower spikes above pale, fingery leaves.

D. hybrid 'Blue Jade'

D. hybs, Large-flowered*★*: Eur–W Asia. Mainly hybs of *D. elatum*, to 7 ft according to cv. Cols white through all shades of blue to rose-pink, red and yellow. Most have pronounced eye. Double-flowered cvs inc 'Alice Artindale'. Prop named sorts by div or cuttings. *Spd:* 30 in; *Fl:* 6–7; *Z:* Arct

D. belladonna hybs*★*: gdn origin. Shorter, bushier, longer flowering; often fl twice. Fls single, pale to violet-blue, white and rose-pink, e.g. 'Pink Sensation'. *Ht:* to 5 ft; *Spd:* 20 in; *Fl:* 6–7; *Z:* Arct

Dianthus

Pink, carnation

Short-lived, little plants including carnations, pinks and Sweet Williams. Most are evergreen with more or less narrow grey or greyish leaves. Many have an intensely sweet scent. All like limy, well-drained soil.

D. Garden pink 'Mrs Sinkins'

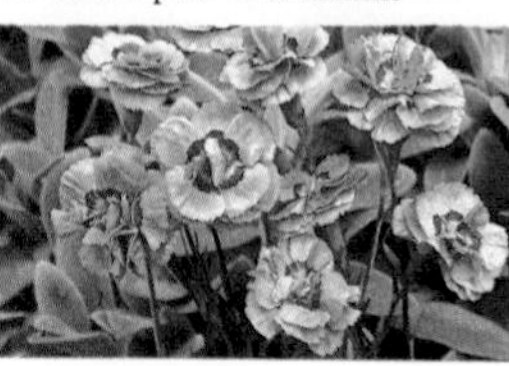

D. Garden pink 'Doris'

D. Border carnations: gdn origin. Range of dependable hardy carnations with wider glaucous lvs and more uprt habit than gdn pinks. Fls frag, white, pale yellow, pink, red or crimson, $1\frac{1}{2}$ in wide, ptls may be flecked. Prop by layers or cuttings (called pipings). *Ht:* 1 ft; *Spd:* to 18 in; *Fl:* 6–9; *Z:* F

D. Garden pinks: gdn origin. Richly frag edge-of-the-border plants derived from sev spp. Evergreen, narrow, glaucous, pointed lvs; fls carnation-like and usually with split sepal ring. Cols white, pink, red or purplish sometimes ringed with a white/crimson centre or flecked. 'Sam Barlow' is a ringed cv. Prop by pipings in July. *Ht:* 1 ft; *Spd:* 2 ft; *Fl:* 6–7; *Z:* PF

Dicentra

Dicentra

D. spectabilis

D. formosa: W N Amer. Tufty; lvs smooth, pale green, ferny. Mauve fls heart-shaped, pendulous, sev per stem. 'Bountiful' has blue-green lvs and plum-red fls. Prop by div. *Ht, Spd:* to 18 in; *Fl:* 4–6; *Z:* Arct

D. spectabilis* Dutchman's breeches, Bleeding heart: Siberia, Japan. V pretty: lvs v cut; locket-shaped rosy-red fls on arched stems. *Ht, Spd:* 18 in; *Fl:* 5–6; *Z:* Arct

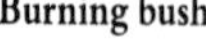

Dictamnus

Burning bush

D. albus: Eur, Asia. Robust with glossy aromatic lvs and v frag white open tubular fls. *D.a. purpureus* is common. *Ht:* 30 in; *Spd:* 2 ft; *Fl:* 6–7; *Z:* Arct

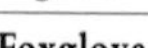

Digitalis

Foxglove

D. purpurea 'Excelsior'

D. grandiflora (= ambigua): Eur. Creamy-yellow 2 in fls and sage-green lvs. Not long-lived but easily renewed by seed or div. *Ht:* to 30 in; *Spd:* 1 ft; *Fl:* 7–8; *Z:* Arct

D. purpurea hybs: Eur. The common purple or white-flowered sp is biennial but some hybs, e.g. 'Excelsior Strain' are longer lived with wider col range. Fls tubular 2 in long on lfy spikes. *Ht:* to 5 ft; *Spd:* 30 in; *Fl:* 6–8; *Z:* Arct

Doronicum

Leopard's bane

A cheerful yellow daisy most notable for being much the earliest of its character—similar plants are more common later on.

D. *'Miss Mason':** gdn origin. Yellow daisy-flowered plant with heart-shaped toothed light green lvs. Fls 2½ in diam. Prop by div. *Ht:* 18 in; *Spd:* 2 ft; *Fl:* 4–6; *Z:* Arct
D. *plantagineum*: W. Eur. In flower early then gets tall and lfy. Lvs smooth, coarsely toothed. *Ht:* 30 in; *Spd:* 2 ft; *Fl:* 4–6; *Z:* Arct
D. *'Spring Beauty'*: gdn origin. Full-petalled yellow fls make solid early splashes of col. Lvs toothed. *Ht:* 18 in; *Spd:* 2 ft; *Fl:* 4–6; *Z:* Arct

D. 'Spring Beauty'

Echinacea

Purple or hedgehog coneflower

E. (= Rudbeckia) purpurea: USA. Lvs dark green, stems stout, branched. Large daisy-like burnished burgundy fls 4 in wide like old wicker beehives with central cone. 'White Lustre' good. *Ht:* 4 ft; *Spd:* 20 in; *Fl:* 8–9; *Z:* Arct

Echinops

Globe thistle

The name globe thistle perfectly describes these easy, tenacious plants with prickly leaves and drumstick flower heads.

***E. ritro**:** E Eur, W Asia. Sturdy plant with jagged lvs and round steely-blue heads of fl 2 in wide which are prickly to touch. For the back of the border. 'Taplow Blue' is lighter blue and taller, reaching 5 ft. Prop by div. *Ht:* to 4 ft; *Spd:* 2 ft; *Fl:* 7–8; *Z:* Arct

E. ritro

Epimedium

Barrenwort

In the department of tasteful understatement. Pretty little smooth green leaves on tall stems with unshowy flowers.

E. grandiflorum: Japan, Manchuria. Slowly spreading; 1 ft lvs have heart-shaped lflts on wiry stems; 1 in fls pale yellow but rose and white forms known. Remove lvs in Jan to show off fls. Prop by div. *Ht, Spd:* 1 ft; *Fl:* 5–6; *Z:* Arct
***E. perralderianum**:** Algeria. Has evergreen lvs and small yellow fls, sev per stem. Prop by div. *Ht:* 1 ft; *Spd:* 18 in; *Fl:* 5–6; *Z:* Arct
E. × versicolor: gdn origin. Young lvs reddish, turning green then bronze. Fls yellow, spls rose, spurs reddish. Sev selected sorts. *Ht, Spd:* 1 ft; *Fl:* 5; *Z:* Arct

E. × versicolor

Erigeron 

Fleabane

Fleabanes have been bred in all colours from pink to purple, single and double. The effect is of early Michaelmas daisies.

E. hybrid 'Mrs F.H. Beale'

E. aurantiacus: Turkestan. Velvety-leaved short-lived per. Fls v full-petalled, bright orange. *Ht, Spd:* 1 ft; *Fl:* 6–7; *Z:* Arct

E. hybrids: gdn origin. Daisy-like fls range in col from mauve, rose-pink to blue-violet or white. Best inc 'Darkest of All' violet-blue; 'Prosperity' mauve-blue. *Ht:* to 30 in; *Spd:* 20 in; *Fl:* 6–8/9; *Z:* Arct

Eryngium  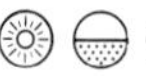 

Eryngium

E. tripartitum*: origin unknown. Splendid tall thistle with dark green basal lvs and spiky steel-blue fls. *Ht:* 4 ft; *Spd:* 3 ft; *Fl:* 8–9; *Z:* Arct

Eupatorium  

Eupatorium

E. purpureum* Joe-pye weed: N Amer. Striking tall late-flowering per; enjoys moist soil. Purplish fls on darker stks in flat heads 5 in wide. Stems lfy, stiff and pointed long into wtr. *Ht:* to 7 ft; *Spd:* 3 ft; *Fl:* 8–9; *Z:* Arct

Euphorbia    

Spurge

Unlikely relations of some fierce cactus-like subtropicals; fashionably low-key in shades of green and (in one case) orange.

E. griffithii 'Fire Glow'

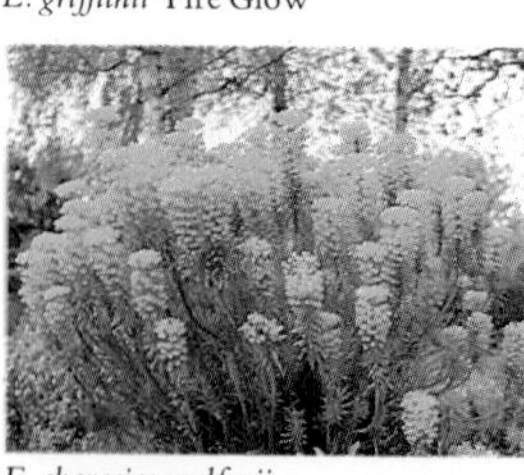
E. characias wulfenii

E. characias*: Eur. Shrubby evergreen, lvs narrow, grey-green finely hry. Sp has green, brown-centred fls unlike *E. c. wulfenii* with yellow-green fls and yellow centres. *Ht, Spd:* 4 ft; *Fl:* 4–5; *Z:* F

E. griffithii 'Fire Glow'*: W Asia. Outstanding for its heads of flame-red fls 4 in wide effective over a long period. V densely bushy, lvs thin. Runs. *Ht:* 30 in; *Spd:* 2 ft; *Fl:* 4–6; *Z:* PF

E. polychroma (= epithymoides)*: Eur. Closely packed stems grow into dense mound of dark green lvs. Fls brilliant chrome yellow. *Ht:* 18 in; *Spd:* 2 ft; *Fl:* 4–5; *Z:* PF

E. robbiae*: Asia Minor. Rosettes of dark evergreen lvs and narrow plumes of light green fls. Invaluable ground cover. Stoloniferous. *Ht, Spd:* 2 ft; *Fl:* 4–5; *Z:* PF

Fascicularia    

Fascicularia

F. bicolor: Chile. A nearly-hardy bromeliad suitable for warm ledges. Lvs narrow, v toothed in rosettes. Fls pale blue in conspicuous flesh-pink bracts. Prop by div. *Ht:* 20 in; *Spd:* 2 ft; *Fl:* 8–9; *Z:* SF

Festuca

Fescue

F. ovina Sheep's fescue: Temp zones. Fine-lvd tuft-forming grass. *F. glauca* is blue-green leaved and best for garden purposes. Good edging plant. Prop by div or seed. *Ht, Spd:* 10 in; *Fl:* 7–8; *Z:* Arct

Filipendula

Filipendula

F. hexapetala Dropwort: Eur, Asia. Neat, clump-forming; lvs finely cut, rich green. Fls creamy-white in flat fluffy heads. 'Flore Pleno' double-flowered more effective. *Ht:* to 3 ft; *Spd:* 18 in; *Fl:* 6–7; *Z:* Arct

F. ulmaria Meadowsweet: Eur, Asia. As above but fls v frag. Young lvs of 'Aurea' golden-green. *Ht:* to 3 ft; *Spd:* 18 in; *Fl:* 6–8; *Z:* Arct

F. ulmaria 'Aurea'

Francoa

Bridal wreath

***F. sonchifolia**:** Chile. Outstandingly graceful plant bearing long stems of delicate pale pink fls over substantial rosettes of fiddle-shaped deeply lobed lvs. Prop by div, seed. *Ht:* 30 in; *Spd:* 18 in; *Fl:* 7; *Z:* SF

Gaillardia

Gaillardia

G. × *grandiflora*: gdn origin. Short-lived but valuable, producing large daisy-like fls, 3 in wide, of yellow, orange or mahogany col over a long period. Lvs oblong, softly hry. 'Ipswich Beauty' orange-red, tipped yellow and 'Wirral Flame' mahogany red, tipped yellow, are good cvs. Prop by root or basal cuttings. *Ht:* to 30 in; *Spd:* 18 in; *Fl:* 6–9; *Z:* Arct

G. × *grandiflora*

Galax

Galax

G. urceolata (= aphylla): E N Amer. Has rounded shiny lvs that become a reddish-bronze in autumn. Fls white in slender spikes. Prop by div. *Ht:* 18 in; *Spd:* 1 ft; *Fl:* 6–7; *Z:* Arct

Galega

Goat's rue

G. × *hartlandii*: gdn origin. Bushy per "sweet pea". Fls small, lilac or white in 1½ in spikes. Lvs grey-green. Prop by div. *Ht:* to 5 ft; *Spd:* 3 ft; *Fl:* 6–7; *Z:* Arct

G. orientalis: Caucasus. A little shorter but otherwise v like above. Fls bluish-white in 1 in spikes. Invasive. Prop by div. *Ht:* 4 ft; *Spd:* 3 ft; *Fl:* 6–7; *Z:* Arct

G. × *hartlandii*

Gazania

Gazania

***G.* × *splendens*:** gdn origin. Lvs narrow, evergreen, rich green above, silvery-white beneath. Daisy-like fls 3 in wide in brilliant yellow, orange and dark red open in sun. *Ht, Spd:* 1 ft; *Fl:* 6–10; *Z:* NF

Gentiana

Gentian

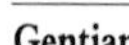

G. asclepiadea

G. asclepiadea Willow gentian: Eur. Arching lfy stems with paired willow-like lvs and rich gentian-blue fls. Prop by seed. *Ht:* 30 in; *Spd:* 18 in; *Fl:* 8–9; *Z:* PF

G. lutea Gentian root: Eur. Robust and v unlike other spp in looks with glaucous, puckered lvs and star-shaped yellow 1 in fls followed by attractive seed heads. Prop by seed. *Ht:* 3 ft; *Spd:* 2 ft; *Fl:* 7–8; *Z:* PF

Geranium

Cranesbill

The cranesbills, not to be confused with the tender South African geraniums (p 16) are hearty, reliable ground-smotherers with dense leafage of great character and a long season of blue, pink or white flowers.

G. 'Johnson's Blue'

G. endressii 'Wargrave Pink'

G. × *magnificum*

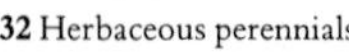

***G. endressii* 'Wargrave Pink':** Pyrenees. Lfy sprawler. Fls bright pink, open, 1 in wide, lvs small, veined, lobed. Prop by div. *Ht, Spd:* 2 ft; *Fl:* 6–7, 10; *Z:* PF

***G.* 'Johnson's Blue':** Gdn origin. Vig, lfy hyb producing generous quantities of luminescent blue fls to 2 in wide. Prop by div. *Ht:* 18 in; *Spd:* 2 ft; *Fl:* 6–9; *Z:* PF

***G. macrorrhizum**:** S Eur. Excellent almost evergreen ground cover plant with pale green aromatic lvs that redden in aut. Fls mauve-pink, 1 in wide. 'Walter Ingwersen' is clear pink; there is also a white form. Prop by div. *Ht:* 1 ft; *Spd:* 18 in; *Fl:* 5–7; *Z:* Arct

***G.* × *magnificum* (= *ibericum, platypetalum*)*:** Caucasus–Iran. Clump-forming hyb with rounded crinkly nettle-green lvs and sticky fl stalks. Fls violet-blue, 1 in diam. Good aut col. Prop by div. *Ht, Spd:* 2 ft; *Fl:* 6–8; *Z:* Arct

G. pratense Meadow cranesbill: N Eur. A clump of deeply divided lvs colouring well in aut. Fls bright blue to 2 in wide. White and blue double-flowered forms available, e.g. 'Caeruleum Plenum'. Prop spp by seed or all by div. *Ht, Spd:* 2 ft; *Fl:* 6–9; *Z:* Arct

Gerbera

Gerbera

G. jamesonii Barbeton daisy: S Africa. Brilliantly coloured daisy, fls 5 in and more across on a plant hry in all its parts. Sp fls bright orange. *G.* × *jamesonii*, the Transvaal daisy, varies from pink to red, yellow and orange shades. Prop from side shoots or seed. *Ht:* 18 in; *Spd:* 15 in; *Fl:* 5–6; *Z:* F

G. jamesonii

Geum

Geum

G. 'Borisii': Bulgaria. Good front-of-the-border hyb. Lvs rounded and hry, 1 in fls like open buttercups but glowing orange. Prop by div. *Ht, Spd:* 1 ft; *Fl:* 6–9; *Z:* Arct
G. chiloense: Chile. Parent of 2 or 3 more useful hybs inc × 'Mrs Bradshaw' bright red; × 'Fire Opal' orange-red; × 'Lady Stratheden' golden yellow. Prop by div, seed. *Ht, Spd:* 2 ft; *Fl:* 5–6; *Z:* PF

G. chiloense × 'Mrs Bradshaw'

Gypsophila

Gypsophila

G. paniculata Baby's breath: Eur, Siberia. A tangle of pale green stems and a froth of white ¾ in fls. 'Bristol Fairy' has double fls; 'Rosy Veil' (18 in) pale pink; likes lime. *Ht:* 3 ft; *Spd:* 4 ft; *Fl:* 6–8; *Z:* Arct

Hedychium

Ginger lily

H. densiflorum: Him. Rhizomatous plant with aspidistra-like soft green lvs clasping the stems. Fls orange-red *c.* 2 in wide in a broad terminal spike. Easy to grow, harder to find. Prop by div, seed. *Ht:* 3 ft; *Spd:* 18 in; *Fl:* 5–7; *Z:* NF

H. densiflorum

Helenium

Helenium

H. autumnale Sneezeweed: Canada, E USA. Valuable spp and cvs for late smr. Single daisy-type fls with pronounced centre disc. 'Moerheim Beauty' mahogany; 'The Bishop' rich yellow. *Ht:* 4 ft; *Spd:* 20 in; *Fl:* 7–9; *Z:* Arct

Helianthus

Sunflower

H. decapetalus: C USA, Canada. Perennial sunflower with coarse lvs and stiff stems. The selection 'Loddon Gold' has deep yellow semi-double fls 3 in wide. Prop by div. *Ht:* to 5 ft; *Spd:* 2 ft; *Fl:* 8–10; *Z:* Arct

Helichrysum

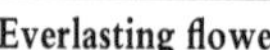

Everlasting flower

H. × 'Sulphur Light' (= × 'Schwefellicht'): gdn origin. Flat heads of sulphur-coloured 1½ in fls over woolly grey-white lvs. One of the few hardy pers of the genus and well worth growing. *Ht, Spd:* 18 in; *Fl:* 6–8; *Z:* PF

Helictotrichon

Helictotrichon

H. sempervirens (= Avena candida): Eur. Splendid blue-grey grass forming neat clumps with graceful arching fl stems effective over a long period. Prop by seed, div in March. *Ht:* 3 ft; *Spd:* 15 in; *Fl:* 6–9; *Z:* Arct

Heliopsis

Heliopsis

H. scabra: N Amer. Lusty coarse-lvd plant. Stiff stems and common yellow daisy-fls 3 in wide. 'Golden Plume' has double fls acceptable to gardening "gentry". Prop by div. *Ht:* 4 ft; *Spd:* 2 ft; *Fl:* 7–9; *Z:* Arct

Heliotropium

Heliotrope, Cherry pie

H. peruvianum

***H. peruvianum**:** Peru. The common heliotrope has flat heads, 3 in or more wide, of deliciously fragrant violet or mauve fls. 'Marina' is deeper in colour. Planted out annually where it is not hardy. Prop by cuttings. *Ht:* to 3 ft; *Spd:* 3 ft; *Fl:* 5–9; *Z:* NF

Helleborus

Hellebore

Stands up to the winter and announces spring with long-lasting flowers of incomparable texture and quality. Most are evergreen.

H. corsicus

H. orientalis

***H. corsicus (= argutifolius, lividus corsicus)**:** Corsica, Sardinia, Balearics. Has cup-shaped apple-green fls 2 in wide and leathery glaucous lvs. Inclined to sprawl; prop by seed. *Ht:* 2 ft; *Spd:* 3 ft; *Fl:* 4–5; *Z:* PF

H. foetidus* Stinking hellebore: Eur. Lvs cut into long thin lflts on almost shrubby stems; 1 in fls cup-shaped, green, edged soft maroon. *Ht, Spd:* 20 in; *Fl:* 2–5; *Z:* PF

H. niger* Christmas rose: Eur, W Asia. Saucer-shaped sol white fls to 2 in wide on short stems. Ptls often pink on their backs, lvs divided, dark. Protect fls to keep them clean; can fl by Christmas. *Ht:* 1 ft; *Spd:* 18 in; *Fl:* 12–2; *Z:* Arct

H. orientalis* Lenten rose: Greece, Asia Minor. True white-fld sp rare but many excellent hybs with up to 4 fls, each 2½ in wide, on a stem; some fls spotted within. *Ht:* 18 in; *Spd:* 2 ft; *Fl:* 2–4; *Z:* PF

Day lily

Each day lily lasts only a day but the supply is endless in all colours from lemon to mahogany over brilliantly green leaves.

***H. flava**:** China. Smaller than *H. fulva* with sweet-scented pale yellow lily-fls 4 in wide and pretty narrow lvs. Fls early. Spreads by runners but not invasive; prop by div. *Ht, Spd:* 2 ft; *Fl:* 5–7; *Z:* Arct
***H. fulva* 'Kwanso Flore Pleno'** Double day lily: Japan. Clumps of smooth bulb-like strap-shaped lvs with green stems each bearing sev burnt orange funnel-shaped semi-double fls 4 in across; indiv fls last only 1 day. Rts a mass of small rhizomes. Prop by div. *Ht:* to 4 ft; *Spd:* 3 ft; *Fl:* 6–8; *Z:* Arct
***H. gdn hybs**:** gdn origin. The existence of the Hemerocallis Society indicates the no of hybs. Mainly to 4 ft × 3 ft but sev dwarf cvs. Fls in all shades of yellow and orange, also pink, maroon and greenish yellow. *Fl:* 6–8; *Z:* PF

H. fulva 'Kwanso Flore Pleno'

H. flava

Hesperis

Hesperis

H. matronalis Sweet rocket: S Eur–Siberia. Sweetly frag short-lived per; enjoys lime. Narrow 4 in lvs and small white, mauve or purple fls in loose 18 in clusters. Some doubles. *Ht:* 3 ft; *Spd:* 18 in; *Fl:* 6–7; *Z:* Arct

Heuchera

Coral flower

Clumps of strong low leaves are the base for airy spikes of bell flowers of various sizes and many colours.

H. × brizoides: gdn origin. Matted clumps of heart-shaped mottled dark green lvs are the foil for dainty stems liberally adorned with little bell-shaped fls brilliantly coloured in shades of pink and red, e.g. 'Coral Plume' coral-red. Prop by div. *Ht:* 2 ft; *Spd:* 1 ft; *Fl:* 6–10; *Z:* Arct
H. cylindrica 'Greenfinch': N Amer. Cv interesting to flower arrangers. Lvs roughly heart-shaped, dull green; fl stems stiff and erect bearing 1 ft spikes of greenish fls. Prop by division. *Ht:* 3 ft; *Spd:* 15 in; *Fl:* 6–10; *Z:* Arct
H. sanguinea Coral bells: SW USA, Mexico. Lvs more mottled than *H. × brizoides* and fl spikes shorter, otherwise sim. Good hybs inc × 'Shere Variety' bright scarlet; × 'Pearl Drops' pearly white. Prop by div after flowering. *Ht:* 18 in; *Spd:* 1 ft; *Fl:* 6; *Z:* Arct

H. sanguinea × 'Sunset'

H. sanguinea 'Red Spangles'

Hibiscus

Hibiscus

H. moscheutos Swamp rose mallow: E USA. Hry-stemmed with soft, toothed lvs hry on the underside. Fls to 11 in across, rose-pink, hollyhock-like with a satin sheen. Hybs range through pink to crimson in colour. Prop from seed. *Ht:* 3 ft; *Spd:* 2 ft+; *Fl:* 6–8; *Z:* SF

Hosta (= Funkia)

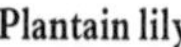

Plantain lily

H. fortunei 'Aureomarginata'

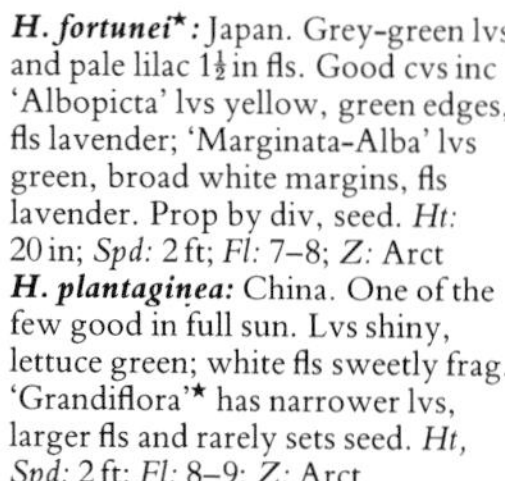

***H. fortunei**:** Japan. Grey-green lvs and pale lilac $1\frac{1}{2}$ in fls. Good cvs inc 'Albopicta' lvs yellow, green edges, fls lavender; 'Marginata-Alba' lvs green, broad white margins, fls lavender. Prop by div, seed. *Ht:* 20 in; *Spd:* 2 ft; *Fl:* 7–8; *Z:* Arct
H. plantaginea: China. One of the few good in full sun. Lvs shiny, lettuce green; white fls sweetly frag. 'Grandiflora'* has narrower lvs, larger fls and rarely sets seed. *Ht, Spd:* 2 ft; *Fl:* 8–9; *Z:* Arct
***H. sieboldiana (= glauca)**:** Japan. V large-lvd sp also good in sun. Glaucous lvs to 1 ft wide; fls a faded lavender. Good buff aut col. *Ht:* 30 in; *Spd:* 2 ft; *Fl:* 7–8; *Z:* Arct
***H. 'Thomas Hogg'**:** gdn origin. One of the best cvs: dark green lvs with narrow white edges, fls lilac (unlike *H. crispula* with undulating lvs and white fls in July–Aug). Prop by div. *Ht, Spd:* 18 in; *Fl:* 6–7; *Z:* Arct

H. fortunei 'Albopicta'

Incarvillea

Incarvillea

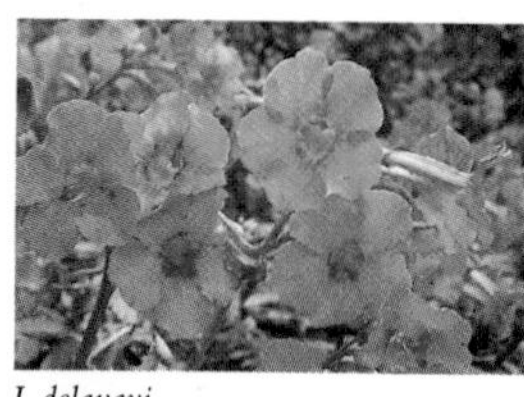

I. delavayi

I. delavayi: W China, Tibet. Lvs deep shining green divided into several lflts. Fls to 3 in, wide-mouthed trumpets of bright rose-red, several on a stem. *I. mairei* 'Bees Ruby' is pale pink and only 7 in tall. Prop by div or seed. *Ht:* 18 in; *Spd:* 1 ft; *Fl:* 5–6; *Z:* PF

Inula

Inula

I. ensifolia

I. ensifolia: Caucasus. Dwarf daisy-flowered front-of-the-border plant. Narrow lvs, yellow 2 in fls, 1 or more per stem. Prop by seed, div. *Ht, Spd:* 1 ft; *Fl:* 8; *Z:* Arct
***I. magnifica**:** Caucasus. Straggling great lfy plant. Stout chocolate-coloured hry stems and flat heads of golden yellow fls. Taller and coarser than *I. helenium* (Elecampane). Prop by div, seed. *Ht:* to 6 ft; *Spd:* 3 ft; *Fl:* 6–8; *Z:* Arct

Iris

Very consistent in design, irises are most diverse in life style, between them flowering all year in conditions from dust to mud.

I. Bearded German iris: gdn origin. Typical border irises. Lvs glaucous, sword-shaped, stems branched, may bear sev large fls each with 3 inner incurved ptls (standards) and 3 larger reflexed ptls (falls). Fleshy rhizomes must not be buried. Select from huge var of cols and combinations. Prop by div. *Ht:* 3 ft; *Spd:* 10 in; *Fl:* 6; *Z:* Arct

I. foetidissima Stinking gladwyn: Eur. Evergreen lvs arching, fls inconspicuous but pods have bright orange seeds. Giant, white varieg and yellow/mauve 'Citrina' forms grown. *Ht, Spd:* 2 ft; *Fl:* 5–6; *Z:* PF

I. germanica Common iris: Eur. Has glaucous lvs and frag purple fls to 5 in wide in gdn form. Sev brown cvs inc 'Brazilia'. Needs lime. *Ht:* to 3 ft; *Spd:* 10 in; *Fl:* 5–6; *Z:* Arct

I. unguicularis (= stylosa)* Winter-flowering iris: Algeria, Med. Bright blue fls to 3 in wide nestle among a dense clump of thin green lvs in mild periods in wtr. Selected forms cherished. Prop by div. *Ht:* 1 ft; *Spd:* 2 ft; *Fl:* 11–3; *Z:* PF

I. germanica 'Brazilia'

I. unguicularis

Kirengeshoma

Kirengeshoma

K. palmata*: Japan. Late-flowering Japanese woodlander enjoying moist soil. Lvs opposite, strikingly vine-like on arching stems. Long, waxy creamy-yellow buds open to shuttlecock-shaped fls up to 1½ in across. Prop by div or seed. *Ht:* 3 ft; *Spd:* 2 ft; *Fl:* 9–10; *Z:* Arct

Kniphofia

Red hot poker, Torch lily

South African plants not guaranteed hardy. They make the most telling exclamation marks in a brimming late summer garden.

K. caulescens*: S Africa. Distinct sp. Lvs in rosettes, evergreen, succ, sword-shaped. Fl spikes to 1 ft, opening soft rose-red, turning pale greenish-yellow. Prop by div or offsets. *Ht:* to 5 ft; *Spd:* 3 ft; *Fl:* 7–10; *Z:* PF

K. dwarf hybs: gdn origin. Many unusual cols inc 'Maid of Orleans'* ivory; 'Jenny Bloom' salmon-peach; 'Dainty Maid' cream and white. Dwarf sp *K. galpinii* has orange fls. *Ht:* 30 in; *Spd:* 2 ft; *Fl:* 7–9; *Z:* PF

K. tall hybs: gdn origin. Sev tall hybs stand out splendidly. 'Bees Lemon' is pale yellow; 'Royal Standard' lemon and scarlet; 'Samuel's Sensation' coral red. *Ht:* 4 ft; *Spd:* 30 in; *Fl:* 7–9; *Z:* PF

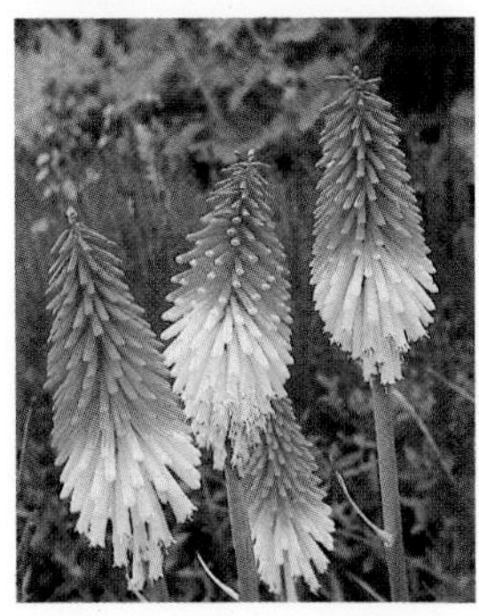

K. tall hybrid 'Royal Standard'

Lamium

Deadnettle

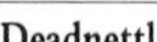

L. maculatum

L. maculatum Dwarf deadnettle: Eur, N Africa, W Asia. Neat ground-covering plant with small nettle-like opposite evergreen lvs each with central white stripe. Fls tubular, 2-lipped, usually purple and *c.* 1 in long. 'Album' white and 'Roseum' pink are good, so are 'Beacon Silver' silvery-white lvs and 'Aureum' golden-yellow but may scorch in sun. Prop by div. *Ht, Spd:* 1 ft; *Fl:* 5–7; *Z:* Arct

Lamiastrum

Lamiastrum Archangel

L. luteum 'Variegatum' (= Lamium galeobdolon, Galeobdolon luteum): Eur. Vig deadnettle spreading widely by stolons. Silver variegated lvs and clustered light yellow fls in axils. *Ht:* to 18 in; *Spd:* 5 ft; *Fl:* 5–7; *Z:* Arct

Lathyrus

Sweet pea

L. vernus

L. (= Orobus) vernus: Eur. Forms a shining clump of vetch or pea-like lfy stems with ½ in purple and blue fls. There are also white and pink-flowered forms. Prop by div or seed. *Ht, Spd:* 1 ft; *Fl:* 5–6; *Z:* Arct

Leonitis

Lion's tail

L. leonorus

L. leonurus: S Africa. Technically a shrub but cut down annually in most countries and thus included as an herbaceous per. Lvs narrow, sage green, hry. Fls tubular in lf axils, bright orange. Prop by cuttings. *Ht:* to 7½ ft; *Spd:* 30 in; *Fl:* 10–12; *Z:* NF

Liatris

Gayfeather

L. spicata Spiked gayfeather: USA. Grassy-lvd, clump forming, producing stout 1 ft spikes of feathery purple fls. *Ht:* 2 ft; *Spd:* 1 ft; *Fl:* 9; *Z:* Arct

Libertia

Libertia

L. formosa: Chile. Narrow grassy lvs and thin stems bearing small pure white saucer-fls in dense clusters. Prop by div or seed. *Ht:* 30 in; *Spd:* 2 ft; *Fl:* 5; *Z:* F

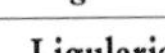

Ligularia

L.* (= *Senecio*) *przewalskii: N China. Striking chocolate-stemmed plant with deeply lobed lvs and terminal 2 ft spikes of little yellow fls. 'The Rocket' is a robust form worth growing. Prop by div. *Ht:* 5 ft; *Spd:* 30 in; *Fl:* 7–9; *Z:* PF

L. przewalskii

Limonium

Sea lavender, Statice

L. latifolium: Bulgaria, S USSR. Has rosettes of wide green leathery lvs and wiry stems carrying a froth of papery lavender-blue fls in groups to 9 in long. 'Blue Cloud' is especially good. Dries well. Prop by div, root cuttings. *Ht:* 18 in; *Spd:* 2 ft; *Fl:* 5–7; *Z:* Arct

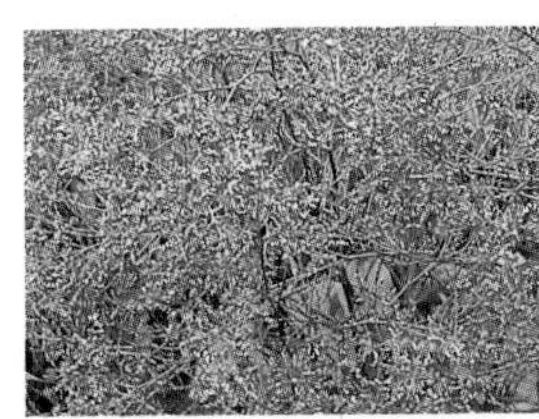

L. latifolium 'Blue Cloud'

Linum

Flax

L. narbonnense: S Eur. An erect sp with fine glaucous lvs and glorious shining blue funnel-shaped fls 1 in wide produced for many weeks. Sev named sorts available. Needs frequent renewing by cuttings or seed. *Ht, Spd:* 18 in; *Fl:* 6–9; *Z:* Arct
L. perenne: Eur. Fls a paler blue and lvs equally fine but greener. Pink and white flowered sorts known, also 'Tetra Red'. *Ht:* to 18 in; *Spd:* 1 ft; *Fl:* 6–8; *Z:* Arct

L. narbonnense

Liriope

Lily turf

L.* (= *Ophiopogon*) *muscari: E Asia. Dark green grassy lvs in dense clumps sometimes used for edging. Fls tiny, rich violet-blue bells crowded on 4 in spikes. Named sorts, also white-flowered and yellow-variegated forms are available. Prop by div. *Ht:* 1 ft; *Spd:* 15 in; *Fl:* 9–11; *Z:* PF

L. muscari

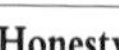

Lunaria

Honesty

L. rediviva* Perennial honesty: Eur. Perennial form of the biennial honesty with sim big basal lvs and paler lavender fls. Produces attractive flat, papery seed pods after flowering. *Ht:* 30 in; *Spd:* 2 ft; *Fl:* 4–6; *Z:* Arct

Lupinus

Lupin

L. hybrid Russell lupins

L. garden hybrids: gdn origin. Best known are the Russell lupins developed from sev spp using *L. polyphyllus* from N Amer as the dominant parent. Prefer a not too rich acid or neutral soil. Fl range includes all cols except green, including bicolours. Lvs are silky, round, divided or pleated. Prop by seed, basal cuttings. *Ht:* to 4 ft; *Spd:* 30 in; *Fl:* 5–6; *Z:* Arct

Lychnis

Campion, Catchfly

L. chalcedonica

L. flos-jovis

L. chalcedonica: E USSR. Tall hry plant with small more or less oval lvs and brilliant orange-red fls in roughly cross-shaped heads 4 in long. Prop by div, seed. *Ht:* to 3 ft; *Spd:* 18 in; *Fl:* 6–8; *Z:* Arct

L. coronaria (= tomentosa, Agrostemma coronaria) Rose campion: Eur. Ever-grey woolly-stemmed plant with grey-white basal lvs and single bright cerise or white fls 1½ in across. Seeds itself freely. *Ht:* 30 in; *Spd:* 20 in; *Fl:* 7–8; *Z:* Arct

L. flos-jovis Flower of Jove: C Alps. Whiter than above and just as woolly. Fls are purple, white or scarlet and ½ in wide. 'Hort's Variety' is shorter and has pink fls. Prop by seed. *Ht:* to 2 ft; *Spd:* 1 ft; *Fl:* 6–7; *Z:* Arct

Lysimachia

Loosestrife

Upright spikes of yellow or white: primula relations not to be confused with the purple loosestrife (*Lythrum*).

L. clethroides

L. clethroides: China, Japan. The white fls are buddleia-like, arched over and turned up at the tips. Lvs undistinguished but col well in aut. Inclined to run; prop by div. *Ht:* to 3 ft; *Spd:* 2 ft; *Fl:* 7–9; *Z:* Arct

L. punctata: Asia Minor. Uprt plant with green pointed oval lvs and whorls of yellow star-like fls in 8 in spikes. Can be invasive. Prop by div or seed. *Ht:* to 3 ft; *Spd:* 2 ft; *Fl:* 6–8; *Z:* Arct

Lythrum

Loosestrife

L. salicaria Purple loosestrife: N temp zones, Aust. Bushy; lvs narrow on slim stems. Long spikes of red/purple fls effective for weeks. 'Robert' rose-carmine a good cv. *Ht:* 3 ft; *Spd:* 20 in; *Fl:* 6–9; *Z:* Arct
L. virgatum: Asia Minor. Smaller and less vig; fls purple. 'The Rocket' is rose-pink; 'Firecandle' rosy red. *Ht:* 2 ft; *Spd:* 15 in; *Fl:* 7–9; *Z:* Arct

L. virgatum

Macleaya

Plume poppy

***M. cordata**:** China, Japan. Invasive architectural plant with magnificent lobed glaucous lvs, milky white beneath with bright orange sap in their veins. Terminal plumes of off-white tubular fls. Prop by div. *Ht:* to 8 ft; *Spd:* 30 in; *Fl:* 8–9; *Z:* Arct
***M. microcarpa* (= *Bocconia cordata*):** China. Tall plumes of pinky-buff fls. 'Coral Plume' is deeper in col. *Ht:* 8 ft; *Spd:* 3 ft; *Fl:* 7–9; *Z:* Arct

M. microcarpa

Malva

Mallow

M. alcea: Eur. Bushy sp with bright green lobed downy lvs and purplish-rose shuttlecock fls to 2 in wide. 'Fastigiata' is more uprt with reddish fls. *Ht:* to 4 ft; *Spd:* 30 in; *Fl:* 7–10; *Z:* Arct
M. moschata Musk mallow: Eur. Finely dissected dark green lvs and long-lasting pink fls 2 in wide. 'Alba' is white. *Ht:* to 30 in; *Spd:* 20 in; *Fl:* 5–10; *Z:* Arct

M. moschata

Meconopsis

Meconopsis

The genus of the fabulous Himalayan blue poppy has members of many colours—all outstandingly beautiful in flower and leaf.

***M. grandis**:** Nepal, Tibet, Sikkim. Easier and longer lived than *M. betonicifolia* (Himalayan blue poppy). Lvs oblong, toothed, slightly bristly in a handsome clump. Fls to 5 in wide, nodding, purple-blue, poppy-shaped. Prop by seed. *Ht:* 3 ft; *Spd:* 2 ft; *Fl:* 5–6; *Z:* PF
M. regia: Nepal. Tall yellow-flowered and usually bi. Lvs hry, silvery or golden, fls sev on a branching stem. Prop by seed. *Ht:* to 5 ft; *Spd:* 6 ft; *Fl:* 6–7; *Z:* PF

M. grandis

Melissa

Balm

M. officinalis Lemon balm: Eur. Deadnettle-like softly hry lvs strongly lemon-scented when crushed. Fls small, white. 'Aurea' has lvs splashed with butter-yellow variegation. *Ht:* 2 ft; *Spd:* 20 in; *Fl:* 6–10; *Z:* Arct

Mertensia

Mertensia

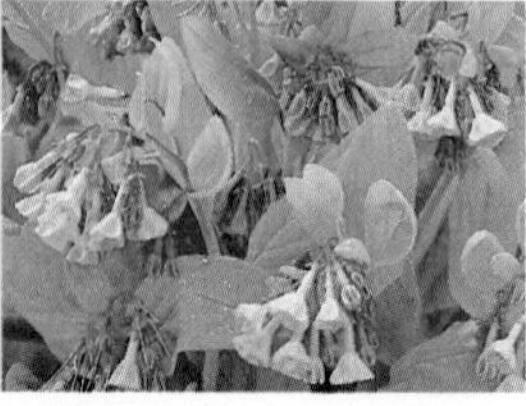

M. virginica

M. virginica Virginia cowslip: Virginia. Purple/blue tubular 1 in fls in drooping heads over smooth blue-grey spatula-shaped lvs in spring. Needs moisture and cool conditions. Prop by div, seed. *Ht:* 18 in; *Spd:* 1 ft; *Fl:* 5–6; *Z:* Arct

Mimulus

Monkey flower

Vivid yellow, orange and red snapdragon-like flowers in profusion, commonly associated with bog gardens.

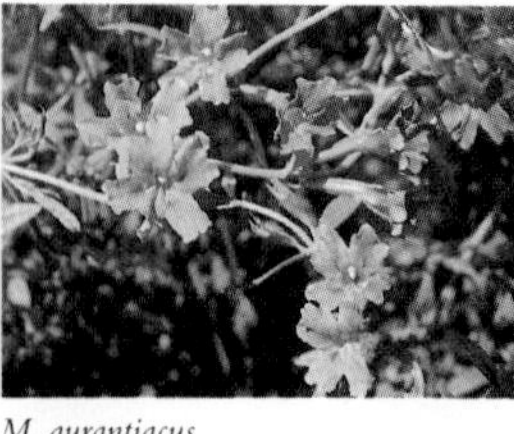

M. aurantiacus

M. aurantiacus (= Diplacus glutinosus): Cal. Shrubby; lvs sticky, fls bright orange funnel-shaped. Prop by cuttings, seed. *Ht:* to 5 ft; *Spd:* 20 in; *Fl:* 6–10; *Z:* F
M. cardinalis: Oregon–Mexico. Colourful, uprt plant with typical snapdragon or "monkey" fls in red or red and yellow. Lvs downy and tacky. 'Rose Queen' has pink fls. *Ht:* to 3 ft; *Spd:* 2 ft; *Fl:* 6–9; *Z:* PF

Mirabilis

Mirabilis

M. jalapa Marvel of Peru: Trop Amer. Has composite lvs and heads of tubular frag fls $1\frac{1}{2}$ in wide opening in afternoon. Fls white, pink or crimson, may be striped or blotched. Prop by seed. *Ht, Spd:* 2 ft; *Fl:* 6–9; *Z:* NF

Miscanthus

Miscanthus

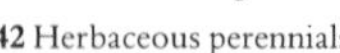

M. sinensis 'Variegatus'

M. sacchariflorus*: Asia, Siberia. Giant grey-green-leaved grass forming bamboo-like clumps. Fls terminal, feathery, brownish. Dies to pale buff; stands up well in wtr. *Ht:* 8 ft; *Spd:* 3 ft; *Fl:* 8–9; *Z:* PF
M. sinensis (= Eulalia japonica): China, Japan. Clump-forming with terminal plumes of silver-white pink-tinged fls. Lvs glaucous. 'Variegatus'* has white-striped lvs; 'Zebrinus'* wider lvs, horizontal yellow bands; 'Gracillimus' thin green lvs. *Ht:* to 5 ft; *Spd:* 30 in; *Fl:* 8–9; *Z:* Arct

Molinia

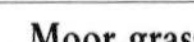

Moor grass

M. caerulea Purple moor grass: Eur, Asia Minor, N Asia. The sp is a dainty clump-forming grass found on wet soils. 'Variegata'* is valued for its yellowish-white striped lvs. Fls bluish. *Ht:* 15 in; *Spd:* 10 in; *Fl:* 7–9; *Z:* Arct

M. caerulea 'Variegata'

Monarda

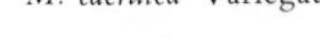

Bergamot

M. didyma* Oswego tea, Bee balm: N Amer. Paired lvs and hooded nettle-like scarlet fls in whorls. 'Cambridge Scarlet' a brighter shade and 'Croftway Pink' rose-pink good cvs. Also grown as a herb. *Ht:* 3 ft; *Spd:* 18 in; *Fl:* 6–9; *Z:* Arct

M. fistulosa*: Virginia. Similar to above. Sp has purple fls; 'Prairie Night' is deeper in col. Prefers dry soil. Prop by div. *Ht:* to 5 ft; *Spd:* 20 in; *Fl:* 6–8; *Z:* Arct

M. didyma

Morina

Morina

M. longifolia*: Nepal. Thistle-like in growth. Shining spiny lvs in whorls. Long-lasting 1 in fls are tubular, initially white, becoming pink then crimson. Prop by div or seed. *Ht:* to 3 ft; *Spd:* 1 ft; *Fl:* 6–8; *Z:* Arct

M. longifolia

Nepeta

Catmint

Coloured like lavender and prefers the same sunny well-drained position. Ideal ground cover for old pink and red roses.

N. × faasenii (= mussinii)*: gdn origin. Common sage-green-leaved aromatic; lavender-blue fls in whorls all smr. Excellent edging, carpeting. Prop by div, cuttings. *Ht, Spd:* 18 in; *Fl:* 5–9; *Z:* Arct

N. × gigantea: gdn origin. Hyb with lavender-blue fls. Like the blue-fld 'Souvenir d'André Chaudron' nearly twice above in height. *Spd:* 2 ft; *Fl:* 6–9; *Z:* Arct

N. × faasenii

Nicotiana

Tobacco plant

N. sylvestris: Argentina. Robust heads of narrow pendulous sweetly frag white 3½ in fls, best in late evening. Can last 2 or 3 years in a warm dry place. Prop by seed. *Ht:* 4 ft; *Spd:* 2 ft; *Fl:* 8–9; *Z:* F

Oenothera

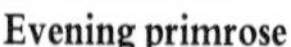

Evening primrose

O. missouriensis

***O. missouriensis (= macrocarpa)**:** SC USA. Sprawling; narrow dark lvs and wide open funnel-shaped lemon fls to 4 in wide. Prop by seed. *Ht:* 10 in; *Spd:* 2 ft; *Fl:* 6–8; *Z:* Arct
O. tetragona (= fruticosa): E N Amer. Dark basal lvs in rosettes; reddish slim stems and buds. Fls bright yellow, 1½ in wide. 'Fireworks' has bronze-red lvs. *Ht:* 18 in; *Spd:* 9 in; *Fl:* 6–8; *Z:* Arct

Omphalodes

Navelwort

O. cappadocica

O. cappadocica (= cornifolia): Lazistan, Cappadocia. Creeping plant with long-stalked, heart-shaped pointed lvs and taller loose sprays of pale blue 5-petalled flowers each ¾ in wide. Prop by div of rhizomatous rts. *Ht:* 9 in; *Spd:* 15 in; *Fl:* 5–7; *Z:* PF

Onopordon

Onopordon

O. acanthium

O. acanthium* Common cotton thistle, Scotch thistle: Eur, Siberia. Huge, sculptural branched white-woolly plant with fierce prickles. Large fls 2 in across are soft purple and thistle-shaped. Prop by seed. *Ht:* to 7 ft; *Spd:* 3 ft; *Fl:* 7; *Z:* PF

Osteospermum (= Dimorphotheca)

Cape marigold, African daisy

O. ecklonis

O. ecklonis: S Africa. Evergreen with shiny lvs and daisy fls 3 in wide on tall slim stems. Fls gleaming white with blue eye and silvery reverse to ptls. Prop by cuttings. *Ht, Spd:* 2 ft; *Fl:* 6–10; *Z:* SF
O. juncundum: S Africa. Paler lvs and smaller fls usually pale pink but sometimes white. Prop by cuttings. *Ht:* 15 in; *Spd:* 18 in; *Fl:* 6–10; *Z:* SF

Oxalis

Oxalis

O. lasiandra (= floribunda) Pink shamrock: Mexico. Blue-green lvs and bright pink fls ¾ in wide, which open in sunshine. Consider before cultivating; once established cannot be eradicated. *Ht, Spd:* 9 in; *Fl:* 6–10; *Z:* SF

Paeonia

Paeony

The aristocrats of the buttercup family with some of the most sumptuous flowers of spring and early summer. They are not hard to grow but like to be left undisturbed. Double forms last longest in bloom.

P. arietina: S Eur, Asia Minor. A less common sp with grey-green lvs and 5 in fls. Try 'Mother of Pearl' dusky pink and 'Northern Glory' a deeper pink. *Ht:* 2 ft; *Spd:* 2 ft; *Fl:* 5; *Z:* Arct

***P. lactiflora*★** Chinese paeony: Siberia, Mongolia. V beautiful with shining lvs and red-tinged stems. Single white frag fls 4 in wide. *Ht:* 30 in; *Spd:* 2 ft; *Fl:* 6; *Z:* Arct

P. officinalis*★*: S Eur. Common deep red single sp of old gdns. 'Rubra Pleno' double red, and double pink and white forms good. *Ht, Spd:* 28 in; *Fl:* 5; *Z:* Arct

P. gdn hybs*★*: Robust plants spectacular in fl. Rec are 'Albert Crousse' double, pink, frag; 'The Moor' single, deep crimson; 'Lemon Queen' anemone-flowered, white, yellow centre. *Ht:* 30 in; *Spd:* 2 ft; *Fl:* 6; *Z:* Arct

P. 'Saunders Hybs'*★*: Range created by Dr A. P. Saunders in the USA. Some, e.g. 'Chalice' single, white; 'Constance Spry' rich rosy-red, are v elegant with 4 in fls and fine lvs. *Ht:* 22 in; *Spd:* 2 ft; *Fl:* 6; *Z:* Arct

P. wittmanniana: NW Caucasus. An excellent taller sp. Lvs vig, puckered and shining, fls 5 in wide, single and light yellowish-green. 'Avant Garde' has soft warm pink fls. *P. mlokosewitschii* equally good with lemon-yellow fls. *Ht:* 3 ft; *Spd:* 2 ft; *Fl:* 4–5; *Z:* Arct

P. hybrid 'Chief Justice'

P. mlokosewitschii

P. officinalis 'Rosea-plena'

Papaver

Poppy

***P. orientale*★** Oriental poppy: Armenia. Tall hairy-leaved per; dies away in mid- to late summer. Huge single or double brilliantly coloured fls 4 in or more across are borne on hry stems to 3 ft high. Spp fiery orange; select cvs inc 'Perry's White' single, white, maroon blotch; 'Stormtorch' single, intense bright red; 'Salmon Glow' double, orange-salmon. Prop by div. *Ht:* to 3 ft; *Spd:* 2 ft; *Fl:* 5–6; *Z:* Arct

P. orientale

Pennisetum

***P. alopecuroides**:** E Asia, E Aust. A soft grass with fluffy spikes of fl to 8 in long which give a purplish-grey effect over grey-white lvs. Prop by seed. *Ht:* 30 in; *Spd:* 2 ft; *Fl:* 8–10; *Z:* PF

Penstemon

Penstemon

An American genus with bright, tubular foxglove-like flowers. On the borderline of hardiness (and in many cases shrubbiness).

P. campanulatus

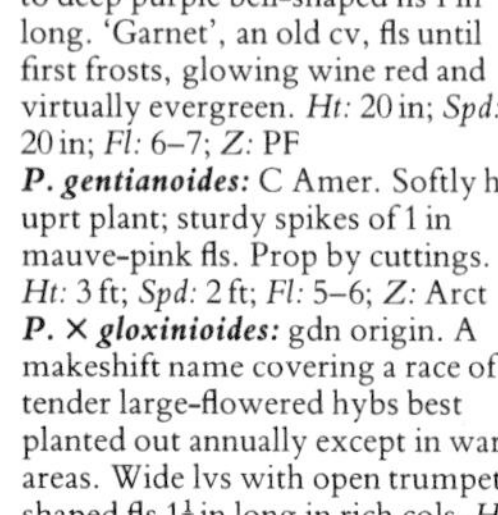

***P. campanulatus*:** C Amer. Narrow-leaved bushy sp with pink to deep purple bell-shaped fls 1 in long. 'Garnet', an old cv, fls until first frosts, glowing wine red and virtually evergreen. *Ht:* 20 in; *Spd:* 20 in; *Fl:* 6–7; *Z:* PF

***P. gentianoides*:** C Amer. Softly hry uprt plant; sturdy spikes of 1 in mauve-pink fls. Prop by cuttings. *Ht:* 3 ft; *Spd:* 2 ft; *Fl:* 5–6; *Z:* Arct

***P.* × *gloxinioides*:** gdn origin. A makeshift name covering a race of tender large-flowered hybs best planted out annually except in warm areas. Wide lvs with open trumpet-shaped fls 1½ in long in rich cols. *Ht:* 2 ft; *Spd:* 18 in; *Fl:* 6–10; *Z:* PF

P. × *gloxinioides*

Perovskia

Perovskia

P. atriplicifolia

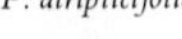

***P. abrotanoides*:** Afghanistan–Tibet. Uprt semi-shrubby plant best hard pruned in March. Slightly hry whitish branching stems, small dissected grey-green lvs and violet-blue fls in 1 ft spikes. 'Blue Haze'* and 'Blue Spire' are good. *Ht:* 4 ft; *Spd:* 2 ft; *Fl:* 8–9; *Z:* Arct

P. atriplicifolia Russian sage: Afghanistan–Tibet. Has sub-shrubby, tapering, white downy stems and fls more violet than blue. Smaller grey-green lvs are coarsely toothed and the whole plant aromatic. Prop by cuttings as *P. abrotanoides*. *Ht:* 2 ft; *Spd:* 4 ft; *Fl:* 8–9; *Z:* Arct

Phalaris

Phalaris

***P. arundinacea* 'Picta'** Gardener's garters, Ribbon grass: Temp N Hem. Vigorous, vivid creeping grass with lvs striped green and white lengthwise. Good in half shade but invasive. *Ht:* 2 ft; *Spd:* 4 ft; *Fl:* 6–7; *Z:* Arct

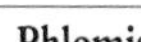

Phlomis

***P. russelliana* (= *samia, viscosa*)*:** Syria. Striking, useful with coarse broad basal lvs and $1\frac{1}{2}$ in fls in whorls up the stems. Fls dry to buff and stay until winter. Prop by seed, div. *Ht:* 3 ft; *Spd:* 2 ft; *Fl:* 6–7; *Z:* Arct

Phlox

North American meadow-flowers much bred for garden use. Almost essential for colour and scent in mid- or late summer. They like fertile soil and need moisture.

***P. maculata**:** E N Amer. Less frequently planted than the summer or gdn phloxes but an especially good plant with lvs pointed in pairs up red-spotted stems and light purple fls *c.* 1 in wide. The cv 'Alpha' is mauve-pink and fragrant. Prop by div, rt cuttings. *Ht:* to 3 ft; *Spd:* 18 in; *Fl:* 7–8; *Z:* Arct

P. paniculata* (= *decussata*) Summer phlox, Garden phlox: E N Amer. The summer phloxes are a range of cvs of the sp ranging in col from white through all shades of pink to red and purple and including orange and mauve to blue sorts. Swooningly scented fl heads of many round 1 in fls often have a deep or contrasting eye. 'Dresden China' is shell pink with a deeper eye, 'Vintage Wine' a rich claret col. Prop by div, basal or rt cuttings. *Ht:* to 3 ft; *Spd:* 2 ft; *Fl:* 7–9; *Z:* Arct

P. paniculata Brigadier'

P. paniculata 'Rheinlander'

Phormium

Essentially shrubby in effect with upright evergreen sword-shaped leaves forming substantial clumps in time.

***P. cookianum**:** NZ. Like a large evergreen iris in habit with green lvs and striking stems of buff-coloured 2 in fls succeeded by twisted seed pods. There are also variegated and tricoloured-leaved forms. *Ht:* 4 ft; *Spd:* 18 in; *Fl:* 7–8; *Z:* SF

P. tenax New Zealand flax lily: NZ. Similar to *P. cookianum* but much bigger, reaching 9 ft × 4 ft. Lvs are a metallic grey-green, fl stems tall and tough bearing warm red 2 in fls followed by shining black seed pods. Worthwhile cvs inc 'Purpureum'* lvs bronze-purple; 'Variegatum' lvs yellowish-white striped and new cvs from NZ: 'Sundowner' lvs grey, green and light red striped; 'Dazzler' lvs yellow and green. Prop sp from seed, cvs by div. *Fl:* 7–9; *Z:* SF

P. tenax

Phygelius

Phygelius

P. capensis

P. capensis* Cape figwort: S Africa. Loosely bushy, sometimes shrubby plant with oval deep green lvs and fascinating terminal heads of several pendulous horn-shaped orange-red fls 1$\frac{1}{2}$ in long. Will thrive in shade in a warm climate. Prop by seed, cuttings. *Ht, Spd:* 3 ft; *Fl:* 8; *Z:* PF

Physalis

Physalis

P. franchetii

P. franchetii Chinese lantern: Japan. Jagged-leaved running per with uninteresting small white fls but seeds enclosed in large bright orange lantern-shaped inflated structures to 2$\frac{1}{2}$ in long which are highly ornamental. Prop by seed, div. *Ht:* 2 ft; *Spd:* 3 ft; *Fl:* 7; *Z:* Arct

Physostegia

Physostegia

P. virginiana The Obedient plant: E USA. Uprt; lvs narrow. Fls pink tubes in terminal 5 in spikes, staying put when touched, hence common name. 'Speciosa' is rose-pink. *Ht:* 3 ft; *Spd:* 18 in; *Fl:* 8–9; *Z:* Arct

Phytolacca

Phytolacca

P. americana

P. americana Virginian poke weed, Red ink plant: Florida. Coarse oval-lvd plant with substantial purplish branching stems and terminal 4 in shrubby spikes of white fls. Juicy, deep purple berries are poisonous. Self-seeds freely. *Ht:* 4 ft; *Spd:* 3 ft; *Fl:* 6–10; *Z:* Arct

Platycodon

Balloon flower, Chinese bellflower

P. grandiflorus

***P. grandiflorus**:** China, Manchuria, Japan. Like a small campanula of notably trim and pleasing design. Fl buds the shape of hot air balloons open into 5-lobed bells *c.* 1$\frac{1}{2}$ in wide. Named forms, e.g. 'Mother of Pearl' can be white, blue or pink. The lvs turn yellow in autumn. Prop by div, seed. *Ht:* to 2 ft; *Spd:* 1 ft; *Fl:* 8–9; *Z:* Arct

Podophyllum

Podophyllum

P. peltatum May apple, Lady's parasol. N Amer. Much prized. Has 1 large round lf with 1 water lily-like 1½ in fl. Plum-shaped fr edible, lvs and rts poisonous. Prop by seed. *Ht:* 15 in; *Spd:* 1 ft; *Fl:* 5–6; *Z:* Arct

Polemonium

Polemonium

P. caeruleum Jacob's ladder, Greek valerian: N Hem. Branching slender stems, bright green divided lvs and blue, bell-shaped ½ in fls freely borne. Also a white form. *Ht:* 2 ft; *Spd:* 18 in; *Fl:* 6–7; *Z:* Arct
***P. foliosissimum**:** W N Amer. Larger all over; a better choice with rich blue or lavender fls. *Ht:* 30 in; *Spd:* 18 in; *Fl:* 6–8; *Z:* Arct

P. caeruleum

Polygonatum

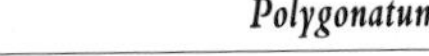

Solomon's seal, Lady's seal

***P. multiflorum of gdns (= P. × hybridus)**:** Eur, N Asia. Graceful arching stems with wing-like horizontal lvs to 5 in long. Fls are greenish-white bells each 1 in long in clusters dangling from the lf axils followed by black berries. Variegated and double-flowered forms also available. Prop by div. *Ht:* 30 in; *Spd:* 1 ft; *Fl:* 6; *Z:* Arct

P. multiflorum

Polygonum

Knotweed

A genus with valuable long and late-flowering members but also some dangerously invasive and weedy ones.

P. affine: Nepal. Mat-forming sp with narrow rich evergreen lvs that col well in aut. Fls red massed in sturdy spikes 6 in long. 'Darjeeling Red' and 'Lowndes's Variety' are recommended. Prop by div. *Ht:* 10 in; *Spd:* 1 ft; *Fl:* 8–10; *Z:* Arct
P. amplexicaule: Him. Vigorous, with long heart-shaped lvs and thin stems bearing narrow 6 in spikes of pink or red fls. 'Atrosanguineum'* is crimson. Prop by div. *Ht:* 3 ft; *Spd:* 3 ft; *Fl:* 7–10; *Z:* PF
P. campanulatum: Him. Pretty non-invasive knotweed with pale pink fls in bunches 3 in wide. Lvs are elliptic, pale green and deeply veined. Prop by div. *Ht:* to 3 ft; *Spd:* 30 in; *Fl:* 7–10; *Z:* PF

P. affine

P. amplexicaule

Potentilla

Cinquefoil

P. gdn hybrid 'Gibson's Scarlet'

P. gdn hybs*: gdn origin. Loud, cheerful mid-smr fls derived from sev more discreet spp. Lvs strawberry-like, fls to 1½ in wide. Good ones include 'Gibson's Scarlet' single, bright scarlet, 1 ft; 'Glory of Nancy' orange-crimson, semi-double, 18 in; 'William Rollison' orange, flame and yellow, 15 in. Prop by div. *Spd:* 1 ft; *Fl:* 6–9; *Z:* PF

Primula

Primula, primrose

The primrose genus, with 500 species, embraces alpines, meadow-flowers and bog plants, all spring flowering and of almost childish charm. All like peaty soil: some drained, some wet, and all are perennials growing rapidly from seed but sometimes short lived. They have a tendency to "mealiness", a floury coating that adds to their crisp, laundered look.

P. denticulata

P. florindae

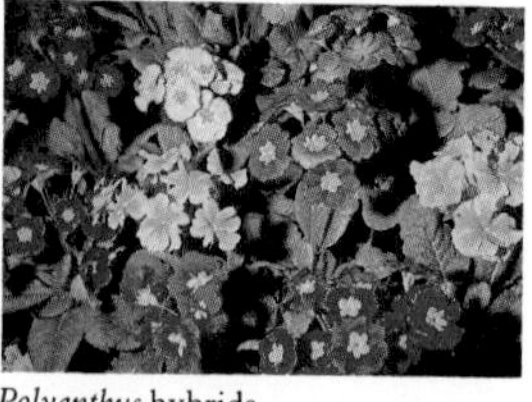

Polyanthus hybrids

P. denticulata Drumstick primula, Himalayan primrose: Him. V early, often starting into fl before lvs. Globular fl heads to 3 in wide are composed of masses of single lilac or pale purple fls each with yellow eye. *Ht, Spd:* 1 ft; *Fl:* 3–5; *Z:* Arct

P. florindae*: Tibet. Tall stems of drooping bell-shaped sulphur-yellow frag ¾ in fls in clusters above broad lvs. Ptls powdered with a white farina. Likes wet ground. *Ht, Spd:* 2 ft; *Fl:* 6–7; *Z:* Arct

P. japonica*: W Him. A type of "candelabra" primula with red, pink or white ¾ in fls arranged in whorls up the stem. 'Miller's Crimson' and 'Postford White' are reliable old cvs. *Ht:* 20 in; *Spd:* 1 ft; *Fl:* 3–5; *Z:* Arct

P. pulverulenta: W Szechwan. Also a candelabra. The ¾ in fls are deep red with a purple eye in whorls up the mealy stems. The lvs are broader at the tip. Likes wet ground. *Ht, Spd:* 1 ft; *Fl:* 6; *Z:* Arct

Polyanthus: gdn origin. Hybs between the primrose (*P. acaulis*) and cowslip (*P. veris*). Fls like bigger primroses and sev on a stem. Many cols inc white, crimson, pink, blue, orange and yellow sometimes laced with gold and occasionally double. *Ht, Spd:* 1 ft; *Fl:* 3–4; *Z:* Arct

Prunella

Self heal

P. grandiflora: Eur. Showy per with divided dark green hry lvs and pink 1 in fls in terminal 3 in spikes. 'Loveliness' is a richer colour. Prop by div. *Ht:* 7 in; *Spd:* 1 ft; *Fl:* 7; *Z:* Arct

Pulmonaria

Lungwort, Soldiers and sailors

P. angustifolia Blue cowslip: Eur. V early; lvs bristly, fls funnel-shaped. 'Munstead Blue' is a deeper col. *Ht:* 10 in; *Spd:* 1 ft; *Fl:* 3–4; *Z:* Arct
P. rubra: SE Eur. More or less evergreen lvs a lighter shade. V early fls brick red. *Ht:* 1 ft; *Spd:* 15 in; *Fl:* 3–4; *Z:* Arct
P. saccharata Bethlehem sage: Eur. Evergreen lvs spotted silvery-pink and grey. Fls pink, becoming blue. *Ht:* 15 in; *Spd:* 2 ft; *Fl:* 3–4; *Z:* Arct

P. saccharata

Ranunculus

Buttercup

R. aconitifolius White bachelor's buttons: Eur. Tall, lfy sp with single white ½ in fls. *Ht:* 30 in; *Spd:* 18 in; *Fl:* 5–6; *Z:* Arct
R. acris* 'Flore-pleno' Yellow bachelor's buttons: Eur, N Asia. Well-behaved; double golden yellow fls with dark green wedge-shaped divided lvs. *Ht:* 30 in; *Spd:* 2 ft; *Fl:* 6–8; *Z:* Arct
R. ficaria Figwort, lesser celandine: Eur. Gdn forms of this weed worth cultivating esp 'Aurantiaca' with bright orange ½ in fls. *Ht, Spd:* 5 in; *Fl:* 3–5; *Z:* Arct

R. acris 'Flore-pleno'

Rheum

Rheum

R. palmatum*: China. Has large green cut or jaggedly-lobed lvs and stout stems of deep red fls in spikes to 3 ft long. The cv 'Atrosanguineum' has the advantage of rich dark red lvs. *Ht, Spd:* 4½ ft; *Fl:* 6–7; *Z:* Arct

Romneya

California tree poppy

R. coulteri*: SW Cal. Running plant with blue-green stems and divided lvs the same lovely col. Large white frag poppy fls to 6 in wide with a boss of golden stamens. *R.* × *hybrida* 'White Cloud' rec. Can be hard to establish. *Ht:* 4 ft; *Spd:* 3 ft; *Fl:* 7–10; *Z:* F

R. × *hybrida*

Roscoea

Roscoea

R. cautleoides: China. Glossy green uprt lvs clasp the fl stems each of which bear several clear yellow orchid-like fls to 2 in long. Prop by div of tubers. *Ht:* to 1 ft; *Spd:* 6 in; *Fl:* 6–8; *Z:* SF, LF

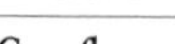

Rudbeckia 

Coneflower

R. fulgida 'Goldsturm'

***R. fulgida var sullivantii* 'Goldsturm'**★ A Black-eyed Susan: E USA. Bristly-lvd with single $2\frac{1}{2}$ in fls like daisies, rich yellow ptls and a central 'eye'. *Ht, Spd:* 2 ft; *Fl:* 7–10; *Z:* Arct

***R. laciniata* 'Golden Glow':** N Amer. Double golden yellow cv. *Ht:* 7 ft; *Spd:* 30 in; *Fl:* 7–9; *Z:* Arct

R. nitida: N Amer. Tall sp to 4 ft; a central black cone prominently displayed by drooping yellow ptls. 'Herbstone'★ pale yellow, green centre is even taller; 'Goldquelle' dwarf. *Spd:* 30 in; *Fl:* 7–10; *Z:* Arct

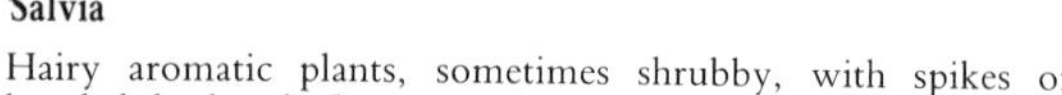

Salvia

Salvia

Hairy aromatic plants, sometimes shrubby, with spikes of hooded deadnettle flowers in almost every colour.

S. nemorosa

***S. nemorosa* (= *S.* × *superba*)★:** SE Eur. Many-stemmed uprt plant with small sage-green lvs. Fls in 8 in spikes are violet-blue with crimson bracts. 'Superba' reaches 3 ft × 2 ft; deeper-coloured 'East Friesland' 18 in × 15 in. *Fl:* 6–9; *Z:* Arct

S. przewalskii: China. Big, lfy plant with large heart-shaped basal lvs and hry stems; $\frac{1}{4}$ in fls purplish-violet. *Ht:* 3 ft; *Spd:* 4 ft; *Fl:* 6; *Z:* Arct

Sanguisorba 

Burnet

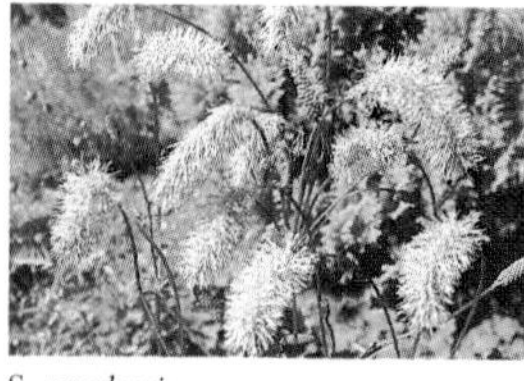

S. canadensis

***S. canadensis* (= *Poterium canadense*):** E N Amer. Strong clump-forming per with eau-de-nil lvs and fluffy 6 in spikes of white fls like bottle brushes. Prop by div, seed. *Ht:* 4 ft; *Spd:* 30 in; *Fl:* 7–8; *Z:* Arct

Saponaria   

Soapwort, Bouncing Bet

S. officinalis: Eur. Sprawler with small opp lvs and spreading rts (stolons). Fls to $1\frac{1}{2}$ in wide are pink or white in frilly heads; double red, white or pink ones are better plants. *Ht, Spd:* 30 in; *Fl:* 7–9; *Z:* Arct

Saxifraga   

Saxifrage

S.* × *umbrosa★ London pride, St Patrick's cabbage: Eur. Rosettes of leathery evergreen lvs and slim fl stems to 18 in with myriads of pink starry fls. 'Variegata' has yellow mottled lvs. *Spd:* 1 ft; *Fl:* 5–7; *Z:* PF

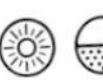   

Scabiosa

Scabious, Pincushion flower

S. caucasica: Caucasus. Long-lived light lavender-blue fls like frilly pincushions on a pale green plant. Lvs on the long stems are divided, at the base lance-shaped. 'Clive Greaves' is a reliable cv; 'Moerheim Beauty' deep blue; 'Miss Willmott' white. Prop by div. *Ht, Spd:* 2 ft; *Fl:* 6–9; *Z:* Arct

S. caucasica

Scrophularia

Figwort

S. aquatica 'Variegata': GB. Spectacular dark green and white variegated lvs make this plant effective from June–Oct. Fls are inconspicuous russet brown. Basal lvs large, white, stem lvs smaller. *Ht:* 3 ft; *Spd:* 18 in; *Z:* Arct

S. aquatica 'Variegata'

Sedum

Sedum

S. 'Autumn Joy'*: gdn origin. Outstanding late-flowerer; flattish pink 8 in fl heads turn to mahogany. *Ht, Spd:* 2 ft; *Fl:* 9; *Z:* Arct
S. maximum 'Atropurpureum': Eur. Maroon lvs and stems with smaller heads of dusky reddish-pink fls. *Ht, Spd:* 18 in; *Fl:* 8–9; *Z:* Arct
S. spectabile Ice plant: China. Forms 7 in domes of pink fls. 'Brilliant' is deep rose-pink; 'Carmen' carmine. *Ht, Spd:* 18 in; *Fl:* 9–10; *Z:* Arct

S. spectabile

Sidalcea

Sidalcea

S. malviflora Prairie mallow: Cal. Silky 2 in fls and abundant fresh green lvs. Many forms, inc 'Elsie Hough' satin pink, 40 in; 'Rose Queen' rose-pink, 30 in; 'William Smith' salmon, 3 ft. *Spd:* 18 in; *Fl:* 7–8; *Z:* F

Sisyrinchium

Sisyrinchium

S. striatum: Chile. Like a small iris in habit but with tiny ½ in fls bell-shaped and creamy-yellow with purple dash on back of each ptl. Frs amber berries. Seeds itself. *Ht:* to 2 ft; *Spd:* 10 in; *Fl:* 6; *Z:* PF

Solidago  

Golden rod

***S. brachystachys* 'Goldenmosa':** Eur. Fluffy yellow golden rod for the front of the border with fl plume to 8 in long and light green lvs. Prop by division. *Ht:* 30 in; *Spd:* 18 in; *Fl:* 8–9; *Z:* Arct

Solidaster  

Solidaster

S. hybridus

***S. hybridus* (= × *Solidaster luteus*, × *Asterago luteus*):** gdn origin. A cross between an aster and a solidago with narrow lvs and flattened heads up to 4 in across composed of numerous small yellow fls which fade to a creamy-yellow. Prop by division. *Ht:* 2 ft; *Spd:* 1 ft; *Fl:* 7–9; *Z:* Arct

Stachys   

Stachys

S. olympica

***S. macrantha* (= *Betonica macrantha*):** Caucasus. Broad, dark wrinkled hry lvs; purple fls. 'Robusta' deeper col. *Ht:* 2 ft; *Spd:* 1 ft; *Fl:* 5–7; *Z:* Arct
S. olympica* Lamb's tongue, Lamb's ears: Iran. Tongue-like woolly lvs and whitish stems with ¼ in fls. 'Silver Carpet' is non-flowering. Good ground cover. *Ht:* 18 in; *Spd:* 1 ft; *Fl:* 7–9; *Z:* Arct

Stokesia    

Stoke's aster

S. laevis

***S. laevis* (= *cyanea*):** N Amer. Narrow lvs form a basal rosette; 3 in fls are open chalices of fringed ptls, blue or mauve with white centres. 'Blue Star' is a better shade. Prop by div. *Ht, Spd:* 18 in; *Fl:* 8–9; *Z:* Arct

Symphytum   

Comfrey

***S. caucasicum*:** Caucasus. Comfreys all have bold hry oval lvs; this one has pale blue tubular 1 in fls rather like borage. *Ht, Spd:* 18 in; *Fl:* 5–6; *Z:* Arct

Tellima   

Tellima

***T. grandiflora**:** N–W Amer. Useful evergreen sp with rounded toothed lvs that redden in winter and sprays of 1 in greenish-yellow bell-like fls in April–June. 'Purpurea' has bronze lvs turning purple in winter. Prop by div or seed. *Ht:* 2 ft; *Spd:* 18 in; *Z:* Arct

Teucrium

T. chamaedrys* Wall germander: Eur. Creeping dark green sub-shrubby edging plant. Fls are pink-mauve like snapdragons with tiny red and white spots. Prop by div, cuttings. *Ht:* 10 in; *Spd:* 1 ft; *Fl:* 7–9; *Z:* Arct

Thalictrum

Meadow rue

Most graceful cousins of the buttercups with complex leaves like rue and small flowers airily displayed.

T. delavayii (= dipterocarpum): W China. Exceptionally elegant; slender branching stems, dainty leaflets and fluffy 6 in heads of deep lilac fls with pronounced pale yellow stamens. 'Hewitt's Double' is a rich rosy mauve but less easy. *Ht:* 3 ft; *Spd:* 18 in; *Fl:* 7–8; *Z:* Arct
T. speciosissimum**:*** N Africa, S Eur. Especially valuable for its blue-green lvs effective from May–aut. Fls pale straw yellow in fluffy pyramids to 9 in long. *Ht:* 4 ft; *Spd:* 28 in; *Fl:* 7–8; *Z:* Arct

T. speciosissimum

Thermopsis

False lupin

T. montana (= fabacea): W N Amer. Almost too easy to grow. Like a slender bright yellow lupin with spikes of fl to 1 ft long. Inclined to run into clumps. Prop by seed. *Ht, Spd:* 3 ft; *Fl:* 6–7; *Z:* Arct

T. montana

Tiarella

Tiarella

T. cordifolia Foam flower: E N Amer. Pretty little ground-covering plant. Pale green lvs rounded, lobed, hry becoming bronze in winter. Fls a creamy white froth of tiny stars on 10 in stems. Prop by div, seed. *Spd:* 6 in; *Fl:* 4–6; *Z:* Arct
T. wherryi: E USA. Lvs similar to *T. cordifolia* but fl stems to 15 in. Fls foaming white or pink tinged in fluffy 10 in spikes. Prop by div, seed. *Spd:* 7 in; *Fl:* 5–6; *Z:* Arct

T. cordifolia

Trachystemon

Trachystemon

T. orientale (= Nordmannia cordifolia): SE Eur, Asia Minor, Caucasus. Giant per borage to 2 ft × 2 ft with long lax lvs and blue fls with prominent anthers. Plant for a wild gdn. Good in dry shade. *Fl:* 3–5; *Z:* Arct

Tradescantia

Tradescantia

T. × *andersoniana*

T. × andersoniana (= virginiana) Spiderwort: gdn origin. Lush, strap-leaved plants often pink-tinged in young growth. Fls have 3 ptls. Most cvs are hybs of *T. virginiana*. Good ones inc: 'J. C. Weguelin' azure; 'Osprey' white, blue eye; 'Purewell Giant' rich purple-red. *Ht:* 22 in; *Spd:* 18 in; *Fl:* 6–9; *Z:* Arct

Tricyrtis

Japanese toad lily

T. hirta: Japan. Graceful and intriguing rather than eye-catching. Lvs to 6 in long are thin and hry, fls narrow-petalled, bell-shaped, white, smothered with purple spots. For moist soil. *Ht, Spd:* 2 ft; *Fl:* 6–7; *Z:* Arct

Trollius

Globe flower

T. × *cultorum* 'Orange Globe'

T. × cultorum: gdn origin. Hybs often listed as *T. europaeum*. Lvs are lobed, fls gold, globe-shaped, 2½ in. 'Alabaster' is pale cream; 'Orange Princess' orange; 'Princess Juliana' yellow. Prop by div. *Ht:* to 3 ft; *Spd:* 18 in; *Fl:* 5–6; *Z:* Arct

T. ledebourii: E Asia. Taller with lvs more deeply divided. 'Golden Queen' is rich orange-yellow. *Ht:* 3 ft; *Spd:* 18 in; *Fl:* 5–6; *Z:* Arct

Valeriana

Valerian

V. officinalis All heal: Eur. Bushy plant beloved of cats. Lvs are bright green, heart-shaped, stems fluted, fls pink in 6 in heads. White and carmine forms are available. Prop spp by seed. *Ht, Spd:* 40 in; *Fl:* 6; *Z:* Arct

X Venidio-arctotis

Venidio-arctotis

× *Venidio-arctotis*

× Venidio-arctotis hybs: gdn origin. Brilliantly coloured daisy flowered hybs of African parents. Cols red, orange, salmon pink, yellow, crimson. Only hardy in frost-free areas in Eur. Prop by cuttings. *Ht:* 18 in; *Spd:* 2 ft; *Fl:* 5–11; *Z:* SF

Veratrum

Helleborine

V. album* White helleborine: Eur, N Africa, Siberia. Exciting pleated lvs with greenish-white waxy fls in branched 1 ft spikes. *V. nigrum* has nearly black fls. Not difficult. *Ht:* 4 ft; *Spd:* 2 ft; *Fl:* 7; *Z:* Arct

Verbascum

Mullein

V. bombyciferum (= broussa): Asia Minor. Eye-catching spire-like biennial with silvery woolly lvs and a 3 ft spike studded with yellow fls. *Ht:* 6 ft; *Spd:* 2 ft; *Fl:* 6–7; *Z:* Arct

V. phoenicium Purple mullein: Eur, N Asia. Basal rosette of deep green lvs; 2 ft spikes of purple fls. Hybs inc 'Cotswold Gem' buff, purple centre; 'Pink Domino' rose-pink. *Ht:* 4 ft; *Spd:* 2 ft; *Fl:* 5–9; *Z:* PF

V. bombyciferum

Verbena

Verbena

V. bonariensis*: S Amer. Long-stemmed lanky per to 4 ft with thin lvs in pairs up branching stems. Tiny bright purple fls in 3 in tufts. *Spd:* 28 in; *Fl:* 7–9; *Z:* PF

V. rigida: S Amer. Tuberous-rooted, often used for bedding out. Lfy stems divided into 3 spikes of frag, purple fls. Prop by div. *Ht:* 2 ft; *Spd:* 18 in; *Fl:* 7–10; *Z:* F

V. rigida

Veronica

Speedwell

Narrow spire-flowers for a long summer season. Easy plants for mixed and herbaceous borders.

V. gentianoides: Caucasus. Lvs a shining deep green, fls pale blue in pointed 10 in spires. There is a creamy-white variegated form. *Ht, Spd:* 2 ft; *Fl:* 5; *Z:* Arct

V. incana: USSR. Silvery-grey hry-lvd plant for front of sunny border. Light blue fls in 6 in spires. *Ht, Spd:* 1 ft; *Fl:* 7; *Z:* Arct

V. spicata: Eur. A neat edging plant with bright blue fls in short spikes. Hybs inc × 'Wendy' blue fls, silvery lvs; × 'Bacarolle' rose-pink; × 'Red Fox' rich plum red; × 'Icicle' white. Prop by div. *Ht, Spd:* 18 in; *Fl:* 6–8; *Z:* Arct

V. virginica (= Veronicastrum virginica, Leptandra virginica): N Amer. Strong spires with regular whorls of horizontal lvs make a unique pattern of light and shade. Fls pale blue but white in the best one 'Alba'*; *Ht:* 4 ft; *Spd:* 18 in; *Fl:* 8–9; *Z:* Arct

V. incana

V. spicata

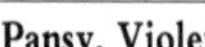

Viola

Pansy, Violet

Little woodland-edge plants with sweet faces best in light shade and leafy soil. Some species flower all summer.

V. cornuta 'Alba'

V. labradorica

V. cornuta: Pyrenees. A plump green cushion of lvs smothered in pale blue 1 in pansy fls. Can also be grown in rock gdns. 'Alba' white and 'Lilacina' pale lilac are good cvs. Prop by div, seed. *Ht:* 1 ft; *Spd:* 18 in; *Fl:* 5–10; *Z:* PF

V. labradorica*: N USA, Canada, Greenland. Small creeping violet with dusky purplish-green lvs and violet-blue fls $\frac{3}{4}$in across. Will tolerate dry shade. *Ht:* 3 in; *Spd:* 10 in; *Fl:* 4–5; *Z:* Arct

V. tricolor Heartsease: Eur. Sprawling wildling with small fls often half black-purple, half yellow. Self-sows. *Ht:* to 6 in; *Spd:* to 15 in; *Fl:* 5–9; *Z:* PF

V. × wittrockiana Garden pansy: gdn origin. Huge range bred for big fls in many cols inc wtr, spr and smr-flowering selections, usually grown as anns and per "tufted pansies" e.g. 'Maggie's Mott' mauve. *Ht:* 9 in; *Spd:* 1 ft; *Z:* PF

Viscaria

Catchfly

V. vulgaris

V. vulgaris: Eur. Siberia, Japan. The name comes from the sticky stem. Sp superseded as a gdn plant by the knicker-pink double-flowered form 'Splendens Plena'. The lvs are narrow. Prop by division. *Ht:* 15 in; *Spd:* 1 ft; *Fl:* 5–7; *Z:* Arct

Zauschneria

Californian fuchsia, Humming bird's trumpet

Z. californica

Z. californica: Cal, Mexico. Sub-shrubby plant also with a place in the rock gdn. Small grey lvs and tall dainty sprays of bright scarlet $1\frac{1}{4}$ in fls. There is a v rare white form. *Z. cana* has needle-like silver lvs and smaller scarlet fls. Prop by cuttings, division or seed. *Ht:* 1 ft; *Spd:* 18 in; *Fl:* 8–10; *Z:* SF

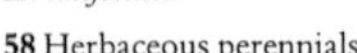

Alpines, rock garden plants

True alpine plants are those that grow naturally on mountains above about 10,000 feet. The plants described in this section as for use in the rock garden are those small bushy or trailing perennials that look at home among rocks, whatever their natural origin. Although spring (after snow melt) is the main flowering season, plants can be found to provide interest all summer.

Acaena

New Zealand burr-weed

A. novae-zealandiae: New Zealand. One of the prettiest of a group of vigorous plants forming bronze carpets to 2 in under reddish fls. All acaenas are ideal for paved areas and difficult sunny sites on poor soil. Fls are petalless but worthwhile, taking the form of club-like burrs on stems held above the lvs. *A. buchananii* has pea-green lvs; the larger lvs of *A. adscendens* are nearly blue. *Spd:* 2 ft; *Fl:* 6–9; *Z:* PF

A. novae-zealandiae

Achillea

Achillea

A. clavenae Alpine achillea: E Alps. Neat, mat-forming. Useful tufty mat of lvs. White fls to ⅓ in diam are held aloft on 6 in stems. Prop by div. Contrasts well with campanulas. *Spd:* 8 in; *Fl:* 5–6; *Z:* Arct

Aethionema

Aethionema, Burnt candytuft

A. 'Warley Rose': Cv found in the garden of Miss Ellen Willmott at Warley, Eng, early this century. The brightest member of a generally rather dim genus, having deep pink fls. Forms shrublets only 6 in high. All aethionemas are attractive for their fls in spikes to 3½ in long and the slightly succulent texture of their tiny leaves. *Spd:* 15 in; *Fl:* 4–5; *Z:* PF

A. 'Warley Rose'

Alchemilla

Lady's mantle

A. erigena (=conjuncta): Swiss Alps. One of the few alpine alchemillas. Forms a neat clump of mid-green lvs with silvery backs and greenish-yellow fls. The genus contains many similar spp, some half dozen of which have gdn value. Prop by seed or div. *Ht:* 6 in; *Spd:* 15 in; *Fl:* 6–8; *Z:* Arct

Allium

Flowering onion

A. beesianum China onion: W China. An onion with china-blue fls to 2 in freely produced on 9 in stems from fibrous clumps rather than true bulbs. Grassy lvs and characteristic onion smell. Prop by div or seed. One of more than 300 ornamental onion spp. *Spd:* 6 in; *Fl:* 7–9; *Z:* Arct

Alyssum

Alyssum

A. saxatile

A. saxatile* Gold dust: Eur. One of the basic rock gdn plants. Forms strong clumps of greyish-green lvs hidden by myriads of brilliant yellow fls in spr. Universally seen in company of blobs of mauve *Aubrieta*. Good cvs include 'Dudley Neville' biscuit-yellow; 'Citrinum' pale yellow; 'Plenum' double yellow, and dwarfs such as 'Compactum'. *Ht:* to 1 ft; *Spd:* to 18 in; *Fl:* 4–6; *Z:* Arct

Androsace

Rock jasmine

A. lanuginosa

A. lanuginosa: Him. The thin stems of this excellent plant link the grey rosettes of lvs and allow them to travel over rocks and crevices showing the ¼ in white fls to advantage. 'Leitchtlinii' has exquisite pink-eyed fls. Sev other forms only suitable for the alpine house. *Ht:* 2 in; *Spd:* to 18 in; *Fl:* 6–10; *Z:* PF

Antennaria

Catsear

A. dioica: Eur, Asia, N Amer. A valuable plant, but uncommon in gdns and the wild. Forms pewter-grey rosettes of lvs with whitish fls to ¼ in diam. Ideal over patches of crocuses. Also a useful carpeting plant for filling pockets in paving. *Ht:* 1 ft; *Spd:* 18 in; *Fl:* 5–6; *Z:* Arct

Arabis

Wall cress, Rock cress

A. caucasica (= A. albida): Eur. A universally grown spring fl with white blooms to ¾ in diam that cool the brassy yellows of the season and continue sporadically into summer. 'Flore Plena' is double, *A. c. variegata* a variegated form. Lvs like grey flannel. *Ht:* 8 in; *Spd:* to 2 ft; *Fl:* 2–6; *Z:* Arct

Arenaria

Sandwort

A. ledebouriana: Armenia. A tufty crevice plant with white fls over narrow grey-green lvs. The shade-loving *A. balearica**, which grows like pale green moss on rock faces, is v pretty but so natural-looking that it fails to attract attention. Deserves wider use. *Ht:* 1¼ in; *Spd:* 1 ft; *Fl:* 5–7; *Z:* PF

Arisarum

Mouse-tail plant

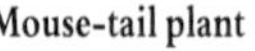

A. proboscidium: Eur Alps. Tuberous-rooted aroid happy in any cool moist spot. Small clumps of arrow-shaped lvs to 4 in partially conceal brownish-white spathes whose tips give the impression of field mice diving for cover. Fascinating for children. *Ht:* 4 in; *Spd:* 6 in; *Fl:* 6; *Z:* PF

Armeria

Thrift, Sea pink

A. maritima: GB. Densely packed narrow lvs form dark mats which are the perfect foil for the light pink fls to 1 in. Gdn forms include 'Laucheana' a rich pink; 'Alba' white and 'Vindictive' a fierce red. All spp are equally at home on the shore and in the mountains. Their use is not confined to the rock gdn— they can form useful cover or edging plants. *Ht, Spd:* to 1 ft; *Fl:* 5–7; *Z:* Arct

A. maritima

Artemisia

Artemisia

A. stellerana* Dusty Miller, Old woman: N Amer NE Asia. One of a genus ranging from tiny alpine house or scree plants to valuable shrubs. Most have lively silver foliage. This one is a trailing plant strong enough to engulf any defenceless neighbours but needs to be replaced by rooted cuttings every 2–3 yrs to preserve its health and vigour. Looks good with scarlet geums or against nodding campanulas. *Ht:* 20 in; *Spd:* 18 in; *Fl:* 8–9; *Z:* PF

A. stellerana

Asarina

Asarina

A. procumbens Trailing snapdragon: Italy, S France. A charming trailer with cream fls and soft grey-green lvs ideal for cool crevices and rock faces. Short-lived but self-seeding. *Ht:* 20 in; *Spd:* 3 ft; *Fl:* 6–9; *Z:* PF

Asperula

Asperula

A. odorata Woodruff: GB. Vigorous members of a pretty minor genus. Forms small rugs of lvs with cross-shaped sweet-scented white or pink $\frac{1}{4}$ in fls. Keep roots cool. *Ht:* to 1 ft; *Spd:* to 18 in; *Fl:* 5–6; *Z:* Arct

Aster

Aster

A. alpinus Alpine aster: Eur Alps. A rock gdn representative of a vast gp inc Michaelmas daisies of the autumn herbaceous border. Easy to grow, reaching 10 in high and twice as wide. Blue and gold fls to $1\frac{3}{4}$ in freely produced in smr. 'Albus' is a useful albino; 'Beechwood' a good purplish cv. *Fl:* 7; *Z:* Arct

A. alpinus

Aubrieta

Aubrieta

A race of about 12 species which have crossed to produce the named cultivars that flower for weeks on end in spring.

A. deltoidea 'Godstone'

***A. deltoidea and gdn hybs**:** Sicily E to Asia Minor. Varieties do not come true from seed so named sorts must be propagated by cuttings. Popular ones include 'Crimson Bedder' red; 'Dawn' rose-pink; 'Gurgedyke' light blue. There is also a less vigorous cream-variegated one with blue fls. *Ht:* 2½ in; *Spd:* to 2 ft; *Fl:* 3–6; *Z:* Arct

Bellis

Daisy

B. perennis 'Pomponette'

B. perennis 'Dresden China': Eur. The prettiest daisy in intentional cultivation, with elegant soft pink double fls. 'Pomponette' is a deeper pink. Much nicer than the once-popular 'Alice'. *B. p. prolifera* the 'Hen and Chicken' daisy has been cultivated since the 17th century. 'White Pearl' is a worthy albino. *Ht, Spd:* to 4 in; *Fl:* 3–10; *Z:* Arct

Borago

Borage

B. laxiflora Baby borage: Corsica. One of the bohemians of the rock gdn, forming trails of clear blue fls among shrubs and heathers. Related to the bigger borage of the herb gdn and like it has hry lvs. Easy from seed and good with yellow alpine hypericums. *Ht, Spd:* to 1 ft; *Fl:* 7–8; *Z:* PF

Campanula

Bellflower

C. garganica

***C. garganica**:** Italy, Yugoslavia. An excellent free-flowering late-summer species found in crevices in the wild and therefore useful for dry walls and similar sites. Star-shaped clear blue fls are in heads to 6 in long. Forms with white centres include 'W. H. Payne'. All are in the white-blue-purple colour range. *Ht:* to 6 in; *Spd:* to 1 ft; *Fl:* 8–9; *Z:* PF

Cerastium

Cerastium

C. tomentosum* Snow-in-summer: Eur. The most rampageous of a v vig bunch but well loved for its sheets of grey-green lvs and waves of white fls to ¾ in. *C. lanatum* is less invasive. *Ht:* to 6 in; *Spd:* 2 ft; *Fl:* 5–7; *Z:* Arct

Ceratostigma

Plumbago, Leadwort

C. plumbaginoides* Perennial plumbago: China. A creeping plant for late smr when the lvs become bronzed as the intense gentian-blue fls begin a lengthy display. Deeper in colour than the shrubby sp *C. willmottianum*. The two look good together. *Ht:* to 1 ft; *Spd:* to 16 in; *Fl:* 7–11; *Z:* PF

C. plumbaginoides

Convolvulus

Bellbind, Bindweed

C. mauritanicus Baby bellbind: N Africa. Inclined to wander but less invasive that the clear pink *C. althaeoides* which is worth growing only where paths or walls stop its trespass. Funnel-shaped fls open and close with the sun. *Ht:* 3 in; *Spd:* 3 ft; *Fl:* 6–9; *Z:* PF

Cornus

Dogwood

C. canadensis* Creeping dogwood: N Amer. The conspicuous bracts form a white layer followed by cheerful red berries over a carpet of dark green lvs. Only 6 in high in fl. Best in semi-shade with an occasional small fern growing through it. *Spd:* 2 ft; *Fl:* 6; *Z:* Arct

C. canadensis

Corydalis

Fumitory

C. wilsonii: China. Forms clumps of prettily dissected grey-green lvs with gps of bright yellow fls over a long period. Sev others weedy but good ones are quite lovely. *Ht:* 10 in; *Spd:* 1 ft; *Fl:* 5–9; *Z:* PF

Cytisus

Broom

C. × beanii Dwarf broom: A hyb found at Kew, London in 1900 and forming a small spreading shrub with pea-like yellow fls to ½ in. *C. × kewensis** taller at 1 ft but also trails and has creamy-white fls. *C. purpureus* has pink and purple fls in frothy sprays. Looks good with heathers. *Ht:* to 10 in; *Spd:* 3 ft; *Fl:* 5–6; *Z:* PF-Arct

C. × beanii

Daphne

Daphne

D. cneorum Garland flower: S Eur. Low spreading shrub smothered with headily frag bright rose-pink fls ½ in. *Ht:* 6 in; *Spd:* 30 in; *Fl:* 5–6; *Z:* Arct

Dianthus

Pink

Country cousins of the carnation with much more natural grace. Invaluable plants for their evergreen leaves, which are often grey and grassy, and for their usually pink, fragrant flowers.

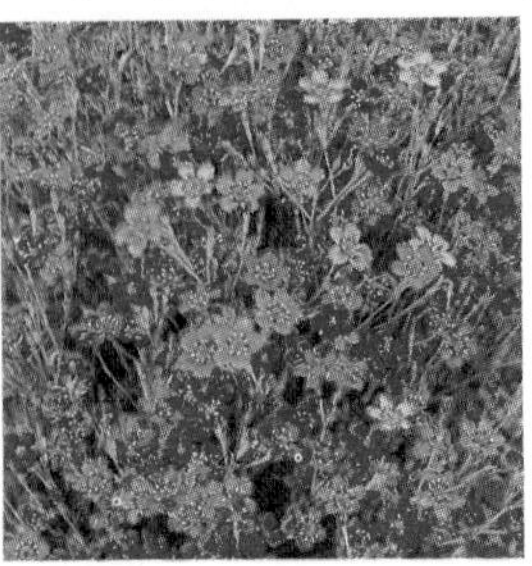

D. deltoides

D. alpinus Alpine pink: Eur Alps. One of the many alpine pinks. Makes low cushions of green lvs with large rosy-red fls to 2$\frac{1}{4}$ in. *Ht:* 4 in; *Spd:* 6 in; *Fl:* 5–8; *Z:* Arct

D. deltoides Maiden pink: Eur. Reaches 6 in high and has a mass of small pink fls to $\frac{3}{4}$ in. Easy from cuttings in July or from seed. *Ht:* 8 in; *Spd:* 10 in; *Fl:* 6–10; *Z:* Arct

Dodecatheon

Shooting star

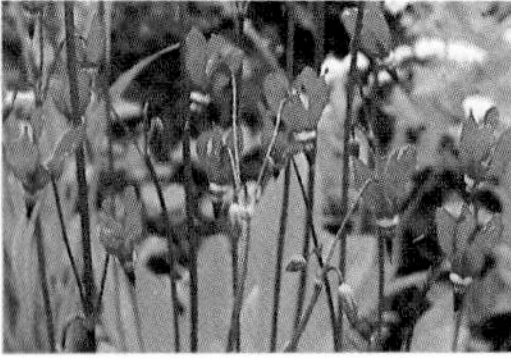

D. maedia

***D. meadia**:** N Amer. Striking and memorable fls from the grassy slopes of mountains, particularly in California. In gdns they like moisture and a little shade. Pink and white fls are poised like tiny comets on long elegant stems to 18 in. Increase by division or seed. *Spd:* 1 ft; *Fl:* 5–6; *Z:* Arct

Dryas

Mountain avens

D. octopetala

***D. octopetala**:** GB. Mat-forming, woody-stemmed. Little oak-like dark green lvs overlap and smother weeds. White, golden-centred single rose-like fls to 1 in arise in spring and summer. Silky seed heads. There is a miniature form *D. o. minor*. *Ht:* to 4 in; *Spd:* 2 ft; *Fl:* 5–6; *Z:* Arct

Erinus

Erinus

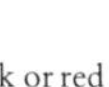

E. alpinus Summer starwort: Eur. Only 2 in high has mauve pink or red starry fls to $\frac{1}{4}$ in. Named forms inc 'Dr Hanelle' crimson and 'Mrs Charles Boyle' pink. *Spd:* 6 in; *Fl:* 3–8; *Z:* Arct

Euphorbia

Spurge

***E. myrsinites**:** S Eur. A fleshy glaucous trailer with terminal heads of greenish-yellow fls in heads to 4 in. Exudes a characteristic milky sap if broken. Easy from seed. *Ht:* 6 in; *Spd:* 18 in; *Fl:* 3–4; *Z:* F

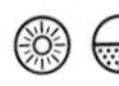  

Gentiana

Gentian

Synonymous with the Alps and rock gardens. Sometimes unpredictable; not all are dwarf. All gardens should have one.

G. acaulis Trumpet gentian: Eur Alps. Pure blue trumpet fls in spr held proudly over mats of green lvs. Likes lime while, as a rule of thumb, autumn-flowering ones (e.g. *G. sino-ornata)* hate it. *Ht:* 3 in; *Spd:* 14 in; *Fl:* 5–6; *Z:* Arct
G. septemfida***:** Caucasus. V easy, smr-flowering. Not fussy about soil. Good from midsmr on, conveniently between spr and aut sorts. *Ht:* 8 in; *Spd:* 1 ft; *Fl:* 7–8; *Z:* Arct

G. septemfida

Geranium

Cranesbill

G. cinereum: Pyrenees. Grey-green lvs are a perfect foil for the rosy-purple fls with dark-veined ptls. *G. dalmaticum* has neat glossy lvs and clear pink fls. *Ht:* 6 in; *Spd:* to 1 ft; *Fl:* 5–10; *Z:* PF

Gypsophila

Gypsophila, Baby's breath

G. repens: Eur Alps. Fleshy-rooted per. Branched stems support frothy clouds of fls. Miniatures of the herbaceous kinds; × 'Letchworth Rose' good long-flowering pink hyb. *Ht:* 10 in; *Spd:* to 2 ft; *Fl:* 6–8; *Z:* Arct

Haberlea

Haberlea

H. rhodopensis: Balkans. Tricky but rewarding plants related to ramondas and like them best grown on their sides in damp walls where their rosettes of lvs can be seen to advantage and water will drain off, preventing rotting. Lf rosettes are dark green and closely packed. Stems of fls *c.* 1 in diam in lavender flecked with gold in spr. *H. ferdinandi-coburgii* is a better form less frequently seen. *Ht:* 5 in; *Spd:* 8 in; *Fl:* 5; *Z:* Arct

H. rhodopensis

Helichrysum

Everlasting flower, Straw flower

H. bellidioides: New Zealand. One of a genus of sun-loving plants mainly grown in alpine houses but this sp is hardier than most gardeners think. Makes silvery lf mats all summer. *Ht:* 3 in; *Spd:* 1 ft; *Fl:* 5–8; *Z:* PF

Hepatica

Hepatica

H. transsilvanica***:** E Eur. The best sp in a genus deserving wider use. Lvs are puckered, kidney-shaped, fls a distinctive blue. Look for rare white, pink or double forms. *Ht:* 6 in; *Spd:* 10 in; *Fl:* 2–4; *Z:* Arct

Hieraceum

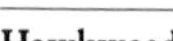

Hawkweed

H. villosum: C Eur. Yellow-flowered sp that can be invasive. Shaggy silvery lvs in rosettes support fl stems to 10 in; *Spd:* 18 in; *Fl:* 6–8; *Z:* Arct

Hypericum

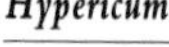

St John's wort

H. olympicum: S Eur. V easy member of a large sun-loving genus. Has blue-grey lvs and freely produced golden-yellow fls. Invasive *H. cerastoides* (= *H. rhodopeum*) also good. *Ht:* 1 ft; *Spd:* 10 in; *Fl:* 7–8; *Z:* PF

Iberis

Candytuft

***I. sempervirens**:** S Eur. Per version of the more colourful border anns. Evergreen fol in substantial mats good in wtr. 'Snowflake' is the best cv with pure white fls. *Ht:* 10 in; *Spd:* to 2 ft; *Fl:* 5–6; *Z:* Arct

Iris

Iris

I. pumila

I. cristata Crested iris: N Amer. A 3 in charmer with blue and gold fls in May and June. The tiny rhizomes like a little sun and cool root conditions. *Spd:* 6 in; *Z:* Arct

***I. pumila**:** Eur, Asia Minor. A wide range of excellent cvs. Cols inc white, pale or indigo blue and yellow. A yellow/brown one received an AGM in 1958 as *I. attica*. *Ht:* to 4 in; *Spd:* 6 in; *Fl:* 4; *Z:* Arct

Leontopodium

Edelweiss

L. alpinum

L. alpinum: C Eur, Asia. An unspectacular plant associated with the high Alps, gentians, yodelling and lederhosen, but not difficult to grow in lowland gdns given sufficient drainage. Fls 2 in wide are whitish-grey with a flannel-like texture, the lvs thin and grey-green. Fls last for sev weeks. *Ht:* 8 in; *Spd:* 9 in; *Fl:* 6–7; *Z:* Arct

Lewisia

Lewisia

L. cotyledon

L. cotyledon: N Amer. Forms rosettes of fleshy green lvs. Best grown in crevices with the rosettes placed vertically to let water drain off. *L. cotyledon* cvs are easiest and will tolerate some lime. Fls are pink to apricot, often striped. Easy from seed but prop cvs by div to maintain their identity. *Ht:* 1 ft; *Spd:* 6 in; *Fl:* 5–6; *Z:* PF

Lithospermum

L. diffusum: Med. Popular spreading sp with small dark green leaves. Produces sheets of exquisite gentian-blue $\frac{1}{2}$ in fls for weeks on end in June through to October. The best form is 'Heavenly Blue'★. The rampant European spp *L. purpureocaeruleum* will tolerate lime unlike the N. American ones. *Ht:* 6 in; *Spd:* 2 ft; *Z:* PF

L. diffusum 'Heavenly Blue'

Lysimachia

Creeping Jenny

***L. nummularia* 'Aurea':** Moneywort: GB. A golden-leaved form less vigorous than the type but good as ground cover. Bears small yellow fls *c.* $\frac{1}{3}$ in across in summer. *Ht:* 2 in; *Spd:* 18 in; *Fl:* 6–7; *Z:* Arct

L. nummularia

Onosma

Donkey plant

O. tauricum: Med. Low clumps with rather coarse lvs from which stems of pendant, tubular, soft yellow fragrant fls arise. Particularly useful for its long flowering season. All onosmas like to grow in rocky fissures and object to being disturbed. *Ht, Spd:* 10 in; *Fl:* 4–8; *Z:* PF–Arct

Oxalis

Oxalis

O. adenophylla: Chile. One of about 1,000 spp, most of which are invasive and should be avoided: never accept one as a gift. Has crinkly grey lvs and lavender or pink fls. The tuber is like a small coconut wrapped in fibrous scales and breaks up into bulbils easily used for propagation after flowering. *Ht:* $2\frac{1}{2}$ in; *Spd:* 6 in; *Fl:* 5–7; *Z:* PF

O. adenophylla

Penstemon

Penstemon

P. rupicola: N Amer. Prostrate woody per with grey-green lvs. Good in sinks and troughs as well as rock gdns. Rosy-carmine fls to 1 in. Prop by seed or cuttings. *Ht:* 4 in; *Spd:* 1 ft; *Fl:* 5–7; *Z:* PF

P. newberryi: W N Amer. Larger than *P. rupicola* with pink or mauve fls. *Ht:* to 18 in; *Spd:* 18 in; *Fl:* 6; *Z:* PF

P. newberryi

Phlox

Phlox

P. *douglasii*

P. douglasii Alpine phlox: Rocky Mts. Hummock-forming. Fls pink, mauve or white. 'Boothman's Variety' is mauve with a violet eye. *Ht:* 2 in; *Spd:* 18 in; *Fl:* 5–6; *Z:* Arct

P. subulata* Moss phlox: E USA. Carpet-forming. Good cvs inc 'Appleblossom' pale pink; 'G. F. Wilson' mauve; 'Temiscaming' magenta. *Ht:* 2 in; *Spd:* to 18 in; *Fl:* 4–5; *Z:* Arct

Polygonum

Knotweed

P. vaccinifolium: Him. From Aug to Oct trailing stems are adorned with pink candles of fls to 2 in. Dense mat of shining evergreen lvs. Useful on flat surfaces or dry walls. *Ht:* 4 in; *Spd:* 3 ft; *Z:* PF

Potentilla

Cinquefoil

P. × 'Tonguei'

P. alba: C, S Eur. Useful as a specimen or in gps as ground cover. Lvs glossy, dark green. Single fls white. *Ht:* 4 in; *Spd:* 15 in; *Fl:* 6–9; *Z:* PF

P. × 'Tonguei': gdn origin. Fls rich apricot, crimson blotched. Plant prostrate. *Ht:* 4 in; *Spd:* 15 in; *Fl:* 8–9; *Z:* PF

Pulsatilla

Pulsatilla

P. vulgaris 'Budapest'

P. vulgaris (= Anemone pulsatilla)* Pasque flower: Eur. Fls borne in Apr and May are 2–3 in across with silky purple ptls and hry stems to 8 in. 'Budapest' is excellent and good nurserymen occasionally offer a red-flowered var. Loves lime. High alpine spp such as *P. alpina* have white or sometimes yellow fls. Raise from seed. *Spd:* 15 in; *Z:* Arct

Ramonda

Ramonda

R. myconi: Pyrenees. Dark green rosettes of thick crinkled lvs with stems of lilac-blue, golden-eyed fls in sprays. Likes peaty soil. Plant on its side in a crevice or dry stone wall. *Ht:* 6 in; *Spd:* 10 in; *Fl:* 4–5; *Z:* Arct

Sanguinaria

Bloodroot

S. canadensis*: N Amer. A crawler of great class. Blue-grey lvs act as wrappers for the buds of exquisite single white fls to 1½ in diam. The rare double 'Flore Pleno' is superb. *Ht:* 6 in; *Spd:* 14 in; *Fl:* 4–5; *Z:* Arct

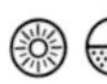   

Saponaria

Soapwort

S. ocymoides: Eur Alps. Good mat or wall-hanging to 20 in. Cheerful pink fls. Hyb × 'Bressingham Pink' is richer col. *Spd:* 1 ft; *Fl:* 6–9; *Z:* Arct

Saxifraga

Saxifrage

Silvery encrusted saxifrages like full sun but *S. umbrosa* and mossy ones need partial shade. All prefer lime.

S. cochlearis: Mar Alps. Forms mounds of silvery lime-encrusted lf rosettes. White fls on 5 in red stems. *S. aizoon* is larger but equally easy. *Spd:* 10 in; *Fl:* 6; *Z:* PF
S. fortunei*: China, Japan. Aut-flowering gem; glossy lvs with mahogany-red backs. Red stems to 18 in bear dainty white fls. 'Wada's Variety' has strikingly red lvs. Needs some shade and much moisture. *Spd:* 14 in; *Fl:* 10–11; *Z:* PF, LF
S. moschata: Eur. Forms soft carpets in partial shade. The many cvs include 'Dubarry' crimson; 'Flowers of Sulphur' yellow; 'Mother of Pearl' white. *Ht:* 6 in; *Spd:* 18 in; *Fl:* 4–5; *Z:* PF
S. stolonifera: China, Japan. Rounded veined lvs with little plantlets on runners. Hardy in gdns. *Ht, Spd:* 1 ft; *Fl:* 7–8; *Z:* PF

S. fortunei

S. moschata 'Edie Campbell'

Sedum

Stonecrop

A vast variety of fleshy rosette plants from a tiny cliff-top one to hearty herbaceous perennials. Many worth growing.

S. spurium: Caucasus. A mat-former. The species has bright crystalline pink fls. 'Schorbusser Blut' is an old deep red cv, 'Green Mantle' rarely flowers but is excellent ground cover. Divides easily. *Ht:* 2½ in; *Spd:* 1 ft; *Fl:* 7–8; *Z:* Arct

S. spurium

Sempervivum

Houseleek

S. tectorum: Eur. The best known of these clump-forming plants with succ lf rosettes. Has red fls and stout stems. *S. arachnoideum** has cobweb-like covering of white hrs. Good for dry places. *Ht:* 6 in; *Spd:* 1 ft; *Fl:* 7; *Z:* Arct

Silene

Campion, Catchfly

S. schafta: Caucasus. Strong magenta-pink fls in sprays to ¾ in freely displayed from July to Oct when they give welcome relief from autumn's orange and gold tints. 'Robusta' is a bit bigger. *Ht:* 6 in; *Spd:* 1 ft; *Z:* Arct

Sisyrinchium

Sisyrinchium

S. angustifolium Blue-eyed grass: N Amer. Has tufts of thin iris-like lvs and charming round fls on 6 in stems. *S. graminifolium*, 8 in, has yellow fls; *S. bermudiana*, 10 in, has violet-blue fls. *Spd:* 10 in; *Fl:* 5–10; *Z:* Arct

Tanacetum

Tanacetum

T. bipinnatum

T. bipinnatum (= densum amani): Asia Minor. The only interesting sp in the genus and one that botanists have continuously renamed. Makes humps of exquisite filigree silver fol. The yellow fls are pleasing but not of great value. Propagate by cuttings. *Ht:* 8 in; *Spd:* 18 in; *Fl:* 8; *Z:* PF

Teucrium

Teucrium, Germander

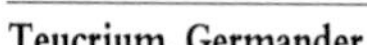

T. chamaedrys* Wall germander: S, C Eur. The best-known sp, often classified as a herb and only suitable for the larger rock gdn or a border edge, but try dwarf 'Nana'. Fls pink. *Ht:* 8 in; *Spd:* 16 in; *Fl:* 7–9; *Z:* PF

Thymus

Thyme

T. serpyllum*: Eur. An absolutely prostrate carpeting herb; lvs dark green. Select from 'Annie Hall' pale pink; 'Pink Chintz' deep pink; 'Coccineus' crimson; 'Albus' white to give a mass of fls. *Spd:* 20 in; *Fl:* 6–7; *Z:* Arct

Veronica

Speedwell

V. prostrata

V. prostrata: Eur–USSR. An easy plant to 4 in with tiny fls in spires of brilliant blue and trailing mats of green lvs. 'Spode Blue' is brighter than the type while 'Mrs Holt' is pink and 'Alba' white. Other spp notorious lawn weeds. *Spd:* 16 in; *Fl:* 5–7; *Z:* Arct

Waldsteinia

Waldsteinia

W. ternata: Eur. A mat-forming sp for the slopes and plains of the rock gdn or as ground cover on a larger scale. Has 3-lobed lvs which colour in autumn and back up the showers of buttercup-yellow fls to ½ in diam. Has surface rooting stems and is easily divided. *Ht:* 2½ in; *Spd:* 18 in; *Fl:* 4–5; *Z:* F

W. ternata

Bog, waterside and pond plants

Plants that live in water or in permanently saturated soil are distinct from those that like moisture, but also need drainage. The latter need oxygen in the soil; the former can dispense with it. Some water plants, in fact, can do without soil altogether and live afloat. This section includes plants for the water itself and for the boggy brink.

Acorus

Acorus

A. calamus Sweet flag: Eur, S Asia, N Amer. Iris-like plant; sword-shaped lvs with wavy edges. Fls curious, greenish-yellow in 4 in spikes like stubby thumbs. *A. c. variegatus* more decorative with creamy-yellow and green lvs. Prop by div. *Ht:* to 3 ft; *Spd:* 2 ft; *Fl:* 6; *Z:* PF

A. calamus

Alisma

Water plantain

A. lanceolatum: N Temp zones. Lvs spear-shaped and veined like lawn plantain. Fls ¼ in wide, pale pink to white in loose clouds on branching stems. Prop by div, seed. *Ht:* to 3 ft; *Spd:* 20 in; *Fl:* 7; *Z:* PF

Aponogeton

Aponogeton

A. distachyus Water hawthorn: S Africa. Floating narrow lively green lvs. Stubby forked fl stems bear white, single-petalled frag fls with brown/purple anthers. *Ht:* 6 in; *Spd:* 20 in; *Fl:* 4–10; *Z:* PF

Butomus

Flowering rush

B. umbellatus: Temp Eur and Asia. Uprt plant with tough narrow pointed lvs with a purplish sheen in infancy, becoming green as they develop. Fls rose-pink, 1 in wide, borne in a terminal umbrella on green stems. Rootstock edible. Prop by div. *Ht:* to 3 ft; *Spd:* 20 in; *Fl:* 6–8; *Z:* PF

B. umbellatus

Calla

Calla

C. palustris Bog arum: E N Amer, N Asia, N Eur. Wandering marginal or shallow-water plant with dark green spear-shaped lvs and white arum-lily-like 4 in fls followed by attractive red berries. Prop by div of creeping rhizomes. *Ht:* to 8 in; *Spd:* 2 ft; *Fl:* 6; *Z:* PF

C. palustris

Caltha

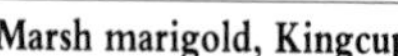

Marsh marigold, Kingcup

C. palustris

***C. palustris**:** Eur, N Amer–Arct, Caucasus. Marginal plant with heart-shaped lvs to 10 in wide when mature. Fls like large golden buttercups 2 in wide on pale green stems. There are single white and an excellent double yellow-flowered form 'Plena'. Prop by div, seed. *Ht:* 1 ft; *Spd:* 18 in; *Fl:* 3–4; *Z:* PF

Cyperus

Sedge

C. papyrus

C. longus Galingale, Umbrella grass: GB. Decorative, grass-like shining green lvs in umbrella-like whorl. Prop by div, seed. *Ht:* to 4 ft; *Spd:* 1 ft; *Fl:* 7–10; *Z:* Arct

C. papyrus Egyptian paper reed: Egypt. Lvs narrow, v small. Stems to 9 ft support mop-like heads of slender threads. Needs warmth. *Spd:* 2 ft; *Fl:* 7–9; *Z:* SF

Eichhornia

Water hyacinth

***E. speciosa (=crassipes)**:** S Amer, Trop Africa. Lvs shiny, heart-shaped; swollen lf stks act as support. Fls funnel-shaped, lavender-blue with gold markings in spikes to 1 ft. Long, trailing purplish rts spread by runners. Prop by div. *Ht:* to 18 in; *Spd:* 1 ft; *Fl:* 6–7; *Z:* NF

Glyceria

Manna grass

G. aquatica variegata: N Hem. Lvs flat, pale green to 3 in wide, striped white. Fls grass-like. *Ht:* to 1 ft; *Spd:* 18 in; *Fl:* 7–9; *Z:* Arct

Gunnera

Gunnera

G. manicata

***G. manicata**:** Brazil. Colossal coarse rhubarb-like lvs to 6 ft wide, on stout, rough, warty stems. Fl spike from base is greenish-brown and club-like to 3 ft long, but the lvs are the main attraction. Prop by div, seed. *Ht:* to 14 ft; *Spd:* 20 ft; *Fl:* 7–10; *Z:* PF

Houttuynia

Houttuynia

H. cordata: Him, China, Japan. Lvs alternate, heart-shaped, bluish-green. Stems uprt, angular, lfy. Fls tiny below elliptical white lflts in 4s. Smells of orange peel when crushed. *Ht:* 18 in; *Spd:* 1 ft; *Fl:* 6; *Z:* Arct

Iris

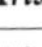

Iris

I. kaempferi*★* Clematis-flowered iris: Japan. Fls to 8 in wide, purple, white, pink or red, may be blotched. *Ht:* 3 ft; *Spd:* 18 in; *Fl:* 7; *Z:* Arct
I. laevigata*★***:** Japan. Tall, fine, strap-like lvs. Fls rich blue, gold mark at ptl base, also white forms. *Ht:* 2 ft; *Spd:* 18 in; *Fl:* 7; *Z:* Arct
I. sibirica*★***:** Eur, USSR. Elegant; narrow lax lvs, neat blue fls. *Ht:* 3 ft; *Spd:* 2 ft; *Fl:* 6; *Z:* Arct

I. kaempferi

Juncus

Rush

J. effusus 'Spiralis' Corkscrew rush: gdn origin. Writhing green stems spiral from the water's surface. 'Vittatus' has lvs striped yellow. Fls insignificant. Prop by div. *Ht:* to 18 in; *Spd:* 15 in; *Z:* Arct

Ligularia

Ligularia

L. dentata (=clivorum): China. Rounded dark green toothed lvs. Fls daisy-like bright orange to 4 in wide. 'Desdemona'★ is magnificent with shining maroon-backed lvs. Prop by div. *Ht:* to 7 ft; *Spd:* 3 ft; *Fl:* 7–8; *Z:* Arct

Lobelia

Lobelia

L. cardinalis Cardinal flower: N Amer. Brilliant rich-scarlet fls, snapdragon-like on 1 side of lfy stems. Lvs smooth, flat, deep green or purple. *L. syphilitica* has clear bright blue fls in lf axils in Aug–Sept and oblong green lvs; there is also a white-flowered form. Prop both spp by div. *Ht:* 3 ft; *Spd:* 1 ft; *Fl:* 7–8; *Z:* PF

Lysichitum (=Lysichiton)

Lysichitum

Dramatic growth of a dazzling yellow or white flower from ground level. Often (wrongly) called Skunk cabbage.

L. americanum Bog arum: W N Amer. Noble bright green lvs, uprt or flopping, to 3 ft × 8 in with sturdy centre rib. Fls like arum lilies to 2 ft, light yellow with green spadix. *Ht:* to 3 ft; *Spd:* 6 ft; *Fl:* 4; *Z:* Arct
L. camtschatcense: Kamtschatka, Japan. Sim to above but white fls 1 ft long. Less easy to prop by seed but both easy by div. *Ht, Spd:* to 3 ft; *Fl:* 5; *Z:* Arct

L. americanum

Lysimachia

Lysimachia

L. punctata: Asia Minor. Erect, lightly hry plant bearing whorls of oblong pointed lvs and bright blue fls in 8 in spikes. Prop by div or seed. *Ht:* 3 ft; *Spd:* 2 ft; *Fl:* 7–9; *Z:* Arct

Mentha  

Mint

M. citrata (=aquatica citrata) Water mint: Eur. Smooth-leaved lemon-scented mint. Fls lavender-blue in 4 in spikes in July–Sept. Prop by division. *Ht:* 1 ft; *Spd:* 2 ft; *Z:* Arct

Mimulus  

Monkey flower

M. guttatus (=luteus guttatus) Monkey musk: N Amer. Spreads and clambers freely. Lvs light green, main stems hollow; 2 in fls are 5-lobed funnels, yellow spotted brown/purple. *Ht, Spd:* 20 in; *Fl:* 6–7; *Z:* PF

Myosotis    

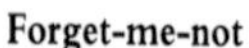

Forget-me-not

M. palustris

M. scorpioides (=palustris) Water forget-me-not: Eur, Asia. Fls to $\frac{1}{2}$ in wide typical forget-me-not-blue with a yellow eye. Rounded lvs a shining rich green. Prop by seed, div or cuttings. *Ht:* to 1 ft; *Spd:* to 18 in; *Fl:* 5–6; *Z:* Arct

Nelumbo   

Lotus

N. nucifera

N. nucifera* E Indian lotus: Asia. Rhizomatous plant for warm water with rounded blue-green wavy-edged lvs to 15 in diam on stems to 6 ft. Chalice-shaped fls white with pink tips or all pink, frag. Seed heads conical, v decorative. *N. lutea* (American lotus) sim but fls yellow. Prop by div or seed. *Ht:* to 6 ft; *Spd:* 30 ft+; *Fl:* 7–9; *Z:* PF

Nuphar   

Water lily

N. advena

N. advena Yellow water lily: N Amer. Tough heart-shaped lvs, stems semicircular in section. Fls chrome yellow, partially open globes held over water surface. *N. lutea* Brandy Bottle has sim but smaller fls with an alcoholic odour. Prop by div, seed. *Ht:* 20 in; *Spd:* to 6 ft; *Fl:* 5–9; *Z:* Arct

Water lily

The loveliest of water-plants are remarkably easy to grow. They can be planted in a weighted sack or perforated container.

N. alba* White water lily: Eur. Young lvs deep red. Fls waxy white, full petalled, green stripe on backs. *Ht:* 1 ft; *Spd:* 6 ft; *Fl:* 7–9; *Z:* Arct
N. gdn hybs*: gdn origin. V many good ones to choose from. Tender/trop sorts inc: 'Mrs G.H.Pring' white; 'St Louis' yellow; 'Mrs C.W.Ward' pink; 'Blue Beauty'; 'Gloire de Temple sur Lot' double; 'Darwin' striped. More vig red cvs are 'Escarboucle'; 'James Brydon'. *Ht:* to 15 in; *Spd:* to 6 ft; *Fl:* 6–9; *Z:* PF
N. × laydekeri: gdn origin. Small hybs with fls *c.* 4 in diam. The two best are 'Lilacea' pink, deepening to crimson and 'Purpurata' red. *Ht:* 15 in; *Spd:* 3 ft; *Fl:* 6–9; *Z:* PF
N. × marliacea: gdn origin. Blanket name for many hybs inc 'Albida' white, frag; 'Chromatella' yellow; 'Rosea' soft pink. *Ht:* to 4 ft; *Spd:* 3 ft; *Fl:* 6–9; *Z:* PF
N. odorata: N Amer. Frag white fls. Cvs inc 'Sulphurea' yellow. *Ht:* 15 in; *Spd:* 3 ft; *Fl:* 6–9; *Z:* PF
N. × pygmaea: gdn origin. Miniatures with fls 2–3 in wide. Rec are 'Alba' white; 'Helvola' yellow. *Ht:* 1 ft; *Spd:* 18 in; *Fl:* 6–9; *Z:* PF

N. gdn hybrid 'Escarboucle'

N. alba 'Gladstone'

N. × *marliacea* 'Rosea'

Peltiphyllum

Umbrella plant

P. peltatum: Cal. Lvs large, nearly circular, lobed, roughly hry. Fls white or pale pink in a flat head on substantial stem before lvs fully developed. Prop by div. *Ht, Spd:* to 2 ft; *Fl:* 4; *Z:* PF

P. peltatum

Pontaderia

Pontaderia

P. cordata Pickerel weed: N Amer. Vigorous plant. Lvs arrow-head-like, smooth green on erect stks. Fls 5-petalled, light blue in 4 in spikes. Prop by div. *Ht:* 18 in; *Spd:* 1 ft+; *Fl:* 7–9; *Z:* PF

P. cordata

Primula

Primula, Primrose

P. sikkimensis: SE Asia. Frag pale yellow fls in long terminal head; lvs oval, glossy green. Many spp listed under herbaceous pers also suitable (except *Polyanthus* hybs). *Ht:* 30 in; *Spd:* 18 in; *Fl:* 5–6; *Z:* Arct

Rheum

Ornamental rhubarb

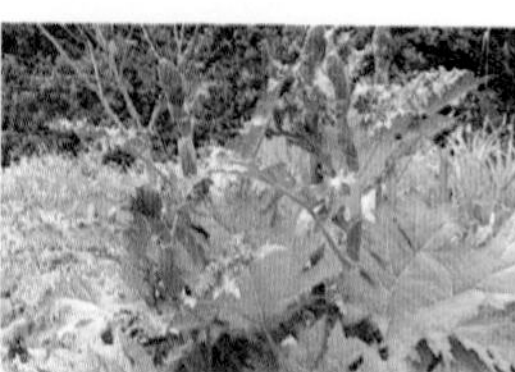

R. palmatum

R. palmatum: China. Elegant rhubarb with large roughly heart-shaped lvs cleanly cut and lobed. Fls red in 3 ft spikes. The cvs 'Atrosanguineum'* and 'Bowles' Form' have rich red young lvs; lf undersides also red fading to green during the season. *Ht:* 8 ft; *Spd:* 6 ft; *Fl:* 6; *Z:* PF

Rodgersia

Rodgersia

R. aesculifolia

R. aesculifolia*: China. Lvs horse-chestnut-shaped to 18 in across, coarsely toothed with brown highlights. Stems covered with brown hrs. Fls tinted white or pink in broadly based panicles to 18 in. Prop by seed, div of rhizomes. *Ht:* to 4 ft; *Spd:* 20 in; *Fl:* 7–10; *Z:* PF

Thalia

Thalia

T. dealbata: Carolina, Texas. Tall, slender plant. Lvs grey/green with whitish bloom. Fls sev per group, violet-purple, hanging from tall stems. Prop by div. *Ht:* to 2 ft; *Spd:* 15 in; *Fl:* 6–9; *Z:* PF

Trollius

Globe flower

T. europaeus: Eur. Bigger, better buttercups; fls globe-shaped to 2½ in wide. Lvs hrlss. Cvs, esp of *C.* × *cultorum* rec, e.g. 'Alabaster' white; 'Canary Bird' yellow. Prop by div. *Ht:* 2 ft; *Spd:* 18 in; *Fl:* 5–6; *Z:* Arct

Zantedeschia

Zantedeschia

Z. aethiopica

Z. (=Calla) aethiopica* Arum lily, Lily of the Nile: S Africa. Bulbous plant with rich dark green arrow-shaped lvs and typical white fl spathes to 9 in with golden yellow spadix. Tender in many areas. Cv 'Crowborough' considerably more hardy. Prop by div. *Ht:* to 4 ft; *Spd:* 2 ft; *Fl:* 6–8; *Z:* SF

Herbs

A non-botanical classification of plants found useful for flavouring, medicinal or cosmetic purposes rather than for actual food or decoration. Most are aromatic and/or flavoursome and few are showy "flowers". They can be shrubby, perennial or annual. Generally the shrubs prefer dry soil, annuals relatively moist conditions and the perennials are not particular.

Allium

Allium

A. sativum Clove garlic: Med. Pungent hardy per. Fls star-shaped, white or purplish. Plant 2 in deep in spr, harvest in late Aug. *Ht:* to 3 ft; *Spd:* 1 ft; *Fl:* 6; *Z:* Arct

A. schoenoprasum Chives: N Hem. Clumps of grassy lvs with onion flavour. Remove mauve fl heads to encourage lf growth. Good edging. *Ht:* 8 in; *Spd:* 1 ft; *Fl:* 6–7; *Z:* Arct

A. schoenoprasum

Anethum

Dill

A. graveolens: Eur. Fennel-like ann to 3 ft. Lvs finely dissected, fls mustard-yellow in flat heads to 3 in wide. Lvs and seeds used in cooking and to flavour vinegar. Prop by seed. *Spd:* 1 ft; *Fl:* 6–8

Angelica

Angelica

A. archangelica*: Eur. Stately short-lived per (sometimes only biennial) usually *c.* 7 ft tall. Stems hollow, lvs rich, fresh green 2 ft or more long. Fls yellow-green in rounded heads 3 in wide. Candied angelica made from stems. Prop by seed in spring or late summer. *Spd:* 3 ft; *Fl:* 7–8; *Z:* PF

A. archangelica

Anthemis

Chamomile

A. nobilis: Eur. Low-growing with rich green lvs. Fls daisy-like. Non-flowering 'Treneague' used as lawns. *Ht, Spd:* 15 in; *Fl: 6–8; Z:* Arct

Anthriscus

Chervil

A. cerefolium: E Eur. Lvs lacy and bright green, slightly aniseed in flavour. Used in sim way to parsley. Stems hollow, fls tiny. Hardy ann or per; prop by seed at regular intervals. *Ht:* 18 in; *Spd:* 1 ft; *Fl:* 6–8

Artemisia

Artemisia

A. dracunculus Tarragon: Eur, Asia. Two types in cultivation—Russian: hardier, to 4 ft, fresh matt green thin lvs; French: More flavour, to 2 ft, lvs darker, glossier. Prop by div, seed. *Spd:* 15 in; *Fl:* 8; *Z:* Arct

Borago

Borage

B. officinalis

B. officinalis: Eur. Easy ann with cucumber-flavoured lvs; an essential garnish for summer drinks. Lvs and stks coarsely hry. True-blue 5-petalled starry fls to 1 in diam can be candied. Sow seed in April, thin out to 15 in. *Ht:* to 3 ft; *Fl:* 6–9

Carum

Caraway

C. carvi: Eur–N India. Slim v branched ann to 2 ft with finely cut lacy green lvs and flat heads of white fls. Lvs and seeds are used for their flavour and are said to "relieve flatulence". *Spd:* 1 ft; *Fl:* 6–7

Coriandrum

Coriander

C. sativum

C. sativum: Eur. Ann *c.* 18 in tall. Finely divided shining green lvs with an aniseed flavour. Fls white or pale lilac in a 5–10-rayed cartwheel. Seeds aromatic but smell unpleasant until dry. Reputedly aphrodisiac. Prop by seed in April. *Spd:* 1 ft; *Fl:* 6–8

Crocus

Crocus

C. sativus

C. sativus Saffron: S Eur–Kurdistan. Aut-flowering small crocus with bright lilac fls 4 in high from whose prominent scarlet stigmas saffron is obtained for use as a flavouring and colouring. Pinch out and dry them. Lvs typically crocus-like to 18 in. Prop by corms planted in July–mid Aug. *Spd:* 4 in; *Fl:* 10; *Z:* PF

Cuminum

Cumin

C. cyminum: Egypt. Ann to 1 ft with v branched stems. Lvs finely cut, deep green. Fls pale rose-pink or white in small heads. Seeds used as flavouring in Arabian, Levantine and Indian cooking. *Spd:* 8 in; *Fl:* 6–7

Foeniculum

Fennel

***F. vulgare**:** Eur. Graceful per. Branched green stems; finely cut rich green lvs and seeds with aniseed flavour. Often used with fish. Fls yellow; prop by seed. Also a good brown-lvd form. *Ht:* 5 ft; *Spd:* 2 ft; *Fl:* 7–8; *Z:* PF

Hyssopus

Hyssop

H. officinalis: S Eur. Semi-evergreen bushy shrub to 2 ft, good as edging plant. Lvs narrow, dark green, aromatic. Fls blue, white or pink *c.* ¾ in wide. Prop by cuttings or sow seed in April. *Spd:* 1 ft; *Fl:* 7–9; *Z:* Arct

H. officinalis

Levisticum

Lovage

L. officinale (= Ligusticum scoticum)**: Eur. Uprt per, celery-like in looks and flavour but taller. Lvs rich green, fls white in July (remove when plant grown as herb). Prop by seed. *Ht:* to 3 ft; *Spd:* 15 in; *Z:* PF

Lippia

Verbena

L. citriodora Lemon or sweet-scented verbena: Chile. Decid shrub with pointed coarse lvs 3–4 in long, intensely lemon-scented. Not often seen more than 5 ft tall but can reach 9 ft in a warm sheltered spot. Fls faded purple in panicles to 4 in long. Prop by cuttings in late smr. *Spd:* 4 ft; *Fl:* 8; *Z:* SF

L. citriodora

Mentha

Mint

M. spicata Spearmint: Eur. The most common mint with smooth lvs. All mints are vig plants: any rooted piece will grow if planted in Feb or March. Most gardeners have a favourite sort. *M. rotundifolia* (Apple mint) with hry lvs and purplish-white fls rec. There is a pretty white-variegated form*. *Ht:* 3 ft; *Spd:* 2 ft; *Fl:* 8; *Z:* Arct

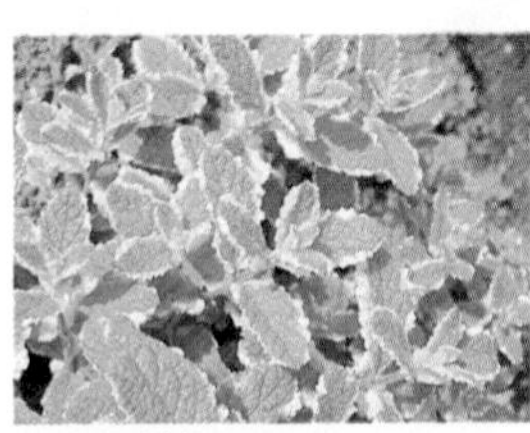

M. rotundifolia 'Variegata'

Myrrhis

Myrrhis

M. odorata Sweet cicely: GB. Hardy per with aromatic pale green foliage like pressed lace. Used in salads and omelettes: not unlike chervil (p 77). Stems 2–3 ft tall bear sev flat heads of white fls in May–June. Prop by seed in March/April. *Spd:* 2 ft; *Z:* Arct

M. odorata

Nasturtium (= Rorippa)

Watercress

N. officinale: Eur. Hardy per salad vegetable or herb. Best in a wet place or shallow stream. Lvs dark green with a peppery flavour. Land or American cress needs less moisture. *Spd:* 2 ft; *Fl:* 6; *Z:* Arct

Ocimum

Basil

O. basilicum Common or sweet basil: Trop Asia. Tall ann. Small oblong lvs have a unique flavour excellent with tomatoes. Fls white, tubular. Prop by seed. Only flourishes in hot smrs. *Ht:* 18 in; *Spd:* 1 ft; *Fl:* 8

Origanum

Origanum

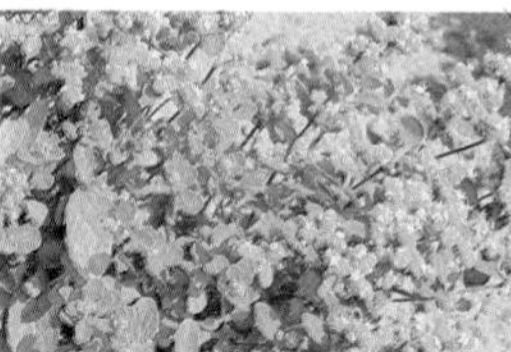

O. marjorana

O. marjorana Sweet marjoram: N Africa. Nearly hardy sub-shrub. Small blunt hry lvs used fresh or dried to flavour poultry or veal. Fls white or faded maroon. Prop by seed under glass in March. Pot marjoram (*O. onites*) is a hardy per; Winter marjoram (*O. heracleoticum*) is less hardy. *Ht:* to 2 ft; *Spd:* 1 ft; *Fl:* 6; *Z:* SF

Petroselinum

Parsley

P. crispum

P. crispum: C, S Eur. Hardy biennial, slow and sometimes hard to germinate, with curled lflts. French or flat-lvd parsley has a better flavour and is easier to grow. Sow only fresh seed. *Ht:* to 2 ft; *Spd:* 9 in; *Fl:* 6–8; *Z:* Arct

Rosmarinus

Rosemary

R. officinalis

R. officinalis*: S Eur, Asia Minor. Shrub with narrow aromatic lvs used particularly to flavour pork and lamb. Usually *c.* 4 ft but can be taller. Fls pale blue, 2-lipped, ¾ in long, on last year's growth in March–April. Prop by cuttings taken in mid-Aug. Uprt and variegated forms grown ornamentally. *Spd:* 6 ft; *Z:* PF

Rumex

Sorrel

R. acetosa: W Asia, N Africa, Eur. Easy strong-growing per to 2 ft. Spear-shaped lvs like spinach pleasantly acid-tasting and make excellent soup. Remove fls. Prop by div or seed in spr. *Spd:* 9 in; *Fl:* 5–8; *Z:* Arct

Rue

R. graveolens: Eur. Small shrub with unpleasant-smelling pungent green lvs. Used medicinally and in claret cup. Fls mustard-yellow in flat heads. Do not confuse with blue-lvd border rue. *Ht, Spd:* 18 in; *Fl:* 6–9; *Z:* Arct

Salvia

Sage

S. officinalis: S Eur. Low evergreen branching shrub 1 ft × 18 in, inclined to layer. Lvs oblong like wrinkled grey-green felt, strong-flavoured and often used with pork. Purple, blue or white 2-lipped fls to 1½ in. Sev coloured-lf forms grown ornamentally but taste the same. Others grown as anns, herbaceous pers. *Fl:* 5–7; *Z:* Arct

S. officinalis

Satureia

Savory

S. montana: S Eur, N Africa. Semi-evergreen sprawling shrub, can be used as an edging plant. Narrow lvs and pale purple fls. Prop by div or seed. *S. hortensis* is a shorter hardy ann. Both can be used as an alternative to thyme. *Ht:* to 15 in; *Spd:* 1 ft; *Fl:* 6; *Z:* Arct

S. montana

Symphytum

Comfrey

S. officinale: Eur, E to Siberia, Turkey. Roughly hry per. Fleshy pale green shoots and sim lvs used in same way as spinach. Fls tubular, white, blue purple or pink in clusters. *Ht:* 4 ft; *Spd:* 20 in; *Fl:* 6; *Z:* Arct

Trigonella

Fenugreek

T. foenum-graecum Classical fenugreek: S France. Uprt ann to 2 ft, many divided lvs. Small white fls followed by seeds with strong celery flavour in sickle-shaped pods. Prop by seed in Apr. *Spd:* 1 ft; *Fl:* 6–8

Thymus

Thyme

T. vulgaris Common thyme: S Eur. Small densely branched wiry spreading bush 6–9 in tall good for edging paths. Tiny deep green lvs, hry on underside, strongly aromatic, excellent for flavouring. Lilac fls in closely packed 2 in heads from June–Aug. Prop by cuttings in May or June in cold frame, or by div, seed. *Spd:* 1 ft; *Z:* Arct

T. vulgaris

Ferns

Flowerless, richly leafy plants reproducing by spores, usually found on their frond undersides. Although suggestive of dank caves several tolerate the worst garden conditions: dry shade.

Adiantum

Maidenhair fern

A. pedatum

A. pedatum American maidenhair fern: N Amer. Perfectly hardy decid fern with pale green lflts on shining black wiry stems to 18 in. Forms light frothy clumps to 10 in wide. Needs moist but well-drained soil. Prop by div or spores. *Z:* Arct

Dryopteris

Dryopteris

D. filix-mas

D. filix-mas* Male fern: Temp zones. Esp useful for dry shady places but naturally better where there is more moisture. Has tapered feather-shaped fronds to 3 ft tall and 9 in wide at the base, making clumps 2–3 ft across. Decid. Prop by division or spores. *Z:* Arct

Matteuccia

Matteuccia

M. struthiopteris* Ostrich plume fern: N Hem. Graceful fern; 3 ft tapering fronds form a green funnel or shuttlecock shape *c.* 2 ft wide at the mouth. Decid but some fronds stay brown until spr. Prop by div, spores. *Z:* Arct

Onoclea

Onoclea

O. sensibilis Sensitive fern, Bead fern: N Amer, N Asia. Good ground cover in moist soils, spreading by rhizomes. Lvs to 18 in, usually arching, thick cut with rounded lobes. *Ht:* 2 ft; *Spd:* 5 ft; *Z:* Arct

Osmunda

Royal fern

O. regalis

O. regalis* Flowering fern: Worldwide except Australasia. Bold stately decid fern esp attractive in early spr when unfurling fronds resemble meditating monks. Lvs 4 ft high with large blades over tough, fibrous rootstock. Prop by div or spores which germinate rapidly when fresh. *Ht, Spd:* 4 ft; *Z:* Arct

Bulbs, corms and tubers

"Bulb" is taken as the group term for plants with swollen underground parts for the storage of supplies, and includes corms (as in crocuses), tubers (as in cyclamen) and rhizomes (as in irises). These parts make a highly convenient package for transplanting and sale, since many have a dormant period when they need no moisture (lilies are an important exception). Most of these plants reproduce by both offsets and seed.

Achimenes

Achimenes

A. hybs: C, S Amer. Curious tuberous plants; those commonly grown are hybs with rough or hairy lvs and funnel-shaped red, pink, white, mauve or deep blue fls. Start in heat. *Ht:* 1 ft; *Spd:* 8 in; *Fl:* 7–8; *Z:* NF

Acidanthera

Acidanthera

A. bicolor: Ethiopia. V like a white gladiolus with fls 2 in wide. It differs in having the tube of ptl-like parts at right angles to the stem and flowers in late Sept–Oct. *A. b. murielae* is hardiest in the gdn and has a purple blotch at the base of each ptl. Prop by corms or seed. Also good in pots. *Ht:* 3 ft; *Spd:* 6 in; *Z:* NF

A. bicolor murielae

Allium

Ornamental onion

A large genus including chives and garlic. All are easy in well-drained borders; most smell of onions if bruised.

A. christophii (= albopilosum)**: Turkestan. The biggest drumstick heads of any onion with 8 in globes of lilac fls. Equally valuable when dry. The strap-shaped lvs are more substantial than others in the genus. Prop by seed or bulblets. *Ht:* 20 in; *Spd:* 8 in; *Fl:* 6; *Z:* Arct
A. giganteum: Him. A splendid globular purplish fl head 4 in wide on a sturdy stem to 4 ft in June. Can be planted to come through low pers. Prop by seed or offsets. *Spd:* 1 ft; *Z:* Arct
A. moly: Med. Has bright yellow clusters of star-fls in July on 8 in stems over bluish-green lvs. Spreads and sows itself freely; easy to naturalize. Prop by seed or division. *Spd:* 1 ft; *Z:* Arct

A. giganteum

A. moly

Amaryllis

Belladonna lily

A. belladonna

A. belladonna: S Africa. Plant these large bulbs *c.* 8 in deep in a warm well-drained place as at the foot of a south facing wall, then leave undisturbed. Pink, mauve-tinted, trumpet-shaped fls 4 in wide with a paler throat appear in Sept–Oct followed by strap-shaped lvs in early spring. Prop by dividing clumps or from seed. *Ht:* 30 in; *Spd:* 1 ft; *Z:* SF

Anemone

Anemone, Windflower

Daisy-like flowers of simplicity and charm. Those listed are woodland plants with rhizomes or tubers flowering in spring.

A. blanda

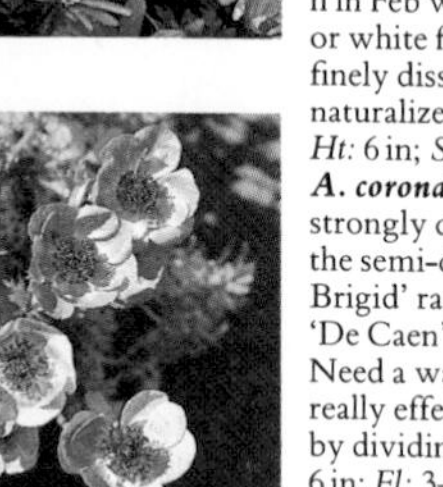

A. coronaria

A. apennina: S Eur. Rhizomatous March–April flowering sp. Naturalizes happily in the light shade of trees or the open border. Has sky-blue circular fls like larger daisies. Prop by division. *Ht:* 6 in; *Spd:* 4 in; *Z:* PF

A. blanda*: Greece–E Eur. Often in fl in Feb with pale to deep blue, pink or white fls 1½ in wide and soft, finely dissected lvs. Best left to naturalize. Divide tubers to increase. *Ht:* 6 in; *Spd:* 4 in; *Z:* F

A. coronaria: S Eur. A range of strongly coloured hybs including the semi-double or full-petalled 'St Brigid' race and the single-flowered 'De Caen' strain plus sev named cvs. Need a warm protected site to be really effective. Good cut fls. Prop by dividing tubers. *Ht:* 1 ft; *Spd:* 6 in; *Fl:* 3–4; *Z:* F

Anthericum

St Bernard's lily

A. liliago*: S Eur (Alpine meadows). Clump-forming, fleshy tuberous-rooted per with narrow 1 ft grass-like lvs and elegant clusters of pure white 1½ in fls. Prop by division. *Ht:* 18 in; *Spd:* 16 in; *Fl:* 6–7; *Z:* PF

Antholyza (= Curtonus)

Antholyza

A. (= Curtonus) paniculata Aunt Eliza: S Africa. Like a giant montbretia with pleated lvs and an arching stem. Burnt orange/red fls are a narrow trumpet shape to 2 in long in a zig-zag. *Ht:* 4 ft; *Spd:* 10 in; *Fl:* 8–9; *Z:* PF

Arisaema

Arisaema

A. candidissimum*: W China. Enchanting sugar-pink and pale green fls to 3 in and 3-lobed lvs make this a v decorative plant. Needs moist but not wet soil. Slow from seed. *Ht:* 10 in; *Spd:* 1 ft; *Fl:* 6; *Z:* Arct

Arum

Flowers arranged on a central proboscis or spadix are shielded by a leafy cloak or spathe—these parts are the main attraction.

A. italicum Italian arum: Eur inc Med. A larger version of the hedgerow Lords and ladies with yellow spathes 7 in high appearing in aut. *A. i. marmoratum* has variegated lvs and a marbled spathe, purplish at the base. Prop by seed or division of tubers. *Spd:* 6 in; *Fl:* 9–10; *Z:* PF
***A. pictum**:** Spain, Corsica. Flowers a little later before lvs appear. Stouter and with larger lvs lasting all winter. Glistening red berries make a striking aut group. Prop by division or seed. *Ht:* 10 in; *Spd:* 6 in; *Fl:* 9–10; *Z:* PF

A. italicum

Babiana

Baboon root

B. stricta hybs: S Africa. Gladiolus-like, open tubular fls for a dry place; wiry stems *c.* 1 ft. Fls are brilliantly coloured and can be blue, violet, pink, crimson or yellow, often with a blotch at the base of each ptl and a sweet scent. Prop by corm offsets. *Spd:* 4 in; *Fl:* 6–5; *Z:* PF

Begonia

Begonia

Two tuberous-rooted begonias are commonly planted in gardens; many others are used in greenhouses or as house plants. The fibrous-rooted sorts are used for edging and carpeting.

B. grandis evansiana Hardy begonia: E Asia. Has heart-shaped lvs green above, red below and single pinks fls to $1\frac{3}{4}$ in wide on lax branching stems to 2 ft in light shade and warmth. Prop by bulblets. *Spd:* 1 ft; *Fl:* 6–9; *Z:* PF
***B. stricta hybs (B × tuberhybrida)**:** gdn origin. The big bedding sorts with fls to 6 in. Many named cvs in a wide variety of colours. *Ht:* 20 in; *Spd:* 16 in; *Fl:* 6–9; *Z:* SF

B. grandis evansiana

Brodiaea (= Tritelia)

Ithuriel's spear

B. laxa: Cal. One of a range of graceful spp and part of the supporting cast of the July gdn. Has agapanthus-like clusters of widely spaced funnel-shaped violet-blue or white fls $1\frac{3}{4}$ in long on slender stems to 2 ft. Prop by offsets. Do not disturb once planted. *Spd:* 4 in; *Z:* PF

Caladium

Caladium

C. bicolor: S Amer. Variable but gorgeous with lvs generally deep pink in the centre merging to white then green. Several cvs also have violet and red stems. Lift in aut when the foliage collapses. Feed often in growth. Should not dry out completely in storage. *Ht:* 1 ft; *Spd:* 10 in; *Z:* NF

Calochortus

Mariposa lily

C. venustus: Cal. Each of the 3 ptls is yellow at the base with a purple blotch and often a pink blotch near top. *Ht:* 2 ft; *Spd:* 1 ft; *Fl:* 5–6; *Z:* Arct

Camassia

Quamash

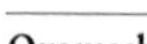

C. *leichtlinii*

C. leichtlinii*: W N Amer. The tallest sp; reaches 3 ft with 1½ in spikes of starry violet-blue, blue or white fls and thin strap-like lvs. Slow from seed but long lived; does not easily produce bulblets. Pretty at the edge of light woodland with *C. quamash* (common quamash). Lasts well when cut. *Spd:* 6 in; *Fl:* 6–7; *Z:* Arct

Canna

Indian shot plant

C. indica hybs: Trop Amer, Asia. Hyb cannas are generally divided into those with green and those with purple lvs. All lvs are broad, shiny and to 4½ ft long. Gladiolus-like fls to 3 in long in spikes may be red, yellow, pink or white. Prop by division. *Spd:* 18 in; *Fl:* 8–10; *Z:* SF

Cardiocrinum

Cardiocrinum

C. giganteum

C. giganteum Giant Himalayan lily: Him. A monster lily to 9 ft with glossy lvs, thick stems and 10 or 12 spectacular glistening white fls each 6 in long hanging from the top. It may take 7 or 8 years from seed to flowering but seedlings give the best flower. *Spd:* 4 ft; *Fl:* 7; *Z:* PF

Chionodoxa

Glory of the snow

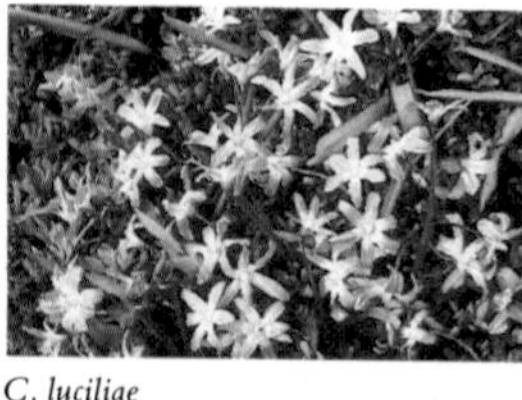

C. *luciliae*

C. luciliae: E Med, Asia Minor. Early bulb 6 in high with up to 10 round starry fls to 1 in diam. Intense blue ptls and a pale to white centre. The strap-shaped lvs are shining green. Will seed itself or thick patches can be divided. Best left to naturalize. *Spd:* 4 in; *Fl:* 3–4; *Z:* Arct

Clivia

Clivia

C. miniata: S Africa. Thick fl stems to 15 in, each bearing a cluster of orange/scarlet open funnel-shaped fls to 3½ in with a yellow throat. Lightly frag, long lasting. Prop by offsets. Tender. *Spd:* 3 ft; *Fl:* 3–8; *Z:* NF

Colchicum

Meadow saffron

Mainly autumn-flowering—the large glossy green leaves do not appear until spring. Petals may have a chequered pattern.

C. autumnale: Eur. Fls are 2 in long and crocus-like but larger and a pale rose-pink. The lvs die away quickly by July. Single white and double rose-pink vars are known. Increase by offsets. *Spd:* 10 in; *Fl:* 9–11; *Z:* Arct

***C. speciosum**:** Caucasus, Asia Minor. The loveliest and most spectacular with chalice-like fls of rosy lilac or even a deep wine col. 'Album' is a desirable albino. *Ht:* 10 in; *Spd:* 1 ft; *Fl:* 9–10; *Z:* Arct

C. speciosum

Convallaria

Lily of the valley

C. majalis: Eur, Asia, N Amer. Hardy genus of a single sp well known as a cut fl of delicious fragrance. Spreading thong-like roots have thick nodes from which sheathed, pointed lvs arise. White, nodding bell-shaped ¼ in fls are borne on arching stems to 8 in. Named forms inc 'Fortin's Giant' pale pink and rare varieg cvs. *Spd:* 2 ft; *Fl:* 4–5; *Z:* Arct

C. majalis

Corydalis

Corydalis

C. solida: Eur. Per with pale green dissected lvs and purple fls. With the blue-flowered *C. cashmeriana** hard to grow but a useful colour change in spr gdn. Prop by seed or division. *Ht:* 6 in; *Spd:* 10 in; *Fl:* 4–5; *Z:* Arct

Crinum

Crinum

***C. × powellii**:** S Africa, S Asia. A hardy hyb except in v cold or badly drained gdns. Has dark green strap-shaped lvs and stout stems to 3 ft with terminal gps of lily-like fls to 6 in wide. *Spd:* 1 ft; *Fl:* 7–9; *Z:* PF

Crocosmia

Crocosmia

C. × crocosmiiflora Montbretia: S Africa. Makes spreading clumps of 32 in sword-shaped lvs. Wiry fl stems have yellow/orange funnel-shaped fls to 1¾ in long in a flat zig-zag cluster in Aug and Sept. *C. masonorum** has larger fls of fierce reddish-orange on curving stems with fls facing upwards. Increase by division or seed. *Spd:* 3 ft; *Z:* PF

C. masonorum

Crocus

Among the most common and loveliest spring flowers. But some crocus species flower in autumn. For easy reference they have been divided into spring flowering species, hybrids and the autumn flowering species often confused with colchicums.

C. tomasinianus

C. Dutch

***C. chrysanthus**:** Greece, Turkey. Fls in mid-Feb are orange or old gold with purplish flecks or feathering outside. Excellent cvs include 'E. A. Bowles' deep yellow; 'Snow Bunting' white inside, cream and deep lilac inside. *Ht:* 3½ in; *Spd:* 4 in; *Fl:* 2–3; *Z:* Arct

***C. Dutch**:** gdn origin. Larger and more flamboyant fls than above in white, mauve or yellow. A number of striped ones, e.g. 'Winston Churchill' are v decorative. *Ht, Spd:* 4 in; *Fl:* 3–4; *Z:* Arct

***C. speciosus**:** S USSR–Iran. Glorious autumn-flowering sp. Slightly globular fls 3½ in high are bright lilac with 3 prominent dark veins and a yellow centre. Plant by July. *Spd:* 4 in; *Fl:* 8–10; *Z:* Arct

C. tomasinianus: Dalmatia. Delightfully invasive spr flowering sp. Slim silvery-mauve buds open to reveal rich purple ptls. 'Whitwell Purple' is darker. *Ht:* 3½ in; *Spd:* 4 in; *Fl:* 2–3; *Z:* Arct

Cyclamen

Cyclamen

Cyclamen vary more in timing than looks. All have typically long-eared flowers and are best increased by seed.

C. coum

C. persicum

C. coum: E Med–N Iran. Rarely over 3½ in in fl with rounded plain dark green lvs. Fls ¾ in long are rich carmine with deep spots at ptl bases. *Spd:* 6 in; *Fl:* 12–3; *Z:* PF

C. europaeum: S Eur. Has deep carmine fls to 1½ in in late smr and often in spr. Distinctive lvs are marked with a silvery zone. *Ht:* 4 in; *Spd:* 6 in; *Fl:* 4, 7–9; *Z:* Arct

***C. hederifolium (= neapolitanum)**:** S Eur. Has angular toothed lvs with variable markings and rose-pink fls 1 in long with a deep carmine blotch at the base. There is also a white form. *Ht, Spd:* to 6 in; *Fl:* 8–11; *Z:* Arct

C. persicum: E Med. Fragrant white or pale pink to carmine fls 1½ in long are held over dark green, often marbled lvs. *Ht:* 10 in; *Spd:* 8 in; *Fl:* 3–4; *Z:* SF

C. repandum Ivy-leaved cyclamen: S Eur. Distinctive lobed lvs have silvery markings and reddish undersides. Frag fls 1 in long are usually bright carmine. *Ht:* 6 in; *Spd:* 8 in; *Fl:* 4; *Z:* PF

Dahlia

Tuberous-rooted daisy-flowered plants, none hardy enough to treat as a perennial in Britain, although tubers will sometimes survive a mild winter. Dahlias are usually classified in 10 groups: Single-flowered; Anemone-flowered; Colarette, Paeony-flowered; Decorative; Ball; Pompon; Cactus; Semi-cactus and Miscellaneous. Some of the groups are further subdivided according to the size of the flowers. All the dahlias generally grown are hybrids of garden origin derived from Mexican species.

D. Single-flowered. Attractive simple fls often used for bedding: 18 in–2 ft tall. Some, e.g. 'Yellow-hammer' have dark coppery foliage, others, e.g. 'Claire de Lune' white fls to 4 in wide with a broad yellow centre disc. 'Bishop of Landaff'*, possibly a form of *D. coccinea*, is scarlet with red lvs—a first class plant. *Ht:* to 5 ft; *Spd:* 2 ft; *Fl:* 8–10; *Z:* SF

D. Anemone-flowered: Fls to 2 in wide have distinctive centre of small tubular ray florets set in a ring of ptls. *Ht:* to 3½ ft; *Spd:* 2 ft; *Fl:* 8–10; *Z:* SF

D. Collarette: Dressy rather prim fls to 4 in wide with 2nd row of short ptls around centre disc. Inner and outer ptls often contrast in col giving a delightful effect. *Ht:* 4 ft; *Spd:* 30 in; *Fl:* 8–10; *Z:* SF

D. Paeony-flowered: Full fls with 2 or 3 rows of undisciplined ptls producing a floppy effect. Heads 3–7 in across according to cv. Dwarfs reach only 30 in, others to 4 ft. *Spd:* 2 ft; *Fl:* 8–10; *Z:* SF

D. Decorative: Subdivided into 4 classes, 3 according to fl size and a dwarf section. All have fully double fls with central disc hidden by ptls and are 3–5 ft tall. 'Gerrie Hoek' is a silvery-pink small decorative with fls 4–6 in diam. The brilliant magenta 'Winston Churchill' is a miniature with fls under 4 in diam. *Spd:* to 4 ft; *Fl:* 8–10; *Z:* SF

D. Ball: The show dahlias with fully double almost round fls over 3 in across. Tightly packed ptls are individually incurved. *Ht:* to 4 ft; *Spd:* 30 in; *Fl:* 8–10; *Z:* SF

D. Pompon: Neat round heads of fl *c.* 2 in diam like pompomed poodles' tails. Vary from miniatures to tall border plants. *Ht:* to 4 ft; *Spd:* 30 in; *Fl:* 8–10; *Z:* SF

D. Cactus: Double fl heads but quill-shaped ptls give a spiky look. Fls 4–10 in diam. Separately grouped as Cactus, Medium Cactus, Small and Semi-cactus. *Ht:* to 5 ft; *Spd:* to 4 ft; *Fl:* 8–10; *Z:* SF

D. Miscellaneous: Do not fit any category, e.g. the tiny star dahlias and those with orchid-like fls. *Ht:* to 3 ft; *Spd:* 2 ft; *Fl:* 8–10; *Z:* SF

D. Decorative 'Polly Peachum'

D. Small cactus 'Klankstad Kerkrade'

D. Collarette 'Grand Duke'

D. Miniature ball 'Rothesay Superb'

Dichelostemma

D. ida-maia (= Brodiaea coccinea) Californian firecracker: Cal. Separated from *Brodiaea* because of its long (2 in) fl tubes, bright yellow tipped green. Of borderline hardiness. *Ht:* 18 in; *Spd:* 6 in; *Fl:* 6; *Z:* SF

Dierama     

Venus' fishing rod, Wand flower

D. pulcherrimum

***D. pulcherrimum*★:** S Africa. From July, often into aut, silvery-pink or purplish bell-shaped 1 in fls are borne on elegantly arching wiry stems 4 ft high. Lvs thin; corms need deep soil. Prop by seed. *Spd:* to 2 ft; *Z:* PF

D. pumilum: S Africa. Shorter at 30 in with stiff uprt stems. A number of named cvs, e.g. 'Ceres' light blue-violet. *Spd:* 18 in; *Fl:* 6–7; *Z:* PF

Dracunculus    

Dracunculus

D. vulgaris Dragon arum: Med. Sinister arum with a 1 ft spathe dull red within and evil purplish-green outside. Fleshy spotted stem, purplish-white tube striped at mouth. Smells fetid. *Ht:* 2 ft; *Spd:* 18 in; *Fl:* 5–6; *Z:* F

Eranthis    

Eranthis

E. hyemalis

***E. hyemalis*★** Winter aconite: Eur. Gleaming buttercup-yellow fls in Feb and March. Single fls 1 in wide on 2–4 in stems backed by a frilled ruff of bright green lvs. Naturalize freely if undisturbed and look well with snowdrops. Soak tubers in water for sev hours then plant 3 in deep. Prop by div or seed. *Spd:* 3 in; *Z:* Arct

Eremurus    

Foxtail lily

Spectacular soaring spikes of little lilies above an eruption of broad green strap-leaves. Sometimes classed as hardy perennials.

E. robustus

E. robustus: Turkestan. Magnificent sp with pokers of peach fls to 8 ft tall over a rosette of lvs each 3 ft × 4 in. Prop by div of starfish-like tuberous rts or fresh seed. *Spd:* 4 ft; *Fl:* 6–7; *Z:* Arct

E. hybs: gdn origin. The 'Shelford Hybrids'★ which fl earlier in June and reach 4–6 ft are frequently seen. Fls buff, pale yellow or shades of pink to white in spikes to 3 ft. Prop by div. *Spd:* 3 ft; *Z:* Arct

Erythronium

E. dens-canis* Dog's tooth violet: Eur–Japan. Violet-like fls purplish-rose, sol, 2 in wide, nodding over beautifully marked lvs. *Ht:* 8 in; *Spd:* 6 in; *Fl:* 3–4; *Z:* Arct
E. revolutum Mahogany fawn lily, Trout lily: N Amer. Cream fls turning purplish. In 'White Beauty'* they remain white, 1–3 per stem. Lvs veined white, faintly mottled. *Ht:* to 1 ft; *Spd:* 6 in; *Fl:* 4–5; *Z:* Arct
E. tuolumnense: Cal. Sim to above but 8–12 smaller yellow fls on a stem. Lvs plain yellowish-green. Prop by div, seed. *Fl:* 4–5; *Z:* Arct

E. revolutum

Freesia

Freesia

F. hybs: S Africa. Fls funnel-shaped, strongly frag, purple, blue, orange, yellow, pink or white on wiry stems to 18 in with narrow lvs. Generally grown under glass or in pots but there are outdoor kinds that need partial shade in a warm gdn. Plant 2 in deep; prop by seed or division of named sorts. *Spd:* 4 in; *Fl:* 3–4; *Z:* SF

F. hybrids

Fritillaria

Fritillary

F. imperialis* Crown imperial: W Him. Spectacular whorl of 2 in nodding orange or yellow bells topped by a tuft of short green lvs. Each fl exquisitely marked inside. Prop by seed. *Ht:* 4 ft; *Spd:* 15 in; *Fl:* 4; *Z:* Arct
F. meleagris Snake's head fritillary: Eur. Of more modest charm. Fls 1–2 per stem, bell-like, veined and checked in varying shades of purple, sometimes white. Lvs narrow. *Ht:* to 15 in; *Spd:* 6 in; *Fl:* 4; *Z:* Arct

F. imperialis

Galanthus

Snowdrop

G. elwesii*: Asia Minor. Among the best spr flowering sp. Big glaucous lvs. Fls $1\frac{1}{4}$ in, each white inner ptl with conspic green blotch at base and tip. Prop by div, seed. *Ht:* 8 in; *Spd:* 8 in; *Fl:* 1–2; *Z:* Arct
G. nivalis* Common snowdrop: Eur–USSR. Ptls white, 1 in, green streaked inside, green marking near tip. Narrow lvs. Sev selected forms and named hybs inc doubles. *Ht:* 8 in; *Spd:* 6 in; *Fl:* 2–3; *Z:* Arct

G. elwesii

Galtonia

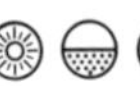

Summer hyacinth

G. candicans

***G. candicans**:** S Africa. Useful Aug/Sept flowering bulb bearing 15–20 white nodding fls each 1½ in long on a 3–4 ft stem. Lvs strap-shaped, uprt, glaucous to 32 in. Slow from seed, better from bulblets. *Spd:* 8 in; *Z:* Arct
G. princeps: S Africa. Shorter and smaller in all its parts. Fls are greenish and useful for cutting. Like *G. candicans* v useful if planted 6 in deep among low pers or ground cover plants. *Ht:* 2 ft; *Spd:* 6 in; *Fl:* 8–9; *Z: Arct*

Gladiolus

Gladiolus

Funnel-flowered relations of the iris, growing from corms. Mostly South African and tender in frost areas, with a few exceptions from the Mediterranean. The showiest are highly bred hybrids, often artificial and plastic-looking, used for summer bedding and as cut flowers. The hybrids want rich but well-drained soil and sun. Many of the species are winter-flowering and need a greenhouse.

G. byzantinus

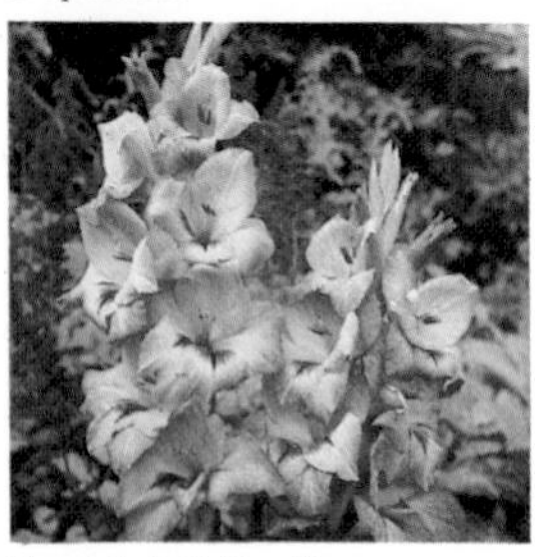

G. gdn hybrid 'Ravel'

G. byzantinus: Med. Good gdn per to 30 in high; 6–10 fierce magenta fls per spike, each 2½ in wide. A highly desirable but less hardy rare white form known. Lvs sword-shaped, grey green. Prop by seed or div of clumps (which tend to spread). *Spd:* 6 in; *Fl:* 6; *Z:* F
G. × colvillei: gdn origin. 'The Bride' is one of the better known of this group of hybs which were some of the first gladiolus crosses made. Colville was the nurseryman who brought them into popularity. White fls 3 in wide with a deep crimson blotch mark. Plant in early aut in mild areas or in pots under glass. Protect in borders in wtr. Prop by cormlets. *Ht:* 30 in; *Spd:* 6 in; *Fl:* 4–6; *Z:* PF
G. × hortulanus gdn hybs: gdn origin. Bulb merchants, catalogues and flower show judges usually list 5 main types of hybs. Large flowered, to 4 ft tall, have roughly triangular fls each to 7 in wide; Primulinas are free-flowering hybs to 3 ft tall with fls to 3 in wide and a hooded top ptl; Miniatures, averaging 18 in high, have smaller fls 2 in wide in Primulina shape and usually attractively ruffled or frilled; Butterfly gladioli to 4 ft tall have close-packed fls often with striking

Gladiolus

contrasting markings in the throat; Mid-season hybs to 4 ft flower in June–July. Between them these hybs cover all shades of the colour card including purple, blue and brown as well as the primary cols. Good examples inc 'Ravel' and 'Red Cascade' as illustrated. Fls to 7 in wide. Each corm can produce 2 spikes each lasting for about 10 days, lvs grow until frosted. Plant 4–6 in deep, lift in aut. *Spd:* to 6 in; *Fl:* 7–9; *Z:* SF

G. tristis Yellow marsh afrikander: S Africa. Elegant but tender May-flowering sp, sweetly frag. To 18 in tall with 3 or 4 pale yellow fls each 2–3 in long and tinted red on ptl reverses. Prop by seed or cormlets. *Spd:* 6 in; *Z:* PF

G. Butterfly gdn hybrid

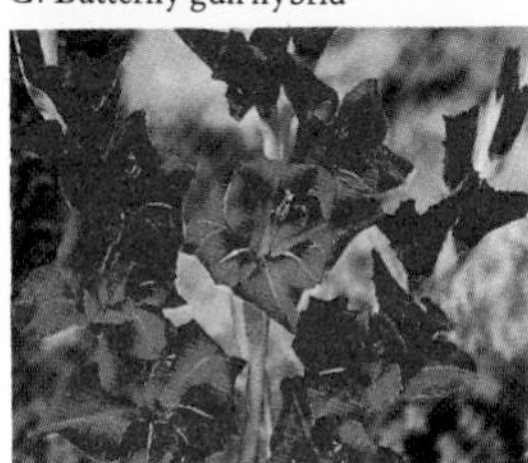

G. gdn hybrid 'Red Cascade'

Gloriosa

Creeping or climbing lily

G. rothschildiana: Africa, Trop Asia. Tender, but can be treated like a dahlia in gdns. Climbs by lf-tip tendrils to 7 ft. Exotic fls 4 in wide with lower half of each ptl yellow, top crimson, reflexed in a turban shape. Start in pots, handle carefully because of brittle rts. Prop by seed, offsets. *Spd:* 2 ft; *Fl:* 6–8; *Z:* NF

G. rothschildiana

Haemanthus

Blood flower, Blood lily

H. coccineus: S Africa. Bulbs produce 2 wide tongue-shaped 18 in lvs dying in smr. Fl clusters 3 in wide in Sept surrounded by fleshy scarlet bracts. Best in pots but will do well in a v warm spot. *Ht:* 10 in; *Spd:* 4 in; *Z:* SF

Hippeastrum

"Amaryllis"

H. hybs: gdn origin. Large funnel-like fl trumpets often 10 in wide; 1–4 on a thick stem 1–2 ft high. Lvs strap-shaped. Easy in pots but only suitable for v warm gdn as they need a minimum temp of 55°F, higher to fl, in Feb–April, and rich, loamy soil. Die down in late smr and need to be dried off in the pots. *Spd:* 6 in; *Fl:* 1–4; *Z:* SF

H. hybrid 'Jenny Lind'

Hyacinthoides (= Endymion)

Bluebell

***H. hispanicus* (= *Scilla hispanica*)★** Spanish bluebell: Spain, Portugal. Fls deep blue to pale pink, ¾in long. Named forms inc 'Mount Everest' white; 'Queen of the Pinks' pink. Prop by div. *Ht:* 1 ft; *Spd:* 6 in; *Fl:* 5; *Z:* Arct

Hyacinthus

Hyacinth

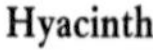

H. Roman 'Eros'

***H. Roman*★:** gdn origin. April-flowering with a loose 4 in gp of white bells on a 9 in stem. Deliciously frag and useful for early forcing in bowls after which they can be planted out and allowed to naturalize. Lvs bright green. Prop by offsets. *Spd:* 9 in; *Z:* PF

Hymenocallis

Spider lily

H. narcissiflora: Peru. Nearly hardy curious bulbous fl with a long white-green faintly striped ptl tube finely feathered at the edge. Fls 1–5 per 18 in stem and 6 in wide. Prop by offsets. *Spd:* 15 in; *Fl:* 3–4; *Z:* PF

Ipheion (= Brodiaea, Milla, Tritelia)

Ipheion

I. uniflorum

I. uniflorum: S Amer. Pretty little spring-flowering bulb bearing 1 (sometimes 2) star-shaped white, pale mauve to deep purple-blue frag fls 2 in wide on a 6 in stem. Lvs thin, pale green and smelling of onions when bruised. V easy in a sunny border. Increase by div of clumps. *Spd:* 3 in; *Fl:* 4–5; *Z:* SF

Iris

Iris

All irises have food-storage organs at or below soil level. The border irises and some others (see p 37) have rhizomes but the miniature winter and spring-flowering and taller summer-flowering English, Spanish and Dutch kinds arise from bulbs. All bulbous irises need good drainage foı a summer period of dry dormancy; moisture is necessary only in the flowering season.

I. danfordiae

I. danfordiae: Turkey. Fls in late Jan–early Feb, deep yellow with a green tinge to 3 in wide and honey fragrance. Plant 3 in deep. Inclined to split into tiny bulblets after flowering. Maintain a clump by adding a few bulbs each year. *Ht:* 4 in; *Spd:* 6 in; *Z:* Arct

I. Dutch: gdn origin. *I. xiphium* × *tingitana* hybs. Fls to 5in wide from mid June–early July make rich

Iris

patches of col in the early border and good cut fls. Wide range of named forms and cols inc white, yellow, orange, blue, purple or bronze and bicolours. Pale blue 'Wedgwood' v popular. Can be left for several years. Prop by seed or separation of bulbs which are smooth unlike the reticulate (wtr/spr flowering) gp. *Ht:* 1–2 ft; *Spd:* to 4 in; *Z:* PF

I. English: gdn origin. Follow on from the Dutch irises in late June and overlap with the Spanish ones in early July. Ptls close, giving elegant appearance, and are white, blue, mauve or purple. Can be left to colonize. Not English: derived from Spanish parents. Prop by seed or division of clumps. *Ht:* to 2 ft; *Spd:* 4 in; *Z:* PF

I. histrioides*: Turkey. Fls before even lf tips show above soil from mid-Jan. Fls to 3½ in wide, intense royal blue with an orange crest and paler spotting are seemingly weatherproof. Fls followed by taller, glaucous lvs. Prop by separation of bulbs or seed. *Ht:* to 4 in; *Spd:* 4 in; *Z:* Arct

I. reticulata: Turkey, Caucasus, Iran. The most reliable and popular winter iris for general gdn planting. Fls to 3 in wide from early Feb, deep violet-purple with gold markings and a velvety sheen. Lvs present at flowering time reach twice the height of the fls and have 4 prominent veins. Sev named cvs available. Prop by seed or separation of bulbs. *Ht:* to 8 in; *Spd:* 4 in; *Z:* Arct

I. Spanish: gdn origin. Succeed Dutch irises in mid-July. Should be treated in the same way but lift and dry bulbs when lvs start to wither. Fls to 4½ in. wide. Cvs offered under names in the following cols: blue, white, yellow and purple, also bicolours, often with a golden blotch as in Dutch types. Plant in Sept. *Ht:* 2 ft; *Spd:* 6 in; *Z;* PF

I. tuberosa (= Hermodactylus tuberosus) Snake's head iris: Eur. Curious rather than beautiful fls with velvety yellow-green standards and purplish-black falls to 2 in. Thin lvs 1 ft tall and fl stems a little shorter. Sometimes a little shy-flowering once established in colonies. Prop by div. *Spd:* to 10 in; *Fl:* 4–5; *Z:* Arct.

I. Dutch

I. histrioides

I. reticulata

I. Spanish

I. tuberosa

Ixia

Corn lily

I. gdn hybs: gdn origin. Brightly coloured fls to ¾ in wide are cream, orange or pink, usually with pronounced central disc, and open only in direct sun. Useful in pots. Plant 3 in deep in aut, protect in wtr, remove in spr. Prop by bulblets or save seed. *Ht:* to 1 ft; *Spd:* 4 in; *Fl:* 5–6; *Z:* PF

Lachenalia

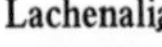

Lachenalia

L. aloides

L. aloides Cape cowslip: S Africa. Barely hardy enough for the gdn but easy in pots if kept frost free. Tubular 1 in fls on 1 ft stems spotted brown like the lvs. 'Lutea' is yellow; 'Nelsonii' green tinged. *Spd:* 6 in; *Fl:* 3–4; *Z:* SF

Leucojum

Snowflake

L. vernum

L. aestivum Summer snowflake*: Eur. Forms large clumps of narrow dark green 2 ft lvs; 2–8 clean white bell-shaped fls 1 in diam, green at ptl tips. 'Gravetye Giant' best. Prop by div. *Spd:* 8 in; *Fl:* 4–5; *Z:* Arct

L. vernum Spring snowflake: Eur. One or 2 white ¾ in fls with pronounced green spot on outer tip of each ptl. Lvs narrow, strap-shaped to 10 in. Naturalizes easily; likes damp. *Spd:* 4 in; *Fl:* 2–3; *Z:* Arct

Lilium

Lily

The most glamorous of bulbs, but also the most demanding. Lilies like a combination of plentiful moisture and rapid drainage, which is often hard to provide. They are vulnerable to disease and suffer from drying out when moved. Woodland conditions and leafy lime-free soil are best for most unless otherwise noted.

L. auratum

L. auratum* Golden rayed lily of Japan: Glorious lily to 8 ft tall with 20+ fls to 1 ft, each ivory white and opening with a central inner gold band and lots of purplish spots. Heavily scented. Plant 4–6 in deep. Stem-rooting; needs support. Prop by scales, bulblets or virus-free stock. *Spd:* 1 ft; *Fl:* 8; *Z:* Arct

L. candidum* Madonna lily: E Med. The common white lily of cottage gdns, 2–6 ft high. Intensely frag 4 in fls with pronounced golden anthers. Transplant bulbs after flowering in early Aug. Plant shallowly; prop by scales or div. Likes sunshine and

some lime. *Spd:* 9 in; *Z:* Arct

L. gdn hybs: gdn origin. Hybrids (there are hundreds) can be more or less divided into categories according to their parentage or to the arrangement and formation of the fls and stem heights. Most are June/July flowering, some Aug. Consult a good catalogue and choose from these divisions: Open-chalice shaped upward-facing; Outward-facing; Pendant; Martagon hybs; Pardalinum hybs; Aurelian (trumpet types); Aurelian (bowl-shaped) and Orientalis (*speciosum* and *auratum*) hybs. *Ht:* to 8 ft; *Spd:* to 1 ft; *Z:* Arct

L. martagon Martagon or Turk's cap lily: Eur. Usually 2–3 ft tall but can reach 5 ft; 30–50 frag purplish-red, purple-spotted fls. There is an enchanting white form. Lvs in whorls up the stem. Plant 4–6 in deep; prop by bulblets, slow from seed. *Spd:* 10 in; *Fl:* 6–7; *Z:* Arct

L. pyrenaicum: Pyrenees. Also "Turk's cap" in type. The acid-greenish-yellow purple-spotted 2 in fls have recurved ptls revealing orange pollen on the anthers. Early June-flowering, unpleasant scent. Lvs narrow, grassy up stems 2–3 ft high. Prop by bulbs, scales or seeds. Likes lime. *Spd:* 10 in; *Z:* Arct

L. regale*: W China. Large trumpet-shaped glistening white fls in July with bright yellow throat and rosy-maroon on ptl outsides. Strongly frag. Excellent border plant reaching 6 ft in good conditions. Remarkably easy to grow and raise from seed, happy on lime. *Spd:* 1 ft; *Z:* Arct

L. tigrinum 'Fortunei'* Tiger lily: sp China, Japan. Distinct orange-red black-spotted 4 in fls on purplish black hry stems to 6 ft bearing bulblets (for prop) in lf axils. *Spd:* 10 in; *Fl:* 8–9; *Z:* Arct

L. candidum

L. regale

L. pyrenaicum

Muscari

Grape hyacinth

M. armenaicum*: N Asia Minor. V easy forming dense clumps with grassy lvs to 18 in. Tiny pitcher-shaped blue fls in clusters 1–3 in long on 8–10 in stems produce a noticeable effect. *M. racemosum* less tall and more common in gdns. Prop by seed, div of bulbs. *Spd:* 4 in; *Fl:* 4–5; *Z:* Arct

M. racemosum

Daffodil

"Daffodils" are narcissi with trumpets as long as their petals (technically perianth segments) or longer. Sixty-odd species, mainly from round the Mediterranean, have produced over 8,000 cultivars, including many of the easiest and hardiest of all the bulbs in the garden.

N. Double 'Mary Copeland'

N. Dwarf (*N. cyclamineus*)

N. Large-cupped 'Ceylon'

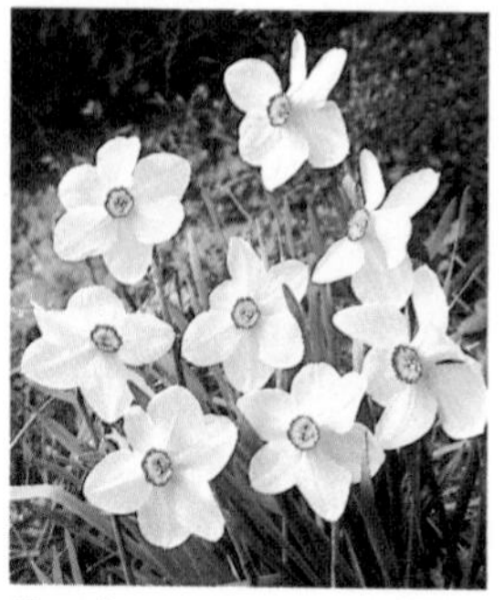

N. poeticus

N. Double daffodils: gdn origin. The plain yellow double daffodil 'Van Sion' found in borders and old orchards is v ancient in cultivation. Newer, better forms, but less weatherproof, inc 'Mary Copeland' with creamy-white ptls interspersed with shorter ones of apricot-buff. *Ht:* 18 in; *Spd:* 6 in; *Fl:* 3–5; *Z:* Arct

N. Dwarf: Spain, Portugal. Botanically *N. bulbocodium* (Hoop petticoat) and *N. cyclamineus*. The former is a March/early April flowering 6 in miniature with a wide-flared trumpet (hence the common name) with only rudimentary ptls. Likes moist soil and naturalizes easily. *N. cyclamineus* is 4–8 in tall with a long, thin perianth tube and swept back ptls. Likes damp soil, can take semi-shade, seeds freely. 'February Gold'* is an excellent cv. *Spd:* 4 in; *Fl:* 2–3; *Z:* PF

N. jonquilla Jonquil: Portugal, Spain–N Africa. Jonquils consist of 5 *Narcissus* spp and sev cvs. Mainly March/April flowering, rush-lvd 6–10 in tall, 1–5 v frag fls per stem. For a sheltered gdn or a cold greenhouse. 'Bobbysoxer' is a cv with yellow ptls and an orange cup. *Spd:* 4 in; *Z:* Arct

N. Large and small cupped: gdn origin. March/April flowering and often 2-coloured. One fl to a stem, the cup is not more than one third the width of the ptls. 'Flower Record' is a good large-cupped one, 'Edward Buxton' a good small-cupped. *Ht:* to 18 in; *Spd:* 6 in; *Z:* PF

N. poeticus Poet's narcissus: S Eur. May-flowering with white ptls forming a flat saucer to 3 in wide (except in *N. p. recurvus*, Pheasant's eye narcissus) and a small red-rimmed yellow or bright red cup. Deliciously frag; valuable as the last narcissus to flower. *Ht:* 18 in; *Spd:* 6 in; *Z:* Arct

N. tazetta: Med–China, Japan. One of the most desirable and sweetly scented of all narcissi but too early and tender for most gdns. Enjoyed best in pots and bowls (for which 'Paper White' is the most common choice) with gps of entirely white fls to 3 in wide on stems to 2 ft tall. *Spd:* 6 in; *Fl:* 3–4; *Z:* F

N. triandrus: Spain. Perfectly hardy little 6 in–1 ft sp with 1–3 nodding white fls per stem. Ptls are about

Daffodil

twice the length of the ½in trumpet and slightly reflexed. Ideal for rock gdns and the front of the border. 'Albus'* white is called Angels' tears; 'Thalia'* is an excellent taller cv with the same grace and is later flowering. *Spd:* 6 in; *Fl:* 4–5; *Z:* Arct
D. Trumpet: gdn origin. Common-or-garden trumpet daffodils comprise a large gp which have 1 large fl on a stem and a trumpet equal in length or longer than the width of the ptls. They may be in 1 or 2 cols and are 18–20 in tall. Plant 6 in deep and leave undisturbed for several years. *Spd:* 6 in; *Fl:* 3; *Z:* PF

N. triandrus

Nerine

Nerine

***N. bowdenii**:** S Africa. Spidery icing-sugar-pink fls in late Sept–Nov in loose terminal clusters 6 in wide on 1–2 ft stems. Strap-shaped fresh green lvs appear at flowering time but die away by following aut. Just about hardy: need warmth to fl really well. Plant no more than 6 in deep. 'Mark Fenwick' is taller. Prop by div but best undisturbed. *Spd:* 6 in; *Z:* SF

N. bowdenii

Ornithogalum

Star of Bethlehem

O. nutans: E Eur, Asia Minor. Drooping white 1 in fls pale green on outside. Floppy lvs to 18 in. Prop by div, seed, naturalizes well. *Spd:* 6 in; *Fl:* 4–5; *Z:* Arct
O. umbellatum: Asia Minor, Eur. 10–20 open starry fls form flat pyramid to 1 ft tall. Fls shining white, green striped ptl backs. *Spd:* 8 in; *Fl:* 4–5; *Z:* Arct

O. umbellatum

Pancratium

Sea lily

P. maritimum: S Eur. V frag white fls 3 in wide in a loose umbel on 1 ft stems in July–Sept. Glaucous lvs virtually ever-grey. Plant 3 in deep, protect in winter. Prop by separation of bulbs. *Spd:* 1 ft; *Z:* F

Pleione

Pleione

P. bulbocodioides: Asia. A group of small hardy orchids often catalogued under older individual names. Lvs narrow, longitudinally pleated. Fls orchid-like to 4 in wide, rose-purple often with whitish lip. Exquisite but not easy. Prop by div of pseudo bulbs. *Ht:* 6 in; *Spd:* 4 in; *Fl:* 3–5; *Z:* SF

Polianthes

Polianthes

P. tuberosa

P. tuberosa Tuberose: Mexico. Rarely seen in gdns nowadays but well worth growing. Strongly frag fls white, open, star-shaped on stems to 4 ft. Lvs narrow, smell v nasty when bruised. Plant new bulbs each season. *Spd:* 5 in; *Fl:* 7–8; *Z:* SF

Ranunculus

Buttercup

R. asiaticus Garden ranunculus, Persian buttercup: Orient. Nearly all double-flowered in a wide range of attractive cols and *c.* 3 in wide. Lvs dissected. Lift and divide annually. *Ht:* to 15 in; *Spd:* 6 in; *Fl:* 5–6; *Z:* F

Rhodohypoxis

Rhodohypoxis

R. baurii: S Africa. Rts fleshy. Brightly coloured white, pink or red fls to 1½ in diam, 6-petalled. Sev named cvs available and many fl from May–Sept. Also good in rock gdns. *Ht:* 4 in; *Spd:* 6 in; *Z:* SF

Schizostylis

Kaffir lily

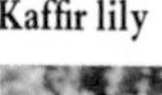

S. coccinea

S. coccinea* Crimson flag: S Africa. Oct–Nov flowering per with fleshy or rhizomatous rtstock. Buds open to form 6-petalled fls 1½ in wide, 10–14 on a spike 18 in–2 ft tall. Pale green lvs sheathing the base of the stem. Good for cutting. Named clones with larger or deep pink or red fls available. Prop by offsets or div. *Spd:* 1 ft; *Z:* SF

Scilla

Squill

Relations of the lily with close-packed little flowers, generally blue. *S. sibirica* is early, easy and in fact essential.

S. peruviana

S. peruviana* Cuban lily: Med. Fine plant with broad green lvs 6–10 in long and domed 6 in heads of lilac-blue fls, 50–100 closely packed. Also a white form. Prop by seed, div. *Spd:* 8 in; *Fl:* 5–6; *Z:* PF

S. sibirica* Siberian squill: E USSR, Siberia. One of the easiest and best early blue fls; 3–4 slightly drooping fls ½ in wide, deep gentian-blue. Lvs squeaky to touch. Prop by seed, offsets. *Ht:* to 8 in; *Spd:* 4 in; *Fl:* 3; *Z:* Arct

Sinningia

Gloxinia

S. speciosa: Brazil. Not hardy but common indoors. Soft hry lvs, bell-shaped 4 in fls deep blue to pink and deep red. *Ht:* 10 in; *Spd:* 1 ft; *Fl:* 5–9; *Z:* NF

S. speciosa

Sparaxis

Sparaxis

S. tricolor Harlequin flower: S. Africa. Most bulbs offered are hybs of this and *S. grandiflora* with the influence of *Streptanthera*. They have 3–6 brightly coloured fls of red, yellow, purple, orange, white or a mixture on wiry stems. Lvs uprt. Prop by seed. *Ht:* 15 in; *Spd:* 4 in; *Fl:* 4–5; *Z:* NF

Sternbergia

Sternbergia

***S. lutea*★:** C Eur. Rather like a yellow aut crocus but lvs and fls appear together. Lvs narrow, deep shining green, gradually reach 6 in; fls 2 in, golden, shining on 5 in stems. Transplant in lf or when dormant in midsummer. Reasonably hardy in all but v cold areas. Prop by div of clumps. *Spd:* 6 in; *Fl:* 8–9; *Z:* F

S. lutea

Tigridia

Tigridia

***T. pavonia*★** Peacock or tiger flower: Mexico, Peru. Exotic 6-petalled fls 4 in wide, inner ptls crimson spotted. Sp orange/scarlet, other forms red, crimson, pink, orange and yellow. Fls last 1 day, but 6–10 in succession. Sadly only hardy in warm gdns. *Ht:* 18 in; *Spd:* 4 in; *Fl:* 7–9; *Z:* PF

Trillium

Trillium

T. erectum Birth root: E N Amer. Symmetrical 3-petalled fls 1½ in wide which can be white, yellow or pink but are usually mahogany; ptls separated by 3 small green sepals. Lvs broad in stalkless whorl of 3 on the stem. Prefers peaty soil. Prop by seed or div of tubers but slow to increase. *Ht, Spd:* 1 ft; *Fl:* 5; *Z:* Arct

T. grandiflorum Wake robin: E N Amer. The best known and most useful gdn plant of the genus producing clean white fls to 3 in wide on a 2 ft single stem. There is also a sumptuous rare double-flowered form★. Prop by div, seed. *Spd:* 1 ft; *Fl:* 4–6; *Z:* Arct

T. erectum

Tritonia

Tritonia

T. *crocata* 'White Beauty'

T. crocata Blazing star: S Africa. Usually best under glass. Glowing orange open fls 1½ in wide, shaded yellow throat. Fls of 'White Beauty' white, may have yellow centre. Lvs narrow. Prop by seed, div. *Ht:* to 2 ft; *Spd:* 6 in; *Fl:* 5–6; *Z:* PF

Tulbaghia

Tulbaghia

T. violacea

T. violacea Violet tulbaghia: S Africa. Tubular fls are violet-coloured and frag, 8–16 at the tip of 1 ft fl stems displayed like a partly opened umbrella. Lvs to 15 in. Prop by seed, offsets. *Spd:* 15 in; *Fl:* 7–9; *Z:* SF

Tulipa

Tulip

Tulips have been garden plants for centuries. Their classification is thus horticultural and artificial, by shape and flowering period. They are normally treated as bedding plants and lifted after flowering. Smaller, often earlier, natural "botanical" species were more recently collected. Many can become permanent.

T. clusiana

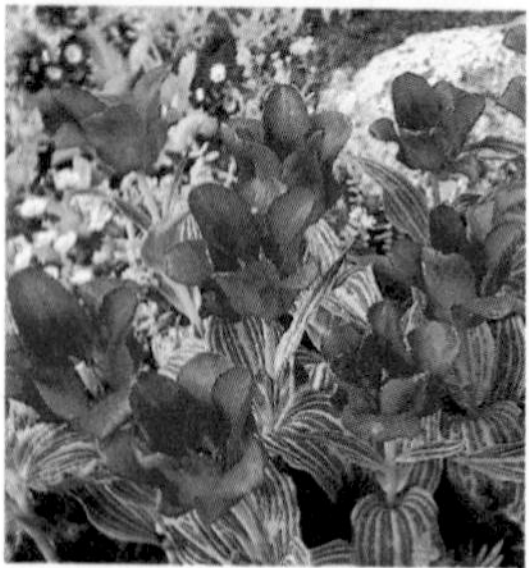

T. greigii 'Red Riding Hood'

T. clusiana Lady tulip: Iran, Iraq, Afghanistan. Slender elegant "botanical" tulip with 1½ in white fls with violet blotch in centre and broad rosy-pink stripe on ptl outside. Lvs to 10 in, slightly glaucous, sometimes with a thread of red along edge. Plant 5 in deep. *Ht:* 8 in; *Spd:* 3 in; *Fl:* 4; *Z:* Arct

T. Darwin: gdn origin. Popular tall May flowering tulips often used for bedding out. Large squarish fls to 5 in across in wide col range from pale yellow through pink, scarlet, crimson, mauve and purple to near-black. Plant 6 in deep in aut. *Ht:* to 2 ft; *Spd:* 8 in; *Z:* Arct

T. fosteriana: Samarkand. V big fls to 9 in wide with long blunt ptls which open flat. Sp is rich shiny scarlet and 8–18 in tall. Cvs have red, pink, yellow or white fls all with characteristic grey lvs. *Spd:* 4 in; *Fl:* 3–4; *Z:* Arct

***T. greigii**:** Turkestan. The sp is brilliant scarlet, its hybs a colourful range 8–10 in tall and long-lasting in fl. The mottled glaucous lvs have attractive brown-purplish streaks. *Spd:* 6 in; *Fl:* 4; *Z:* Arct

Tulip

T. kaufmanniana Water lily tulip: Turkestan. The sp is cream with a pink and yellow flush; hybs range from yellow to scarlet and have 3–5 lvs, the longest, lowest ones to 10 in. All are *c.* 1 ft tall with $3\frac{1}{2}$ in fls in March–early April according to type and severity of wtr. Can be left to colonize. *Spd:* 6 in; *Z:* Arct

T. Lily-flowered: gdn origin. Tall late-flowering tulips with distinct long, slightly waisted fls to 8 in diam and pointed reflexed ptls. Good col range, mainly in deep shades. *Ht:* 2 ft; *Spd:* 6 in; *Fl:* 5; *Z:* Arct

T. Parrot*: gdn origin. Tulips 18 in–2 ft tall with large fringed and ruckled ptls forming heavy, often floppy fls 8 in wide. Brightly coloured and inc strange mixtures such as salmon-pink with streaks of green, orange and yellow. *Spd:* 8 in; *Fl:* 5; *Z:* Arct

T. kaufmanniana

T. Parrot 'Sunshine'

Vallota

Vallota

V. capensis Scarborough lily: S Africa. Like a more elegant amaryllis with 4 in fls of similar funnel shape but smaller with up to 10 fls per 18 in stem. Broad lvs 18 in at flowering time. *Spd:* 1 ft; *Fl:* 8–9; *Z:* NF

Veltheimia

Veltheimia

V. capensis: S Africa. Something like a squat red hot poker. Many strap-shaped, bright green wavy-edged lvs to 1 ft. Fls reddish-pink or yellowish, spotted pendulous tubes on purplish spotted stems. *Spd:* 18 in; *Fl:* 4–7; *Z:* SF

Watsonia

Watsonia

W. pyramidata (= rosea): S Africa. Botanically close to gladioli. Can be divided for gdn purposes into decid and evergreen sorts. *W. pyramidata* is decid with red fls, *W. beatricis*, one of the best evergreens, also with red fls in spikes to 5 ft. Prop from corms. Not reliably hardy; can be lifted in aut. *Spd:* 8 in; *Fl:* 6; *Z:* F

W. pyramidata

Zephyranthes

Zephyranthes

Z. candida Flower of the West Wind: S America (along La Plata River). Single white funnel-shaped fls $1\frac{1}{2}$ in wide and narrow green lvs. Colonizes readily in warm borders. Prop by offsets. *Ht:* 8 in; *Spd:* 6 in; *Fl:* 9–10; *Z:* SF

Roses

The conventional classification of roses, with such evocative terms as China and noisette, Portland and damask, reflects their ancient history in cultivation. In modern practice, broader distinctions are sufficient guide to general character. Here we classify them simply into natural species and old-fashioned shrubs; modern (mainly 20th century) shrubs; hybrid teas; floribundas, with the similar grandifloras; climbers and ramblers; and miniatures.

Species and old roses

These roses may not be such efficient "flowering machines" as the latest bedding varieties but have more grace and charm, distinction of habit, leaf and fragrance, and more character. Most flower only once but many produce ornamental hips.

R. × *alba* 'Semi-plena'

R. centifolia

R. gallica 'Versicolor'

R. damascena 'Madame Hardy'

***R.* × *alba*★** "White Rose of York", "Jacobite Rose": gdn origin. Famous old rose, long in cultivation. Flat semi-double richly frag white fls to 3 in wide. Lvs pale, 5–7 greyish-green lflts. 'Celestial' clear pink double; 'Great Maiden's Blush' pale pink double. *Ht:* 6 ft; *Spd:* 6 ft; *Fl:* 6–7; *Z:* Arct

***R. centifolia*★** Cabbage or Provence rose: gdn origin. Head of a group of richly scented forms and cvs. Fls of sp deep pink, round, 3 in wide. Lvs have 5–7 lflts. 'Muscosa' the Moss rose sim, fls double, sticky glandular "mossy" buds and shoots. *Ht, Spd:* 4 ft; *Fl:* 6–7; *Z:* Arct

***R. chinensis*★** China rose: China. Elegant sp, seemingly always in fl. Ptls translucent, crimson or old rose pink. Form 'Old Blush' China, fls to 2½ in wide, most common. Lvs have 3–5 lflts. *Ht:* to 5 ft; *Spd:* 3 ft; *Fl:* 6–9; *Z:* PF

***R. damascena*★** Damask rose: Asia. V old in cultivation, many forms and hybs. Lvs greyish-green, 5–7 lflts; stems prickly. Fls richly frag, red, 3 in wide. 'Versicolor' is the semi-double white-striped "York and Lancaster" rose. *Ht, Spd:* to 6 ft; *Fl:* 6–7; *Z:* Arct

***R. gallica*★** French rose: S Eur–W Asia. Dwarf, bushy spp. Stems bristly, lvs coarse, leathery, 3–5 lflts. Fls single, deep pink to crimson, 3 in wide. Hips (frs) round, brick red. *R. g. officinalis* the "Apothecary's Rose" or "Red Rose of Lancaster" has frag, semi-double, bright crimson fls with prominent yellow stamens. Lvs dark green. *R. g.* 'Versicolor' or "Rosa Mundi" is a sport of *R. g. officinalis* with semi-double fls but in deep rosy red splashed and striped blush pink. *Ht, Spd:* 3 ft; *Fl:* 6; *Z:* Arct

***R. hugonis*★:** China. Fls pale yellow, single, to 2½ in wide. Lvs have 5–11 lflts. Hips round, dark red. Forms delicate arching shape. *Ht, Spd:* 6 ft; *Fl:* 6; *Z:* Arct

R. moyesii* China. Vig, uprt shrub. Fls single, blood red, 2 in wide followed by bottle-shaped red hips to 2½ in. Parent of shorter 'Geranium' with lighter, brighter red fls. *Ht:* to 12 ft; *Spd:* 8 ft; *Fl:* 6–7; *Z:* Arct

R. pimpinellifolia* *(= spinosissima)* Scotch or Burnet rose: Eur–USSR. Suckering prickly-stemmed bush; lvs have 5–9 small, apple-green lflts. Fls small but generously produced and with exquisite scent, white or pale pink in sp. Hips round, blackish, shiny. Cvs inc double, pink, red, white and yellow forms, e.g. 'William's Double Yellow'. *Ht:* 3 ft; *Spd:* 5 ft+; *Fl:* 5–6; *Z:* Arct

R. rubiginosa (= eglanteria)* Sweet briar, Eglantine: Eur. Thorny, stout shrub, good hedging. Fls small, single, bright pink; lvs deliciously frag, esp after rain. Lvs have 5–9 lflts. Hips oval, orange. *Ht, Spd:* 8 ft; *Fl:* 6; *Z:* Arct

R. rubrifolia*: C, S Eur. Decorative in lf, fl and fr. Lvs have 5–9 steely blue-grey lflts with hint of crimson. Fls single, 1½ in wide, rose-pink, paler towards centre. Hips oval, glistening browny-red. Comes true from seed. *Ht:* 7 ft; *Spd:* 6 ft; *Fl:* 6; *Z:* Arct

R. rugosa* Ramanas rose: E Asia. Suckering on light soils. Lvs have 5–9 handsome round, veiny dark green lflts with useful yellow aut col. Fls single, red or white, 3 in diam. Hips orange-red, tomato-shaped. Sev excellent (AGM) cvs inc 'Fru Dagmar Hastrup' dwarf, single, pale pink; 'Roseraie de l'Hay' semi-double crimson-purple; 'Blanc Double de Coubert' semi-double white; 'Sarah van Fleet' masses of semi-double mallow-pink fls. *Ht:* to 7 ft; *Spd:* 6 ft; *Fl:* 6–7; *Z:* Arct

'Frau Karl Druschki'*: gdn origin. Hybrid perpetual. Splendid white repeat-flowering uprt rose with bright green lvs. Fls to 4 in wide. *Ht:* 5 ft; *Spd:* 4 ft; *Fl:* 6–10; *Z:* PF

'Hugh Dickson'*: gdn origin. Hybrid perpetual. Wonderfully vig. Long shoots can be wall-trained. Fls bright scarlet-crimson to 4 in wide. *Ht:* 9 ft; *Spd:* 10 ft+; *Fl:* 6–9; *Z:* PF

'Mrs John Laing'*: gdn origin. Hyb perpetual. V popular. Strong growth and large pink frag fls freely borne. *Ht:* 5 ft; *Spd:* 5 ft; *Fl:* 6–9; *Z:* PF

'Reine des Violettes'*: gdn origin. Hyb perpetual. Fls burgundy-purple to 4 in wide, fading to a wine-stained col. *Ht:* 6 ft; *Spd:* 5 ft; *Fl:* 6–9; *Z:* PF

R. hugonis

R. moyesii

R. moyesii fruits

R. rugosa 'Sarah van Fleet'

'Frau Karl Druschki'

'Reine des Violettes'

The bedding roses par excellence, in which individual flowers 4–6 in wide, from long pointed buds, have been brought to perfection in the nursery; flowering is almost continuous all summer and autumn. Disadvantages are awkward little angular bushes and proneness to disease.

Hybrid tea 'Fragrant Cloud'

Hybrid tea 'Peace'

Hybrid tea 'Super Star'

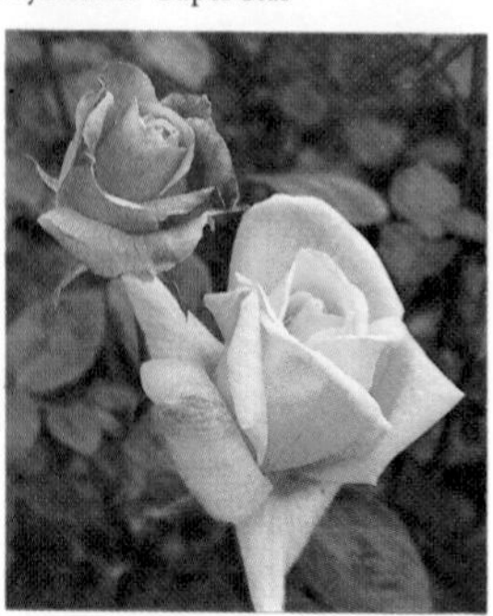

Hybrid tea 'Sutter's Gold'

***'Beauté'**:** Long pointed buds open to apricot/orange frag fls. Lvs glossy, dark green. *Ht, Spd:* 5 ft; *Fl:* 6–7(–9); *Z:* PF

***'Blessings'**:** Uprt rose. Fls frag, clear coral pink, freely borne, weather resistant. *Ht, Spd:* 3 ft; *Fl:* 6–7(–9); *Z:* PF

***'Duke of Windsor'**:** Strong, vig. Fls brilliant orange, frag; lvs glossy, dark green. *Ht:* 3 ft; *Spd:* 30 in; *Fl:* 6–7(–9); *Z:* PF

***'Eden Rose'**:** Robust, healthy bush bearing rich carmine fls with paler ptl reverses. Lvs medium green. *Ht:* 5 ft; *Spd:* 4 ft; *Fl:* 6–7(–9); *Z:* PF

***'Fragrant Cloud'**:** V frag coral red fls. A good bush seemingly resistant to all weathers and diseases. *Ht:* 3 ft; *Spd:* 30 in; *Fl:* 6–7(–9); *Z:* PF

***'Gaujard'**:** Ptls white, edged in silver-pink. Fls frag. Lvs have bronze hue. *Ht:* 5 ft; *Spd:* 3 ft; *Fl:* 6–7(–9); *Z:* PF

***'Grand'mère Jenny'**:** Fls of florist's shape, long, pointed in bud, yellow suffused pink. Frag. *Ht:* 5 ft; *Spd:* 3 ft; *Fl:* 6–7(–9); *Z:* PF

***'Josephine Bruce'**:** Much loved old favourite. Slim buds open to richly frag gorgeous rich crimson fls with deeper sheen. Lvs dark green, shining. Prone to mildew. *Ht, Spd:* 30 in; *Fl:* 6–7(–9); *Z:* PF

***'Lady Sylvia'**:** Well tried and proven. Frag fls soft pink, shaded yellow. *Ht:* 3 ft; *Spd:* 4 ft; *Fl:* 6–7 (–9); *Z:* PF

***'Peace'**:** Strong growing. Large frag fls yellow with ptls edged pink. Lvs dark shining green. *Ht, Spd:* 6 ft; *Fl:* 6–7(–9); *Z:* PF

***'Super Star'**:** Frag fls a fluorescent vermilion—an overpowering col needing careful placing. *Ht:* 5 ft; *Spd:* 3 ft; *Fl:* 6–7(–9); *Z:* PF

***'Sutter's Gold'**:** Frag rose of good stamina for bedding. Fls rich yellow, buds and ptl backs shaded reddish-orange. Lvs dark green, glossy coppery hue. *Ht, Spd:* 3 ft; *Fl:* 6–7(–9); *Z:* PF

***'Wendy Cussons'**:** Cerise ptls with scarlet reverses. *Ht:* 3 ft; *Spd:* 30 in; *Fl:* 6–7(–9); *Z:* PF

***'Whisky Mac'**:** Warm yellow/ toasted bronze frag fls of good shape and size. Lvs v dark. Also 'Yellow Whisky Mac' with coppery lvs. *Ht:* 3 ft; *Spd:* 30 in; *Fl:* 6–7(–9); *Z:* PF

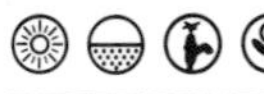

Old-fashioned roses had a narrow range of ancestors. Modern shrubs draw on the inheritance of a wide range, including recently-introduced species, to produce plants of great character, some flowering repeatedly. The hybrid musks, nearest to floribundas, are ideal as shrubs for bedding.

'Canary Bird'*: Rich yellow early single making tall vase-shaped bush. Lvs have 7–13 pretty little lflts. *Ht:* 8 ft; *Spd:* 6 ft; *Fl:* 5–6; *Z:* Arct

'Complicata'*: Forms dome-shaped bush of sage green lvs. Fls single, bright pink, to 4 in wide. *Ht:* 5 ft; *Spd:* 8 ft; *Fl:* 6–7 ft; *Z:* Arct

'Constance Spry'*: Uprt; lvs dark green. Fls double, rose-pink, v frag, inclined to nod. *Ht:* 7 ft; *Spd:* 5 ft; *Fl:* 6–7; *Z:* PF

'Fritz Nobis'*: Has beautifully formed bright shell-pink clove-scented fls in profusion and orange hips. One main burst of fls then continues blooming sporadically until autumn. *Ht:* 6 ft; *Spd:* 5 ft; *Fl:* 6(–9); *Z:* PF

'Fruhlingsgold'*: Tall arching shrub rose. V free flowering, once. Fls creamy-yellow, frag, single. Its sister plant called 'Fruhlingsmorgen' less tall and has clear yellow in centre with maroon stamens. Produces a few dark hips. *Ht, Spd:* 7 ft; *Fl:* 5–6; *Z:* PF

'Golden Wings'*: Large single yellow fls over a long period and matt green lvs. *Ht:* 6 ft; *Spd:* 5 ft; *Fl:* 6–7; *Z:* PF

'Marguerite Hilling'*: Vig modern shrub rose making a large dense bush. Fls rich pink, deeper in bud, single with a few extra ptls. A sport of 'Nevada' (below). *Ht, Spd:* 8 ft; *Fl:* 5–6; *Z:* PF

'Nevada'*: Strong grower with few thorns and graceful arching stems. Buds pale pink, fls creamy white flushed pink in heat, single with prominent stamens. Dying fls hang on which is the only disadvantage. *Ht:* 6 ft; *Spd:* 8 ft; *Fl:* 5–6; *Z:* PF

'Nymphenburg'*: Strong-growing rose with arching shoots that can be wall trained. Glossy deep green lvs and frag salmon-pink fls with orange shading, yellowish at base. Decorative orange hips. *Ht:* 6 ft; *Spd:* 8 ft; *Fl:* 6–7; *Z:* PF

Hybrid musks

'Buff Beauty'*: Dark green lvs start coppery. Soft apricot fls fade to buff. Makes a spreading bush or good against a wall. *Ht, Spd:* 6 ft; *Fl:* 6–7(–9); *Z:* PF

'Cornelia'*: Tight buds open to rosette-shaped fls of coppery apricot which fade to pink. *Ht:* 5 ft; *Spd:* 7 ft; *Fl:* 6–7(–9); *Z:* PF

Modern shrub 'Canary Bird'

Modern shrub 'Complicata'

Modern shrub 'Fruhlingsgold'

Modern shrub 'Golden Wings'

Modern shrub 'Nevada'

Hybrid musk 'Buff Beauty'

Hybrid musk 'Prosperity'

***'Felicia'*★:** One of the most rewarding of all shrubs. More compact than other hyb musks and bearing great quantities of shapely double fls, apricot-pink in bud, opening to clear silvery pink. *Ht:* 5 ft; *Spd:* 6 ft+; *Fl:* 6–7(–9); *Z:* PF

***'Penelope'*★:** Deep pink buds open to creamy pink, then fls become off-white. Hips coral pink with a grey bloom. *Ht:* 4 ft; *Spd:* 5 ft; *Fl:* 6–7 (–9); *Z:* PF

***'Prosperity'*★:** Dark green lvs on stems with a reddish cast. Fls borne in large trusses with pale yellow tinge in centre. *Ht:* 6 ft; *Spd:* 4 ft; *Fl:* 6–7(–9); *Z:* PF

***'Wilhelm'*★:** Semi-double rich maroon fls fade to a pleasing crimson-purple. Persistent orange hips. No scent. *Ht:* 6 ft; *Spd:* 5 ft; *Fl:* 6–7(–9); *Z:* PF

Floribundas and Grandifloras

In contrast to the hybrid teas with their emphasis on the single, perfect bloom on each shoot, floribundas carry smaller flowers, $2\frac{1}{2}$–$3\frac{1}{2}$ in wide, in greater numbers, usually in clusters, over an equally long period. In practice the distinction between the two classes is rapidly being eroded by further breeding.

Floribunda 'All Gold'

Floribunda 'Elizabeth of Glamis'

***'All Gold'*★:** V reliable long-established bedding rose with glossy lvs and unfading, frag, semi-double bright yellow fls. *Ht:* 3 ft; *Spd:* 30 in; *Fl:* 6–10; *Z:* PF

***'Apricot Nectar'*★:** As good as it sounds. Vig, free-flowering; big, shapely full-petalled fls of soft apricot. Deliciously frag. *Ht:* 4 ft; *Spd:* 3 ft; *Fl:* 6–10; *Z:* Arct

***'Chanelle'*★:** Creamy shell-pink double fls and deep green shining lvs. Bushy, reliable, frag. *Ht, Spd:* 30 in; *Fl:* 6–10; *Z:* PF

***'Chinatown'*★:** Vig, full-flowered. Strongly frag custard-yellow fls may be tinged rhubarb-pink. *Ht, Spd:* 4½ ft; *Fl:* 6–10; *Z:* PF

***'Dearest'*★:** Fls contradictory: flat like an old fashioned rose but bright chorus-girl pink. Excellent frag bedding rose. *Ht, Spd:* 2 ft; *Fl:* 6–10; *Z:* PF

***'Elizabeth of Glamis'*★:** Handsome in bud. Frag fls coral-pink and hold their col well. Good fol. *Ht, Spd:* 30 in; *Fl:* 6–10; *Z:* PF

***'Frensham'*★:** Fls rich crimson red but no scent. Lvs dark green, glossy. Bushy shrub that maintains its vigour. *Ht, Spd:* 3½ ft; *Fl:* 6–10; *Z:* PF

***'Gruss an Aachen'*★:** Good mixer in any company. Fls frag, double, pearly-white ageing to parchment col. Low bushy habit; clean fol. *Ht, Spd:* 30 in; *Fl:* 6–10; *Z:* PF

***'Iceberg'*★:** Strong growing; good shining lvs, shapely buds and clean white fls sometimes developing pink flush with age. Sweetly frag. 'Ice White' more fully double. *Ht, Spd:* 3 ft; *Fl:* 6–10; *Z:* PF

***'Masquerade'*★:** Yellow in bud, opening to salmon-pink and becoming deep red. The effect is so striking that it must be used with great care to avoid loud col clashes. *Ht, Spd:* 4 ft; *Fl:* 6–10; *Z:* PF

***'News'*★:** Rose of unique hue—the col of beetroot juice in bud, opening and fading to light purple. Associates well with, and extends the effect of, old roses. *Ht, Spd:* 30 in; *Fl:* 6–10; *Z:* PF

***'Queen Elizabeth'*★:** Head and shoulders above other floribundas at 7 ft with tapering buds opening to clear pink, frag fls. Lvs clean dark green. Also good hedging. *Spd:* 4 ft; *Fl:* 6–10; *Z:* PF

***'Violet Carson'*★:** Frag peach pink fls yellow on ptl reverses. Lvs a clean mid-green. *Ht, Spd:* 4 ft; *Fl:* 6–10; *Z:* PF

Floribunda 'Iceberg'

Floribunda 'Masquerade'

Floribunda 'Queen Elizabeth'

Climbers and ramblers

Climbers are roses that produce relatively few very long and stiff stems and often flower repeatedly over a long period. Ramblers usually have more pliable and shorter shoots in large numbers and flower only once but with overwhelming generosity. Again there is no hard and fast distinction, particularly among the huge-growing sorts.

***R. banksiae*★** Banksian rose: China. V vig small-flowered climber for warm (and high) walls, blooming in late spr. Sev forms: 'Lutea' double, yellow with tight rosettes in generous bunches, is hardiest but least frag; *R. b. normalis* (the wild subsp) is single, white, v frag and rather tender; 'Albo-plena' is double, white, frag; *R. b. lutescens* single, pale yellow, frag. Lvs pale with 7–9 lflts; few thorns. *Ht:* 20 ft; *Spd:* 20 ft; *Fl:* 5–6; *Z:* PF

***R. bracteata*★** Macartney rose: China, Formosa. Rather tender white rose, evergreen with v dark

R. banksiae 'Lutea'

Rambler 'American Pillar'

Rambler 'Albertine'

Climber 'Dorothy Perkins'

Climber 'Golden Showers'

Climber 'Mermaid'

glossy lvs divided into 5–11 lflts with unusual blunt tips. Habit like a tall shrub; downy shoots with thorns in 1s and 2s. Single fls 3 in wide, prominent stamens, lemon scent. Named for the lfy bracts behind fls. Parent of the excellent 'Mermaid' (see below). *Ht:* 15 ft; *Spd:* 8 ft; *Fl:* 6–9; *Z:* PF

***R. filipes**:** W China. Sensationally vig climber capable of 20 ft shoots. Small creamy-white single fls in sprays of 100 or more at a time have prominent stamens and musk fragrance. Lvs have 5–7 narrow green lflts. 'Kiftsgate' has copper new wood and extra vigour in fl. Small oval red hips. *Ht:* to 60 ft; *Spd:* 30 ft; *Fl:* 6–7; *Z:* PF

R. wichuraiana* Memorial rose: E Asia. Trailing evergreen rambler. Excellent ground cover, easily trained. Fls white, yellow stamens, frag, in small clusters, v late. Important parent of many cvs inc 'Dorothy Perkins' (see below). *Ht:* to 25 ft; *Spd:* 10 ft; *Fl:* 7–8; *Z:* PF

***'Albertine'**:** Rambler especially good when allowed to froth over a wall or down a bank. Free flowering. Semi-double fls open coppery-pink from deep red buds. Well scented, prone to mildew. *Ht, Spd:* 20 ft; *Fl:* 6; *Z:* PF

***'Albéric Barbier'**:** Rambler widely planted since 1900 and still highly rec. Exceptionally vig. Persistent dark glossy green lvs with obvious coppery-red lf stks. Fls open milky-white with warm creamy centre. Buds creamy-yellow. Sweet scent. *Ht, Spd:* 25 ft; *Fl:* 6–7; *Z:* PF

***'American Pillar'**:** Rambler excluded from some gdns and books because of its dazzling shocking-pink single fls each with white eye, borne in extravagant clusters. No scent. For best results prune hard immediately after flowering. Best on a pergola. *Ht:* to 15 ft; *Spd:* to 30 ft; *Fl:* 6–7; *Z:* PF

***'Dorothy Perkins'**:** Well established old favourite rambler, hyb of *R. wichuraiana*. Covered in bright rose-pink double or semi-double fls in full smr. Blooms once. Mildew-prone. *Ht, Spd:* 10ft; *Fl:* 6–7; *Z:* PF

***'Gloire de Dijon'**:** Early, richly frag climber; v vig but needs some support. Fls double, quartered, soft buff with warm apricot flush. *Ht, Spd:* 12 ft; *Fl:* 5–10; *Z:* PF

***'Golden Showers'**:** Weatherproof with rich golden-yellow, double, lightly frag fls. Clean, glossy, deep green fol. *Ht:* 12 ft; *Spd:* 8 ft: *Fl:* 6–8; *Z:* PF

'Madame Grégoire Staechelin'*: Climber. Firm favourite producing generous quantities of sweetly scented clear pink fls, with deeper col on ptl reverses, for about 3 weeks from early June. Lvs deep green. At home on a stately balustrade or cottage gdn wall. Good on a N-facing wall. *Ht, Spd:* 20 ft; *Z:* PF

'Mermaid'*: V vig climber. Coppery young lvs become glossy green. Fls single, pale yellow; pronounced boss of deep buff stamens. *Ht, Spd:* to 25 ft; *Fl:* 6–10; *Z:* PF

'New Dawn'*: Strong, recurrent-flowering rambler. Lvs glossy. Fls full petalled, soft pink with silvery sheen v attractive when half open. Shorter than average if grown against a tree or allowed to sprawl. *Ht, Spd:* 20 ft; *Fl:* 6–7; *Z:* PF

'Paul's Scarlet Climber'*: Moderately vig with 1 main flowering in late June and a few late blooms. Lightly frag rich crimson-scarlet fls becoming purplish with age. *Ht:* 20 ft; *Spd:* 15 ft; *Z:* PF

'Zéphirine Drouhin'*: Tall shrub. Cerise-pink perpetual-flowering semi-double deliciously frag rose. Stems virtually thornless; young shoots reddish. Useful hedging. *Ht, Spd:* 10 ft; *Fl:* 6–10; *Z:* PF

Rambler 'New Dawn'

Climber 'Paul's Scarlet Climber'

Climber 'Zéphirine Drouhin'

Miniatures

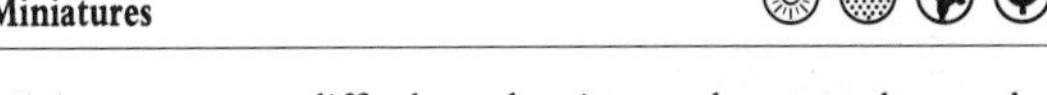

Miniature roses are difficult to place in a garden scene, but can be enchanting grown in pots. They are mainly derived from a dwarf perpetual China rose which gave them a long flowering season.

'Baby Masquerade'*: Smaller in all its parts but otherwise an exact copy of the flame and gold floribunda of the same name (p 108). Like other miniatures it needs full sun and good drainage. *Ht:* to 1 ft; *Spd:* 8 in; *Fl:* 6–7; *Z:* PF

'Mr Bluebird'*: Fls purple-blue, semi-double to 2 in wide. *Ht:* 1 ft; *Spd:* 8 in; *Fl:* 6–7; *Z:* PF

'Ocaru' (= 'Angela Rippon')*: A shapely, frag salmon pink rose with fls to 2 in wide. *Ht:* 1 ft; *Spd:* 8 in; *Fl:* 6–7; *Z:* PF

'Pixie' (= 'Little Princess'): Double white fls prettily flushed in shades of deep and pale pink. *Ht, Spd:* 9 in; *Fl:* 6–7; *Z:* PF

'Yellow Doll': Double fls opening yellow, fading to ivory-white. *Ht:* to 1 ft; *Spd:* 9 in; *Fl:* 6–7; *Z:* PF

Miniature 'Baby Masquerade'

Miniature 'Ocaru'

Climbers

The gardener's idea of a climber is a plant best suited for walls and fences. In nature such plants are adapted for climbing trees (where many hang on with above-ground or aerial roots) or for scrambling through shrubs to the light. They sometimes twine but often just throw out long shoots needing support. Roots in shade, head in light is a good rule for cultivation.

Aconitum

Monkshood

A. volubile: SE Asia. Unusual slender herbaceous climber with typical helmet-shaped purple-blue 3 in fls in a loose gp. Valuable in late smr. Likes shade at rts. *Ht:* 14½ ft; *Spd:* 4 ft; *Z:* PF

Actinidia

Actinidia

A. kolomikta

A. chinensis Chinese gooseberry: China. Shs and young lvs v hry. Parchment-coloured fls and (in heat) edible frs if ♂, ♀ plants grown. *Ht:* 30 ft; *Spd:* 15 ft; *Fl:* 6; *Z:* PF

***A. kolomikta**:** China, Japan. Curious, decorative with oval lvs green at base then red with white band at tip. Fls lightly frag. *Ht:* 20 ft; *Spd:* 15 ft; *Fl:* 6; *Z:* Arct

Akebia

Akebia

A. quinata

***A. quinata**:** China, Japan. Elegant, easy semi-evergreen with pale green lflts and vanilla-scented purplish-green and light crimson fls in drooping gps. Frs elongated. Prop by cuttings, seed. *Ht:* 32 ft; *Spd:* 20 ft; *Fl:* 4–5; *Z:* Arct

Allamanda

Allamanda

A. cathartica

A. cathartica: S Amer. Spectacular tropical climber. Yellow fls 3 in wide, periwinkle shape on a plant to 13 ft once established. Needs pinching out to make it branch low down; best trained on wires inside. More exotic forms like 'Grandiflora' best grafted on to common stock. *Spd:* 20 ft; *Fl:* 7–9; *Z:* NF

Aristolochia

Dutchman's pipe

A. macrophylla (= durior): N Amer. Vig, climbs by twining. Fls yellowish-purple, pipe-shaped, lidded, 1½ in long and concealed by mass of rounded lvs. Can reach 30 ft on a tree or wall. *Spd:* 8 ft; *Fl:* 6; *Z:* Arct

Berberidopsis

Berberidopsis

B. corallina Coral plant: Chile. Barberry-like tough lvs, deep green with a pale underside, contrast prettily with the orange/coral red fls in Aug and Sept. Has no grip of its own; needs support on a sheltered wall or in partial shade. Prop by seed, layers, cuttings. *Ht:* 20 ft; *Spd:* 10 ft; *Z:* SF

B. corallina

Bougainvillea

Bougainvillea

Tall scramblers needing support. Brilliant bracts make them most spectacular for hot gardens or conservatories.

B. glabra: Brazil. V showy with richly coloured pointed deep magenta bracts. Sev recent hybs with pale blue, white, orange or pink bracts. Perfectly hardy in S France and quite happy in pots (outdoors in smr) in cooler climates. *B. spectabilis* has hooked spines, hry lvs and rosy bracts. *Ht:* to 13 ft; *Spd:* 20 ft; *Fl:* 8–9; *Z:* NF

B. spectabilis

Campsis

Trumpet vine, Trumpet creeper

C. radicans: SE USA. Vig, lfy, climbs with aerial rts. Intense orange and scarlet 3 in fls in a hot spot. Seedlings variable. *Ht:* 13 ft+; *Spd:* 10 ft; *Fl:* 8–9; *Z:* Arct

C. × tagliabuana 'Madame Galen'*: gdn origin. The best clone of the hyb with bunches of salmon-red trumpet-shaped 3 in fls. Best if given reflected heat of a hot wall. *Ht:* 13 ft; *Spd:* to 25 ft; *Fl:* 8–9; *Z:* Arct

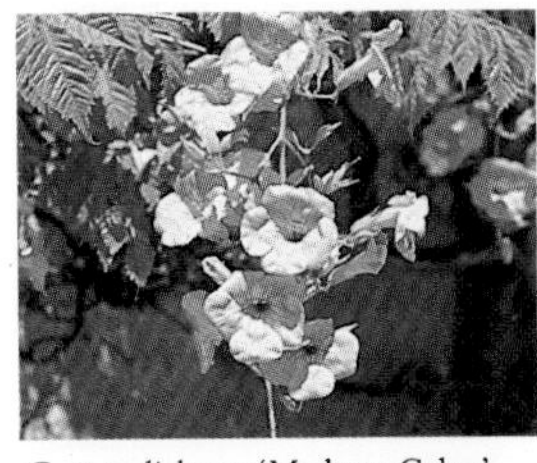

C. × tagliabuana 'Madame Galen'

Celastrus

Staff vine, Climbing bittersweet

C. orbiculatus: NE Asia. Splendid vig climber happiest growing over a tree. Wonderful in aut when lvs turn yellow and brown/red frs split to reveal scarlet seeds against bright yellow skins. Fls green, inconspic, in June–July. Prop by seed, not fussy about soil. *Ht:* to 40 ft; *Spd:* 18 ft; *Z:* Arct

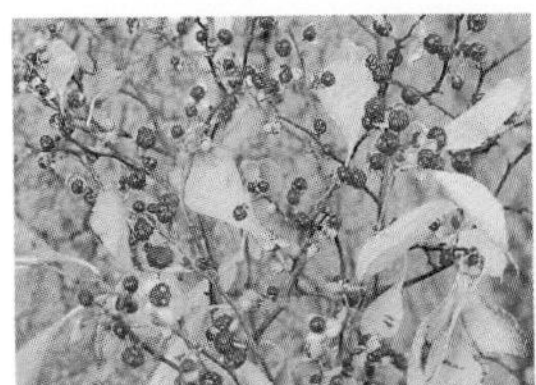

C. orbiculatus

Clematis

Garden hybrid clematis are conventionally classified in botanical groups according to their known or supposed parentage which dictates whether they flower on young or old wood (or both) and hence when they should be pruned. All large-flowered clematis are such hybrids and bloom in early, mid or late summer. A number of smaller-flowered species extend flowering from late winter into autumn. Nearly all can be pruned in late winter.

C. jackmanii

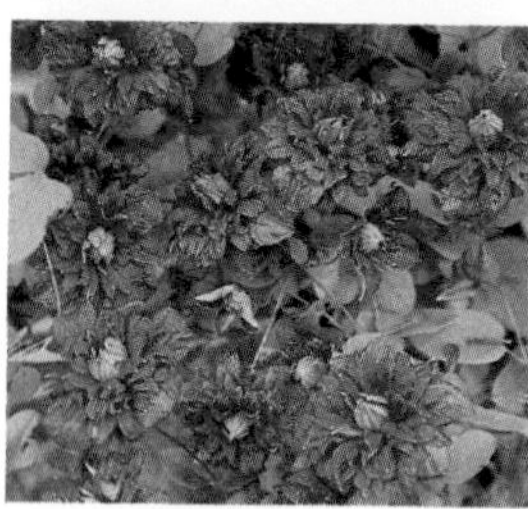

C. viticella purpurea 'Plena Elegans'

C. orientalis

C. alpina: Eur, N Asia. Pale blue fls 1½ in wide, white stamens. 'Frances Rivis' is excellent. *C. macropetala* sim, the 2 spp are known as "atragenes". Prune. *Ht:* 8 ft; *Spd:* ft; *Fl:* 4–5; *Z:* Arct

C. armandii: China. Leathery-lvd evergreen; clusters of white fls 2½ in wide. 'Appleblossom' and 'Snowdrift' (both AGM) worth searching for. Try not to prune. *Ht:* to 30 ft; *Spd:* to 10 ft; *Fl:* 4–5; *Z:* PF

C. flammula* Virgin's bower: S Eur. From Aug–Oct the little creamy-white strongly frag fls are produced on a tangled mass of stems. Prop by seed; prune. *Ht:* 16 ft; *Spd:* 8 ft; *Z:* PF

C. jackmanii*: gdn origin. Intense violet-purple fls. Prune. Try 'Jackmanii Superba'. *Ht:* 13 ft; *Spd:* 10 ft; *Fl:* 7–10; *Z:* Arct

C. montana*: Him. Vig. Pale dusky pink buds, anemone-like white fls 2 in diam. 'Elizabeth' (AGM) soft pink; 'Rubens' (AGM) rose-pink fls. Do not prune. *Ht:* 30 ft; *Spd:* 20 ft; *Fl:* 5; *Z:* PF

C. orientalis*: Caucasus, Him–N China. Mod vig; finely cut pale green lvs, thick-petalled yellow fls 1½ in wide. Hard prune. *C. tangutica* sim. *Ht:* 16 ft; *Spd:* 10 ft; *Fl:* 8–10; *Z:* PF

C. viticella*: Eur. Vig but elegant. Crimson-violet fls 2½ in diam. 'Royal Velours' (AGM) deeper col; 'Alba Luxurians' (AGM) white fls, green or mauve ptl tips; 'Kermesina' wine red. Hard prune. *Ht:* 11 ft; *Spd:* 10 ft; *Fl:* 7–9; *Z:* Arct

C. puniceus

C. puniceus Parrot's bill, Lobster's claw: NZ. Exotic-looking climber or wall-trained shrub for a warm garden or a conservatory or sun room. Has brilliant scarlet fls like parrots' beaks in 4 in clusters. Prop by seed or cuttings. *Ht:* 12 ft; *Spd:* 8 ft; *Fl:* 5–6; *Z:* SF

Cobaea

C. scandens Cup-and-saucer plant: C, S Amer. Can survive mild wtrs but best as an ann. Will fill a large space either temporarily or annually. Has cup-and-saucer-like bell-shaped 3 in fls beginning green and gradually becoming purplish. Easily reaches 15 ft in a season. Prop by fresh seed. *Spd:* 15 ft; *Fl:* 5–10; *Z:* SF

C. scandens

Cucurbita

Ornamental gourd

C. pepo: Trop Amer. Blanket name for sev sorts highly prized for their frs which harden easily and last for months in wtr. Easily grown annually from seed over twiggy branches or arches; also good ground cover, behaving (but not tasting) like marrows. *Ht:* 10 ft; *Spd:* 8 ft; *Fl:* 7–9; *Z:* SF

Eccremocarpus

Chilean glory flower

E. scaber: Chile. Almost instant climber for the impatient gardener but rather untidy. Tubular 1 in fls can be orange, yellow or scarlet and are followed by small inflated pods generously packed with seed. Clear yellow fls and claret-coloured forms sometimes seen. *Ht:* to 10 ft; *Spd:* 6 ft; *Fl:* 6–10; *Z:* SF

E. scaber

Hedera

Ivy

The most adaptable evergreen climbers, equally effective as ground cover, in a huge range of leaf sizes, shapes and colours.

H. canariensis Canary Is ivy: Canary Is. Vig; lvs often bronze in aut with pronounced veins. 'Variegata' (= 'Gloire de Marengo') has white-edged lvs splashed green and silver-grey. *Ht:* 40 ft; *Spd:* 20 ft; *Z:* PF

H. colchica* Persian ivy: Iran, Caucasus. V big glossy drooping lvs. 'Dentata' (AGM) lvs irregularly toothed; 'Dentata Variegata' cream/green variegated and 'Paddy's Pride' yellow-centred lvs netted gold all rec. *Ht:* 40 ft; *Spd:* 20 ft; *Z:* Arct

H. helix Common ivy: Eur, Asia Minor. Among many cvs are: 'Buttercup' (AGM) lvs small, yellow; 'Glacier' lvs silver-grey, white edges; 'Goldenheart' (AGM) central gold splash; 'Hibernica' (Irish ivy) vig plain green lvs; 'Marmorata' mottled lvs, rosy-grey/green effect. *Ht:* to 100 ft; *Spd:* 18 ft+; *Z:* Arct

H. colchica

H. helix 'Glacier'

Holboellia

Holboellia

H. (= Stauntonia) latifolia: Him. Deliciously frag climber needing shelter in all but mildest areas. Greenish-white ♂ and greenish ♀ fls in separate clusters on same plant. *Ht:* 12 ft; *Spd:* 10 ft; *Fl:* 6–7; *Z:* SF

Hydrangea

Hydrangea

H. petiolaris

H. petiolaris* Climbing hydrangea: Japan–Korea. Bushy shrub with aerial rts to climb trees. Ideal for a north wall but will do equally well in a sunnier spot or up a tree. Large heads 10 in wide of white fls like well-known Lacecaps (p 139). Prop by cuttings or pieces with aerial rts. Slow to establish. *Ht:* to 80 ft; *Spd:* 20 ft; *Fl:* 6; *Z:* Arct

Ipomoea

Morning glory

I. rubro-caerulea: Trop Amer. Half-hardy ann best grown from seed (chip outer shell) and planted out after last spr frosts. Vivid sky-blue fls to 5 in diam. Needs support; good in pots. *Ht:* 8 ft; *Spd:* 10 ft; *Fl:* 7–9

Jasminum

Jasmine

The jasmines are small-flowered but extremely valuable for their scent in summer and colour in winter. They are easy to grow and not fussy about soil.

J. nudiflorum

J. officinale

J. nudiflorum Winter jasmine: W China. Sprawling green-stemmed shrub with myriads of yellow (sadly scentless) fls 1 in wide from mild periods in early winter to early March. Has no climbing equipment but can be wired to a wall, or looks good on a bank. Prune after flowering; prop by cuttings or layers. *Ht:* to 14 ft; *Spd:* 15 ft; *Z:* PF

J. officinale* Common white jasmine: Caucasus–China. Vig, twining climber, needs strong support; tends to be top heavy. Sweetly frag white fls to 3 in. Prop by cuttings, layers. *Ht:* 20 ft; *Spd:* 18 ft; *Fl:* 6–9; *Z:* PF

J. polyanthum: China. The jasmine of Arabian Nights, powerfully frag fls pale pink in bud. Not hardy but a strong candidate for indoors where it flowers from Nov–April. Prop by cuttings. *Ht:* 24 ft; *Spd:* 18 ft; *Fl:* 4–6; *Z:* SF

J. × stephanense: gdn origin. Vig hyb with frag pale pink fls in 3 in gps. Strongly growing shs often look yellowish and sick but this is natural. Prop by cuttings. *Ht:* to 25 ft; *Spd:* 18 ft; *Fl:* 6; *Z:* PF

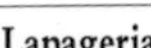

Lapageria

L. rosea Chilean bell flower: Chile, Argentina. Lustrous waxy bell-shaped 3 in fls of a bright light red in drooping clusters. Needs shade and insists on a lime-free soil. The rare white form is less hardy. Prop by seed. *Ht:* to 16 ft; *Spd:* 8 ft; *Fl:* 7–10; *Z:* NF

L. rosea

Lathyrus

Sweet pea

L. latifolius Everlasting sweet pea: Eur. Per useful against a wall, over a tough shrub or on a trellis. Large trusses of frag pink fls. Best cvs, e.g. 'White Pearl' have larger fls. *Ht:* 10 ft; *Spd:* 5 ft; *Fl:* 8; *Z:* Arct

Lonicera

Honeysuckle

L. japonica: China, Japan. Semi-evergreen, rapidly twining. Flared tubular 1½ in fls white, V frag. 'Aureoreticulata' (AGM) lvs gold-netted, few fls. *Ht:* 20 ft; *Spd:* 12 ft; *Fl:* 6; *Z:* Arct

L. periclymenum* Woodbine: Eur, N Africa. Creamy-white fls with purple tinge and heady frag in June–Sept. 'Belgica' fls crimson-purple outside, yellowish inside in May, June; sim 'Serotina' fls July–Oct. *Ht:* 12 ft; *Spd:* 12 ft; *Z:* Arct

L. japonica 'Aureoreticulata'

Mandevilla

Chilean jasmine

M. suaveolens: Argentina. White fls like periwinkles with sweet smell and elongated heart-shaped lvs. For warm gdns or conservatory. Rarely reaches more than 10 ft. Prop by seed. *Spd:* 4 ft; *Fl:* 8–9; *Z:* SF

Parthenocissus

Virginia creeper

Leafy self-clinging vigorous climbers often seen covering houses with brilliant red autumn colour. Flowers are insignificant.

P. henryana*: China. Velvety dull green lvs silver-veined turning purplish then bright red. *Ht:* 15 ft+; *Spd:* 18 ft; *Z:* F

P. quinquefolia: E USA. The true Virginia creeper. Spectacular aut col when large lvs (each with 5 lflts) turn scarlet. Prop by cuttings. *Ht:* 30 ft+; *Spd:* to 30 ft; *Z:* Arct

P. tricuspidata Boston ivy: China, Japan. Lvs as above but smaller and coarsely toothed. Burning red aut col. *Ht:* 30 ft+; *Spd:* to 30 ft; *Z:* Arct

P. quinquefolia

Passiflora

Passion flower

P. caerulea

P. caerulea★: C, SW Amer. The only sp commonly grown. Pliant tendrilled climber needing support. Intricate lightly frag fls opening to a saucer shape with prominent central stk holding stigmas and anthers. Named from the elements of the Crucifixion. Frs orange, egg-shaped in a hot year. Prop by cuttings. *Ht:* 20 ft; *Spd:* 18 ft; *Fl:* 7–10; *Z:* F

Pileostegia

Pileostegia

P. viburnoides★: India, China. V desirable woody self-clinging shrub. Heads of white fls best in Aug–Sept are appealing in bud when they look pale green against darker lvs. Prop by cuttings. *Ht:* 20 ft; *Spd:* 18 ft; *Z:* PF

Plumbago

Plumbago, Leadwort

P. capensis

P. capensis★ Blue or Cape plumbago: S Africa. Delightful semi-evergreen pale-lvd wall-trained shrub with pale blue phlox-like fls in gps to 1 ft long all smr. Tender, so only suitable under glass or in portable tubs except in warm countries. Prune hard in wtr, prop by cuttings. *Ht:* to 12 ft; *Spd:* 15 ft; *Fl:* 5–11; *Z:* SF

Polygonum

Knotweed

P. baldschuanicum Russian vine: Turkestan. Rampageous smotherer. Masses of white fls tinged icing-sugar pink. Easily confused with *P. aubertii* which has plain white fls. *Ht:* 40 ft; *Spd:* 100 ft+; *Fl:* 7–10; *Z:* Arct

Schizophragma

Schizophragma

S. integrifolia: China. Hydrangea-like decid climber growing well in shade but producing more fls in sun. Fls white in gps to 1 ft wide, lvs rounded, toothed. Good on stumps. *Ht:* to 40 ft; *Spd:* 18 ft; *Fl:* 7; *Z:* Arct

Solanum

Solanum

S. jasminoides 'Album'

S. crispum Climbing potato: S Amer. Long-stemmed semi-evergreen; many bluish-purple yellow-eyed fls. 'Glasnevin' (AGM) fls more freely. Needs support. *Ht Spd:* to 20 ft; *Fl:* 7–9; *Z:* F

S. jasminoides: S Amer. Less hardy but more vig with grey-blue $\frac{3}{4}$ in fls. Best on a sunny wall. The white form 'Album'★ is outstandingly beautiful. Prop by cuttings. *Ht:* to 15 ft; *Spd:* 20 ft; *Fl:* 7–10; *Z:* SF

Thunbergia

Thunbergia

T. alata Black-eyed Susan: S Africa. Graceful fast-growing ann summer climber with startling black-centred orange funnel-shaped fls 2 in diam. Prop by seed (save your own). *Ht:* 10 ft; *Spd:* 10 ft; *Fl:* 6–10

Trachelospermum

Trachelospermum

T. asiaticum: Korea, Japan. Tidy, self-clinging, reasonably hardy. Fls small, jasmine-like, cream with buff eye, ravishing fragrance. *T. jasminoides* has larger fls but is less hardy. *Ht:* 20 ft; *Spd:* 10 ft; *Fl:* 7–8; *Z:* PF

Tropaeolum

Nasturtium

T. peregrinum Canary creeper: Peru. Ann; lemon-yellow fls over pale green lvs. Good on a wire fence or twiggy site. Prop by seed. *Ht:* 10 ft; *Spd:* 15 ft; *Fl:* 6–10

T. speciosum* Flame flower: Chile. Lightweight per needing cool moist soil. Myriads of bright scarlet fls 1½ in wide. Plant in shade. *Ht:* 10 ft; *Spd:* 5 ft; *Fl:* 7–10; *Z:* SF

T. peregrinum

Vitis

Grape vine

V. 'Brandt'*: Asia Minor, Caucasus. V good hardy fruiting vine with delicious blue-black grapes. Lvs turn rosy-crimson in aut. *Ht:* 30 ft; *Spd:* 20 ft; *Z:* PF

V. coignetiae Glory vine: Japan. Handsome huge round lvs woolly below and black grape-like inedible frs. Spectacular orange/yellow-crimson aut col. *Ht:* to 70 ft; *Spd:* to 40 ft; *Z:* Arct

V. vinifera 'Purpurea'* 'Teinturier grape': gdn origin. Medium claret-coloured lvs crimson in aut. V dark fr, rarely sweet. Green-lvd 'Incana' (Miller grape) good. *Ht Spd:* 22 ft; *Z:* PF

V. coignetiae

Wisteria (= Wistaria)

Wisteria

W. sinensis* Chinese kidney bean: China. Strong stems turn anticlockwise (unlike *W. floribunda*); 6 in racemes of pale lilac honey-scented pea fls. White fld forms of both known. Smr prune. Can make a small tree. *Ht:* to 70 ft; *Spd:* to 50 ft; *Fl:* 5–6; *Z:* Arct

W. venusta: Japan. Less well known and smaller, denser racemes v pale pink. Lvs and shs downy. Prop by layers. *Ht:* 30 ft; *Spd:* to 30 ft; *Fl:* 5–6; *Z:* Arct

W. sinensis

Shrubs

Shrubs are defined here as any plants with woody, permanent, above ground parts that are not trees. Some of the shrubs described in this section can grow as trees, particularly in warmer climates, but are often seen in gardens as big bushes with many stems, not one long trunk. Trailing, ground-covering woody plants are also included.

Abelia

Abelia

***A. × grandiflora**:** gdn origin. Arching evergreen of delicate beauty in late smr. Lvs pointed, oval, pale undersides. Bell-shaped 1 in fls palest pink and white with hry throat and reddish-purple veins. Also a variegated form. Prop by cuttings. *Ht, Spd:* 5 ft; *Fl:* 7–10; *Z:* Arct

Abutilon

Abutilon

Fast-growing, soft-wooded tree mallows of great character. *A. vitifolium* with big fragile flowers and jagged leaves is one of the great "instant" shrubs, given moisture and warmth.

A. megapotamicum

A. megapotamicum: Brazil. Lax evergreen. Spls crimson, anthers purple. Lvs of *A. m. variegatum* yellow-blotched. *Ht, Spd:* 8 ft; *Fl:* 5–10; *Z:* SF

A. vitifolium: Chile. More substantial; splendid vine-lvs. Fls of 'Album' white; of 'Veronica Tennant' pale lavender. *Ht:* 12 ft; *Spd:* 8 ft+; *Fl:* 6–7; *Z:* SF

Acacia

Wattle

A. dealbata Silver wattle, Mimosa: Aust. Silvery-green feathery lvs. Fls frag, soft yellow, fluffy 9 in balls. Good in conservatories in cold zones. Prop by seed, cuttings. *Ht:* 60 ft; *Spd:* 18 ft+; *Fl:* 1–4; *Z:* SF

Acer

Maple

A. japonicum Japanese maple: Japan. Slowly forms round bush to 20 ft. Lvs serrate, nearly round; fls wine red in bunches; frs key-like. Glowing aut col. Sev cvs of great quality inc 'Aconitifolium' (AGM) lvs deep cut; 'Aureum' (AGM) lvs soft yellow. *Spd:* 20 ft; *Fl:* 4–5; *Z:* Arct

Aesculus

Horsechestnut

A. parviflora

***A. parviflora**:** SE USA. Shrubby, spreading horsechestnut with typical compound hand-shaped lvs. Elegant white candles of fls to 1 ft high, stamens pink and showy. Prop by suckers, seed. *Ht:* to 13 ft; *Spd:* 13 ft+; *Fl:* 8; *Z:* Arct

Amelanchier

Snowy mespilus, June berry

A. canadensis* Shadbush: E N Amer. Large bush/small tree. Lvs oblong, emerging woolly, fiery in aut. Fls starry, white in pendulous bunches to 4 in. Frs purple in June. *Ht:* to 30 ft; *Spd:* 15 ft; *Fl:* 4; *Z:* Arct

Aralia

Aralia

A. elata Angelica tree: Asia. Spiny-stemmed suckering shrub/small tree. Oversize palm-like lvs; white fls in long plumes. Lf markings in 'Aureovariegata' yellow; 'Variegata' white. *Ht, Spd:* 15 ft; *Fl:* 8–9; *Z:* Arct

Arbutus

Arbutus

A. × andrachnoides: gdn origin. Big bush/small tree. Stems warm cinnamon col. Fls white, pitcher-shaped, bunched; frs small, orange-red. *Ht, Spd:* 15 ft; *Fl:* 4–5; *Z:* PF

A. menziesii Madrona: W N Amer. Bark peeling, stems richer col. Frs orange. Acid soil. *Ht:* 25 ft; *Spd:* 20 ft; *Fl:* 4–5; *Z:* PF

A. unedo* Strawberry tree: Eur, Asia Minor. More lfy and bushy, lime-tolerant. Red frs and white fls borne together. *Ht:* 10 ft+; *Spd:* 8 ft+; *Fl:* 8–10; *Z:* F

A. menziesii

Arctostaphylos

Manzanita, Bearberry

A. manzanita: Cal. Uprt shrub, stems reddish, lvs evergreen, hard, bluish-grey, pointed. Fls pitcher-shaped in nodding 2 in bunches. Frs small, brown. *Ht:* to 20 ft; *Spd:* 9 ft; *Fl:* 2–4; *Z:* PF

A. uva-ursi: N Hem. Prostrate evergreen, lvs glossy, fls pale pink, vase-shaped; frs round, bright red. Prop by seed, cuttings. *Ht:* 4 in; *Spd:* 2 ft; *Fl:* 4–5; *Z:* Arct

A. manzanita

Artemisia

Artemisia

Fine-foliage shrubs related to wormwood, absinthe, tarragon and sage-brush. Good in sun and dry soil.

A. abrotanum Southernwood, Lad's love: S Eur. Uprt sub-shrub often used for low hedges. Lvs grey-green, finely cut, v aromatic. Fls insignificant. Prop by cuttings. *Ht:* to 4 ft; *Spd:* 30 in; *Z:* Arct

A. arborescens: S Eur. Grown for the intricate fol which is shining pewter-grey, white below. Stems whitened. Soft fluffy shrub tender in hard wtrs. Prop by cuttings. *Ht, Spd:* 3½ ft; *Z:* F

A. abrotanum

Arundinaria  

Bamboo

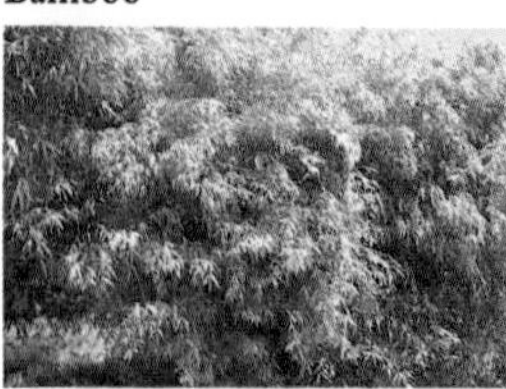

A. nitida

A. japonica (=Bambusa metake): Japan. Forms broad suckering clump of dull green canes under pale brown sheaths. Lustrous lvs to 1 ft. *Ht:* 15 ft; *Spd:* 20 ft+; *Z:* PF

A. (=Sinarundinaria) nitida: China. Makes clump of purplish stems. Paler shining evergreen lvs in 2nd yr greyish below. Prop by div. *Ht, Spd:* 10 ft; *Z:* PF

Aucuba   

Aucuba

A. japonica Spotted laurel: Japan. V striking shiny-lvd shrub. Type has rather pale lvs. Frs handsome waxy red, fls white. 'Crotonifolia' (AGM) best cv, lvs yellow-blotched. *Ht, Spd:* 7 ft; *Fl:* 3–4; *Z:* PF

Azara   

Azara

A. serrata: Chile. Rather tender. Lvs in 2s or 3s on downy shoots. Fls yellow, frs whitish, plant uprt. Hardier *A. microphylla* has mustard-yellow vanilla-scented fls in Mar. *Ht:* 10 ft; *Spd:* 5 ft; *Fl:* 7; *Z:* F

Ballota   

Ballota

B. pseudodictamnus: Med. Low scarcely woody sub-shrub with woolly white stems, rounded sage-green lvs and whorls of white purple-spotted ½ in fls that appear pink. Prop by cuttings. *Ht, Spd:* 2 ft; *Fl:* 7; *Z:* F

Berberis  

Barberry

A huge genus of wickedly prickly shrubs, evergreen and deciduous with masses of small yellow or orange flowers in spring.

B. darwinii

B. × stenophylla

B. candidula: China. Forms dense, glossy, evergreen dome. Lvs close-packed, stems fiercely prickly. Fls single, pale yellow. *Ht, Spd:* 2–3 ft; *Fl:* 4–5; *Z:* Arct

B. darwinii: Chile. V popular evergreen. Spiny 3-pointed lvs, v many orange-yellow fls. Frs oval, glistening, bluish-black. *Ht:* 6 ft; *Spd:* 4 ft; *Fl:* 4–5; *Z:* PF

B. × stenophylla: gdn origin. Graceful arching evergreen bush. Stems spiny, profuse yellow fls. *Ht, Spd:* 10 ft; *Fl:* 4–5; *Z:* Arct

B. thunbergii: Japan. Decid, densely prickly bush. Clustered yellow fls. Brilliant red aut col, small red frs. *B.t. atropurpurea* most reliable purple-lvd shrub. Lvs of 'Aurea' yellow; 'Rose Glow' purple, mottled silver and pink. *Ht:* 6 ft; *Spd:* 6 ft; *Fl:* 4–5; *Z:* Arct

B. wilsoniae: China. Arching, decid. Frs. lvs soft coral in aut. *Ht:* 3 ft; *Spd:* 4 ft; *Fl:* 4–5; *Z:* PF

Beschorneria

B. yuccoides: Mexico. Exotic grey-green lvd yucca-like plant. Lvs 18 in × 2 in in rosette. Fls nodding, vivid green with coral-red bracts. Needs shelter. Prop by div, seed. *Ht:* 4 ft; *Spd:* 3 ft; *Fl:* 5–6; *Z:* SF

Buddleia

Fast-growing soft-wooded shrubs making angular patterns with opposite branching. Honey-smelling flowers are a great attraction to butterflies. Most have flowers in stiff or soft spikes.

B. davidii Butterfly bush: China. Stiff common shrub wildly popular with butterflies. Lvs long, pointed, soft green, white beneath. Sp has panicles to 20 in of mauve fls surpassed by sev good named cvs inc: 'Black Knight' (AGM) violet; 'Empire Blue' (AGM); 'Royal Red' (AGM). Prune hard in Mar. *Ht, Spd:* 9 ft+; *Fl:* 7–10; *Z:* Arct

B. fallowiana*: China. Finer but less hardy with white woolly lvs and panicles of honey-scented lavender-blue fls to 10 in. 'Alba' is a white-flowered cv. Needs shelter. Prop by cuttings. *Ht:* 10 ft; *Spd:* 6 ft; *Fl:* 6; *Z:* PF

B. globosa Orange ball buddleia: Chile, Peru. More substantial semi-evergreen bush. Fls orange-yellow ball-shaped, 2–10 in a branched terminal head. Prop by cuttings. *Ht, Spd:* 10 ft; *Fl:* 5–6; *Z:* PF

B. davidii

B. globosa

Box

B. sempervirens Common box: Eur, W Asia, N Africa. Smells of ancient gdns. Lvs oval, close-packed, dark glossy green. Tiny fls look yellow but are green with prominent anthers. Rabbit-proof. *B.s.* 'Suffruticosa' (Edging box) neat, lighter green dwarf form to 5 ft usually clipped. *Ht:* to 20 ft; *Spd:* to 20 ft; *Fl:* 4; *Z:* Arct

B. sempervirens 'Suffruticosa'

Callicarpa

C. bodinieri: China. Uprt shrub grown for its small, round vivid bluish-lilac frs borne in bunches in Oct–Nov. Lvs slim, purplish in aut. Prop by seed, cuttings. *Ht:* 6 ft; *Spd:* 3 ft+; *Fl:* 7; *Z:* PF

C. japonica: Japan. Smaller; lvs oval, fls pink, frs shiny, lilac. Both spp fr more freely in gps. *Ht:* 4 ft; *Spd:* 3 ft; *Fl:* 8; *Z:* PF

C. japonica

Callistemon

Bottle brush

Graceful wavy shrubs with vivid bottle-brush flowers in summer. In this characteristically Australian flower design the "bristles" are the stamens.

C. citrinus

C. citrinus: Aust. Tall shrub/small tree. Lvs narrow, fls in cylindrical 4 in spikes, prominent red stamens and flattened oval woody frs. 'Splendens' (AGM) bright crimson. Prop by cuttings. *Ht:* to 15 ft; *Spd:* 10 ft; *Fl:* 6; *Z:* SF

C. salignus: Aust. Young growth silky, finely hry. Stamens creamy yellow, may be pale pink. One of the hardiest spp. Prop by cuttings. *Ht:* 15 ft+; *Spd:* 10 ft+; *Fl:* 6; *Z:* SF

Calluna

Heather, Ling

C. vulgaris 'Elsie Powell'

C. vulgaris: Eur, Asia Minor, E N Amer. Densely bushy; lvs massed, tiny. V many white-purple fls. Some cvs have coloured fol, eg: 'Blazeaway' lvs red in wtr, fls lilac-mauve; other good cvs inc 'Peter Sparkes' (AGM) fls pale pink, double; 'Tib' fls rosy red, double. (See also pp 130, 132.) *Ht, Spd:* 30 in; *Fl:* 7–11; *Z:* Arct

Camellia

Camellia

The most sumptuous of winter and spring flowers and remarkably hardy. Best in acid soil and light woodland shade.

C. japonica 'Magnolii flora'

C. reticulata

C. japonica*: Japan, Korea. Fls single, semi-double, double, paeony or anemone-like, red in sp. Cvs reds, pinks to white and striped. Rec (all AGM): 'Adolphe Audusson' blood red; 'Contessa Lavinia Maggi' double, white or pink striped cerise; 'Lady Clare' peach-pink semi-double. *Ht:* to 30 ft; *Spd:* 6 ft+; *Fl:* 4–6; *Z:* PF

C. reticulata: China. Fls deep rose pink, single. Semi-double cvs inc 'Captain Rawes' (AM); 'Trewithen Pink' (AM). *Ht:* to 25 ft; *Spd:* 8 ft+; *Fl:* 2–4; *Z:* F

C. sasanqua: Japan. Fls white or pale pink, frag, single. Cvs inc 'Crimson King' red; 'Narumi Gata' (AM) white tinged pink. *Ht:* 15 ft; *Spd:* 6 ft+; *Fl:* 10–4; *Z:* F

C. × williamsii: gdn origin. Superb, free-flowering. Fls pink or white single, pink semi-double in 'Donation' (AGM). *Ht:* 10 ft; *Spd:* 6 ft; *Fl:* 11–5; *Z:* F

Caragana

Pea tree

C. arborescens: Siberia, Manchuria. Pretty uprt shrub/small tree. Lvs small, compound, fls yellow, pea-like. 'Lorbergii' more elegant, narrow-lvd. Prop by seed, cuttings. *Ht:* to 15 ft; *Spd:* 6 ft+; *Fl:* 5; *Z:* Arct

Carpenteria

Carpenteria

***C. californica**:** Cal. Handsome shrub for a warm spot. Lvs narrow, pointed. Frag fls 3 in wide, single, white, with prominent golden anthers. Prop by seed, layers, cuttings (slow). *Ht:* to 8 ft; *Spd:* 3 ft; *Fl:* 6–7; *Z:* PF

C. californica

Caryopteris

Caryopteris

***C. × clandonensis 'Arthur Simmonds'**:** gdn origin. Small rounded shrub, many greyish stems. Lvs dull grey in bud opening soft grey-green. Fls bright blue in 2 in clusters. *Ht:* 3 ft; *Spd:* 4 ft; *Fl:* 8–9; *Z:* Arct

Cassia

Cassia

C. corymbosa: S Amer. Tender sp for sheltered place or cool greenhouse. Lvs have pairs of lflts. Fls in clusters rich yellow single, cup-shaped, 3 in wide. Prop by seed, cuttings. *Ht, Spd:* 6 ft; *Fl:* 8–9; *Z:* F

Ceanothus

Californian lilac

Fast-growing shrubs from the dry hillsides of California, invaluable for their blue flowers, a rare colour in shrubs.

***C. 'Autumnal Blue'**:** gdn origin. Probably the hardiest of the rather tender evergreen hyb ceanothus. Lvs blunt, oval, rich green. Fls fluffy, china blue. Fast growing, prop by cuttings. *Ht, Spd:* 11 ft; *Fl:* 7–9; *Z:* PF

C. dentatus: Cal. Fast-growing uprt evergreen. Lvs small, thick, dark green, pale below. Fls bright blue in thimble-shaped clusters 1½ in wide. Name often used for larger-lvd *C. × veitchianus*. *Ht:* 11 ft; *Spd:* 6 ft; *Fl:* 5; *Z:* PF

C. 'Gloire de Versailles': gdn origin. Decid hyb. Lvs larger, young stems pale jade green. Masses of powder-blue fls in loose panicles to 8 in. *Ht, Spd:* 6 ft; *Fl:* 7–10; *Z:* PF

***C. impressus**:** Cal. Spreading small evergreen. Deeply furrowed lvs slightly hry. Fls deep blue in 1 in clusters. *Ht, Spd:* to 5 ft; *Fl:* 4–5; *Z:* F

C. dentatus

C. impressus 'Puget Blue'

Ceratostigma    

Ceratostigma

***C. willmottianum**:** China. Low soft-wooded shrub with long late-smr season. Lvs light green, bristly, may redden in aut. Fls brilliant blue, open, tubular in groups 2½ in diam. *Ht, Spd:* 3 ft; *Fl:* 7–10; *Z:* F

Cercis  

Cercis

C. siliquastrum Judas tree: E Med. Small branchy tree; pale lvs almost round. Rich pink pea-fls from bare branches and even trunk. *C. canadensis* (American redbud) sim. *Ht:* 20 ft; *Spd:* 20 ft+; *Fl:* 5; *Z:* PF

Chaenomeles (=Cydonia)  

"Japonica", Flowering quince

C. × *superba* 'Crimson and Gold'

C. speciosa (=C. lagenaria, Pyrus japonica): China. Rounded bush, can be wall-trained. Brs spiny, angular, lvs oval. Rose-like fls over a long season 2 in diam, single, semi-double or double with prominent anthers. Frs yellowish, round. Cvs inc 'Moerloosii' (AM) pale pink and white; 'Nivalis' (AM) white; 'Sanguinea Plena' double red. *Ht, Spd:* to 8 ft; *Fl:* 2–5; *Z:* Arct

C. × superba: gdn origin. Smaller, equally vig. Fls Jan–Feb if sheltered and intermittently to Aug. Best cvs (all AGM) inc 'Crimson and Gold'; 'Knap Hill Scarlet'; 'Rowallane' crimson red. *Ht, Spd:* to 5 ft; *Z:* Arct

Chimonanthus  

Winter sweet

***C. praecox (=fragrans)**:** China. Deliciously frag fls on bare wtr brs. Waxy pale yellow fls 1 in wide with inner ring of short purple ptls. Good on chalky soils and against walls. *Ht, Spd:* to 11 ft; *Fl:* 12–3; *Z:* PF

Chionanthus   

Fringe-tree

C. virginicus: E N Amer. Tall shrub or bushy small tree grown for its abundant loose fluffy frag fls with fringe-like creamy white ptls. Best on deep lime-free loam. *Ht:* 20 ft+; *Spd:* 15 ft; *Fl:* 6; *Z:* Arct

Choisya  

Mexican orange flower

C. *ternata*

***C. ternata**:** Mexico. Highly rec rounded shrub with glossy green 3-lobed lvs and heads of white star-shaped frag fls each to 1½ in wide in Apr–May and intermittently to Dec. Lvs unpleasantly pungent if crushed. Prop by cuttings. *Ht:* to 10 ft; *Spd:* to 8 ft; *Z:* PF

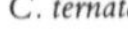

Cistus

Rock rose

Aromatic, often gummy, Mediterranean evergreens with myriads of short-lived fragile flowers. For dry soil. Increase all types by cuttings.

C. × aguilari: Spain, Morocco. Natural hyb, plain white fls. 'Imaculatus' (AGM) better form bearing myriads of large white purple-blotched fls. Lvs sticky. *Ht:* 4 ft; *Spd:* 30 in; *Fl:* 6–7; *Z:* F

C. × cyprius: gdn origin. One of the hardiest hybs. Lvs sombre dark green. Fls white, 3 in wide, with crimson blotch at base of each ptl. Inclined to arch and build up solid mass of fol. *Ht:* to 8 ft; *Spd:* 5 ft; *Fl:* 6–7; *Z:* PF

C. × cyprius

C. laurifolius: Eur. Hardiest sp. Lvs hrlss, oval, pointed, sticky. Fls plain white 2 in wide in generous clusters. Sim size to above but more uprt. *Fl:* 6–8; *Z:* PF

C. populifolius: Eur. Slightly less hardy with larger, paler long-stkd poplar-shaped lvs. Fls white, conspic yellow base to each ptl. *Ht:* 6 ft; *Spd:* 4 ft; *Fl:* 6–7; *Z:* F

C. laurifolius

Citrus

Lemon

C. ichangense Ichang lemon: China. Nearly hardy lemon and decorative small shrub with single white frag fls and bright yellow edible lemon frs. Worth trying in correct zone. *Ht:* 10 ft; *Spd:* 5 ft; *Fl:* 5–6; *Z:* SF

Clerodendrum

Clerodendrum

***C. trichotomum**:** Japan. Large lfy dome-shaped bush grown for its lurid turquoise-blue frs. Lvs have fetid smell if crushed but fls v frag, star-like with persistent maroon spls. *Ht, Spd:* 18 ft; *Fl:* 7–9; *Z:* PF

Clethra

Clethra

C. alnifolia Sweet pepper bush: N Amer. Uprt, twiggy. Wonderfully frag fls in 6 in spikes. Lvs oval, nearly smooth. 'Paniculata' (AGM) best cv. Prop by layers, suckers. *Ht, Spd:* 7 ft; *Fl:* 8; *Z:* Arct

C. barbinervis: China, Japan. Sim to above but to 9 ft. Good aut col. Fls fluffier, young lvs downy. *Spd:* 9 ft; *Fl:* 7–9; *Z:* Arct

C. alnifolia

Colutea

Bladder senna

C. arborescens: S Eur. Amusing inflated pea-pod bladders (fun to pop) follow yellow pea-like ¾ in fls. Lvs grey-green, compound. Quick growing, good for new and seaside gdns. *Ht:* 6 ft; *Spd:* 5 ft; *Fl:* 6–9; *Z:* Arct

Convolvulus

Convolvulus

***C. cneorum**:** S Eur. Shining ever-grey shrublet. Fls funnel-shaped, 1 in wide, v pale pink. Best at foot of a warm wall or against a sunny rock. A plant to cherish. Prop by cuttings. *Ht:* 30 in; *Spd:* 3 ft; *Fl:* 5–9; *Z:* SF

Cordyline

Cabbage tree, Cabbage palm

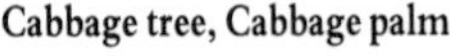

C. australis

C. australis: Aust, NZ. Palm-like with mop heads of 3 ft sword-shaped lvs, deep maroon in 'Atropurpurea'. Fls frag, white, frs bead-like, cream, blue-tinged. *Ht:* to 40 ft; *Spd:* 8 ft; *Fl:* 5; *Z:* SF

C. indivisa: NZ. Sim but bigger lvs. Fls grey-white flushed purple in 4 ft plumes. Frs purplish. *Ht:* to 25 ft; *Spd:* 10 ft; *Fl:* 5; *Z:* NF

Cornus

Dogwood, Cornel

Most valuable genus for flowers, autumn colour, fruit, variegated foliage, interesting habit and bark colour (not all, alas, on the same plant). Increase plants by cuttings.

C. alba 'Spaethii'

C. mas

C. alba: Siberia. Clump-forming. Slim, uprt blood red stems best in wtr. Lvs col in aut. Fls in flat heads, fr white, tinged blue. Rec cvs 'Elegantissima' (AGM) lvs white margins; 'Sibirica' stems scarlet; 'Spaethii' (AGM) lvs yellow varieg. *Ht, Spd:* 8 ft; *Fl:* 5–6; *Z:* Arct

C. florida: E USA. Glorious in N Amer with white pink or red ptl-like bracts but rarely fls in N Eur. *Ht, Spd:* 20 ft; *Fl:* 5; *Z:* Arct

C. kousa: Japan, Korea, Big, bushy. Fls abundant, creamy-white bracts to 1½ in in 4s, frs like strawberries. *C.k. chinensis** taller, both superb aut col. *Ht, Spd:* to 20 ft; *Fl:* 5–6; *Z:* Arct

C. mas Cornelian cherry: Eur. Excellent wtr-flowering twiggy shrub/small tree. Fl heads 1 in wide, acid-yellow with yellow-green bracts. Frs red, oval. Also a pretty white-varieg form*. *Ht, Spd:* to 25 ft; *Fl:* 2–3; *Z:* Arct

C. nuttallii Pacific dogwood: W N Amer. Rare but superb: 6–8 creamy-white bracts round purplish-green central boss. Frs orange-red. Brilliant aut col. No lime. *Ht, Spd:* 20 ft; *Fl:* 5; *Z:* PF

Corokia

Wire-netting bush

C. cotoneaster: NZ. Like a tangle of wire-netting with small narrow dark green lvs like white suede below and dusting of bright yellow star-shaped fls. Frs small, round, red. *Ht:* 7 ft; *Spd:* 5 ft; *Fl:* 5; *Z:* SF

Corylopsis

 ***C. pauciflora:*** Japan. Hazel-like lvs pink tinted when young and in aut. Fls frag, pale yellow in 2s or 3s, large pale bracts. *C. spicata* (AM) less pretty. *Ht:* 6 ft; *Spd:* 6 ft+; *Fl:* 3–4; *Z:* Arct/PF

Corylus

C. maxima* 'Purpurea' Purple filbert: S Eur (sp). Dark purple lvs broad oval to 5 in long, downy when young. Caterpillars can make them shabby in smr. Bears purple 4 in catkins in Feb–Mar. Fr typical cobnut with long husk. Prop by suckers, layers. *Ht:* to 20 ft; *Spd:* to 10 ft; *Z:* Arct

C. maxima 'Purpurea'

Smoke tree

C. coggyria (=Rhus cotinus)* Venetian sumach: S Eur–China. Bushy, branchy. Lvs round/oval. Fl heads soft frothy masses to 8 in. 'Notcutt's Variety' (AGM) deep purple lvs, purple-pink fls; 'Royal Purple' (AGM) paler. Best aut col in poor soil. *Ht, Spd:* 10 ft; *Fl:* 7–8; *Z:* Arct

Cotoneaster

Easy, hardy, immensely varied shrubs unremarkable in flower but useful for their varied habits and usually brilliant fruits.

C. conspicuus (=C.c. 'Decorus')*: Tibet. Small-lvd evergreen. Fls small, white; berries bright red. Good on banks. *Ht:* 4 ft; *Spd:* 8 ft; *Fl:* 5; *Z:* PF

C. 'Cornubia': gdn origin. Tall spreading semi-evergreen. Masses of brilliant red berries. *C.* × 'Rothschildianus' (yellow frs) less attractive to birds. *Ht, Spd:* 20 ft+; *Fl:* 5–6; *Z:* PF

C. dammeri (=humifusus): China. Prostrate evergreen, lvs oval, frs glistening red. Tolerates shade. 'Skogholm' pop ground cover. *Ht:* 9 in; *Spd:* 5 ft+; *Fl:* 5–6; *Z:* Arct

C. horizontalis Herringbone cotoneaster: China. Spreading, decid, herringbone brs. V good varieg form*. *Ht:* to 5 ft; *Spd:* 8 ft; *Fl:* 5–6; *Z:* Arct

C. microphyllus: Him, China. Tiny-lvd evergreen; young shoots woolly. Good on banks or in rock gdn. *Ht:* 3 ft; *Spd:* 4 ft+; *Fl:* 5–6; *Z:* Arct

C. simonsii: Assam. Decid, stiff, uprt. Frs large, scarlet. Makes hedge with a little pruning. *Ht:* 8 ft; *Spd:* 6 ft; *Fl:* 5–6; *Z:* PF

C. conspicuus

C. horizontalis

Broom

The most varied of the three genera of "brooms" (the others are *Genista* and *Spartium*) includes colours other than yellow.

C. battandieri

C. × praecox

C. multiflorus (=albus) White Spanish broom: SW Eur, N Africa. Tough, uprt. Masses of pea-like white fls. *Ht:* 10 ft; *Spd:* 5 ft; *Fl:* 5–6; *Z:* Arct

C. battandieri* Moroccan broom: Morocco. Silver-silky laburnum-like lvs; fls golden-yellow in uprt plumes, strong pineapple frag. *Ht, Spd:* 12 ft; *Fl:* 6–7; *Z:* PF

C. × praecox Warminster broom: gdn origin. V prolific creamy ½ in fls. 'Albus' is white; 'Gold Spear' and 'Allgold' smaller, fls deeper yellow. *Ht, Spd:* 5 ft; *Fl:* 5; *Z:* Arct

C. scoparius: Eur. Brilliant yellow, free-flowering. Hybs in wide col and bicol range, eg × 'Andreanus' yellow/brownish-crimson; × 'Killiney Salmon' orange/pink. *Ht:* 12 ft; *Spd:* 5 ft; *Fl:* 5; *Z:* Arct

Daboecia     

Daboecia

D. cantabrica: St Dabeoc's heath, Connemara heath. Low-growing heath. Buds egg-shaped opening into bright, clear purple bells. 'Alba' (AGM) fls white, lighter green lvs; 'Atropurpurea' (AGM) deep purple; 'Praegerae' glowing pink. *Ht:* 2 ft+; *Spd:* 18 in; *Fl:* 6–11; *Z:* Arct

Daphne     

Daphne

Dignified small shrubs with intensely fragrant flowers. Even in cool, limy, well-drained soil they may be short-lived.

D. retusa

D. mezereum

D. blagayana: SE Eur. Deliciously frag creamy-ivory tubular fls in massed head. Lvs evergreen. Likes to run between stones. *Ht:* 2 ft; *Spd:* 3 ft; *Fl:* 3–4; *Z:* Arct

D. cneorum Garland flower: Eur. Trailing stems, many short evergreen lvs. Fls pink or rosy red in dense gps 2 in wide with sweet frag. May fl in aut. *D. × burkwoodii* taller semi-evergreen hyb to 4 ft. 'Somerset' (AGM) better. *Ht:* 1 ft; *Spd:* 18 in; *Fl:* 4–5; *Z:* Arct

D. mezereum* Mezereon: Eur. Pop wtr-flowering cottage-gdn plant; memorable cloying frag. Pinky-grey fls ½ in wide can be rich purple/red. Fr red, poisonous. White forms with amber fr to be treasured. *Ht:* 4 ft; *Spd:* 3 ft; *Fl:* 2–3; *Z:* Arct

D. retusa: China. Dense evergreen shrublet. Fls rose-purple, pale throat, red fr. *Ht, Spd:* 3 ft; *Fl:* 5–6; *Z:* PF

Datura

Thorn apple

D. sanguinea: Peru. Tender, exotic. Fls pendulous, tubular, flared to 8 in, rusty orange-red. Lvs hry, oval. Prop by cuttings. *Ht, Spd:* to 10 ft; *Fl:* 5–6; *Z:* NF

D. suaveolens Angel's trumpet: Mexico. Sim in habit but lvs variable, often longer; fls frag, white. Both hardy in S Eur. *Ht, Spd:* to 15 ft; *Fl:* 6–8; *Z:* NF

D. suaveolens

Desfontainea

Desfontainea

 **D. spinosa (=hookeri):** S Amer. Usually small-medium bush but taller in warm regions. Lvs holly-like; fls scarlet, tubular to 1½ in, open yellow throat. Frs small, fleshy. *Ht:* 8 ft+; *Spd:* 5 ft+; *Fl:* 7–9; *Z:* SF

Deutzia

Deutzia

Deciduous early-summer shrubs of extreme pink-and-white charm but rarely making a landmark and sadly without scent.

D. × rosea (=gracilis rosea): gdn origin. Dainty; v many flared, bell-shaped pale pink fls, no frag. 'Carminea' (AGM) deeper col. *Ht, Spd:* 3 ft; *Fl:* 5–6; *Z:* Arct

D. scabra (=crenata): China, Japan. To 10 ft, peeling bark. Doubles inc 'Pride of Rochester' and 'Candidissima' pure white. *Spd:* 4 ft; *Fl:* 6–7; *Z:* Arct

D. scabra 'Candidissima'

Disanthus

Disanthus

D. cercidifolius*: Japan. Quietly attractive, lvs can be brightest of all reds in aut. Fls tiny, frs nut-like. *Ht, Spd:* 8 ft; *Fl:* 10; *Z:* PF

Dorycnium

Dorycnium

D. hirsutum (=Lotus hirsutus)* Hairy Dorothy: S Eur. Hry silver-grey sub-shrub. Circular heads of pale pink-flushed pea-fls and chocolate brown seed pods. Prop by seed. *Ht, Spd:* 3 ft; *Fl:* 6–10; *Z:* Arct

Drimys

Drimys

D. winteri (=Wintera aromatica) Winter's bark: Andes. Handsome sp made famous by Sir Francis Drake's Captain William Winter. Lvs long, shining, glaucous below. Fls waxy white, sweetly frag in loose gps. Bark grey-brown aromatic. *D. w. andina* reaches 3 ft and will fl when small. *Ht:* 20 ft; *Spd:* 15 ft; *Fl:* 5; *Z:* SF

D. winteri

Elaeagnus

Elaeagnus

Most valuable vigorous hardy shrubs, evergreen and deciduous, with fragrant flowers and foliage ideal for screening.

E. pungens 'Maculata'

E. angustifolia Russian olive: Near E. Silvery willow-lvd small tree, young twigs white. Edible frs. *Ht, Spd:* to 15 ft; *Fl:* 6; *Z:* Arct

E. pungens: Japan. Bushy evergreen. Varieg cvs inc: 'Dicksonii' wide, yellow margin; 'Maculata' central yellow dash; 'Aurea-variegata' (AGM) thin yellow margin. *E.* × *ebbingei* more vig. *Ht, Spd:* 15 ft; *Fl:* 10–11; *Z:* PF

Embothrium

Fire bush

E. coccineum (=lanceolatum, longifolium): Chile. Tall, uprt, startling in fl with bottle-brushes of vivid orange-scarlet tubes. *E. c. lanceolatum* (AM) hardier, scarlet fls. *Ht:* 35 ft; *Spd:* 10 ft; *Fl:* 5–6; *Z:* F

Enkianthus

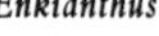

Enkianthus

E. campanulatus: Japan. Enchanting uprt twiggy, decid bush. Fls waxy, bell-shaped, cream suffused and shot with reddish-brown. Superb aut col. *E. perulatus* white-fld. *Ht:* 8 ft; *Spd:* 5 ft; *Fl:* 5; *Z:* Arct

Erica

Heath, Heather

The hardy European heaths range from dwarfs to small trees. One or another flowers almost every month. All have masses of minute evergreen leaves and prominent, often coloured, petal tubes which die on the plant, remaining a good brown colour. Both flower and foliage colour seem infinitely variable. Most demand acid soil and all are best propagated by cuttings.

E. arborea

E. cinerea

E. arborea*: Med, N Africa. Usually seen as 'Alba' with whitish sweetly frag fls and soft fol. *Ht, Spd:* 10 ft; *Fl:* 4; *Z:* PF

E. carnea (=herbacea)*: Alps. Good ground cover. Lvs pale green, fls white or pink. Takes lime. *Ht:* 9 ft; *Spd:* 18 in; *Fl:* 11–5; *Z:* Arct

E. ciliaris Dorset heath: SW Eur. Pitcher-shaped rose-pink fls. Lvs downy except in taller 'Mawaeana'. *Ht:* 1 ft; *Spd:* 18 in; *Fl:* 7–11; *Z:* PF

E. cinerea Bell heather: W Eur. Dense mats of lvs. Some, e.g. 'Golden Hue' have golden fol. Cvs for wide col range inc 'Alba Minor' white; 'C.D.Eason' (AGM) deep pink; 'Rosea' (AGM) bright pink. *Ht:* 15 in; *Spd:* 18 in; *Fl:* 6–9; *Z:* Arct

E. × darleyensis: gdn origin. Lime tolerant, bushy. 'A.T.Johnson' (AGM) rich rose-red; 'George Rendall' (AGM) deeper pink. *Ht, Spd:* 3 ft; *Fl:* 11–5; *Z:* PF

Heath, Heather

E. erigena (=mediterranea): SW Eur. Takes lime but not dryness. Fls white, pink or deep red. 'W.T. Rackliff' white, chocolate anthers. *Ht, Spd:* 18 in; *Fl:* 3–5; *Z:* PF

E. lusitanica Portuguese heath: SW Eur. Spikes of frag white fls pink in bud. *Ht, Spd:* to 10 ft; *Fl:* 1–4; *Z:* SF

E. tetralix Cross-leaved heath: Eur. Fls pink, white or crimson. 'Mollis' (AGM) white. *Ht, Spd:* 18 in; *Fl:* 6–10; *Z:* Arct

E. vagans Cornish heath: S Eur. Long 9 in pokers of fl. 'Lyonesse' (AGM) creamy white. *Ht, Spd:* 4 ft; *Fl:* 6–9; *Z:* Arct

E. terminalis (=stricta): Eur. Rose-pink fls, happy on chalk, hardy. *Ht, Spd:* 4 ft; *Fl:* 6–9; *Z:* Arct

E. erigena

E. tetralix 'Mollis'

Eriobotrya

Loquat

E. japonica* Loquat: China, Japan. One of the biggest-lvd semi-hardy evergreens. Lvs to 9 in, fls frag, yellowish-white. Frs soft orange, apricot-like, delicious. *Ht:* to 30 ft; *Spd:* 10 ft; *Fl:* 11–4; *Z:* PF

Erythrina

Erythrina

E. crista-galli Common coral tree: Brazil. Usually wall-trained, often cut back in frost. Waxy, pea-like 2 in fls in long gps. Lvs green, divided into 3. Prop by cuttings. *Ht, Spd:* 8 ft; *Fl:* 5–6; *Z:* NF

Escallonia

Escallonia

E. 'Donard' hybs: gdn origin. Among hardiest hybs; bell-shaped fls in profusion. Lvs shiny, often clammy. Fls in red-pink, e.g. 'Slieve Donard' apple-blossom pink. *E.* 'Iveyi' with bigger lvs needs protection, fls white. Prop by cuttings. *Ht:* 8 ft; *Spd:* 6 ft; *Fl:* 6–9; *Z:* F

E. 'Donard Seedling'

Eucryphia

Eucryphia

E. glutinosa (=pinnatifolia): Chile. Lvs cut into 5 toothed lflts. Fls white, 2½ in wide, boss of golden stamens. Rich aut col. *Ht:* 15 ft; *Spd:* 10 ft+; *Fl:* 7–8; *Z:* F

E. × nymansensis 'Nymansay'*: gdn origin. Fast-growing lime tolerant noble uprt evergreen hyb. Fls sim. *Ht:* 18 ft; *Spd:* 6 ft; *Fl:* 8–9; *Z:* F

E. glutinosa

Euonymus

Spindle

Shrubs with bright seed capsules splitting to reveal even brighter seeds. Deciduous ones may colour well in autumn.

E. japonicus

E. alatus

E. europaeus

E. alatus Winged spindle: China, Japan. Unique cerise to rose-red aut col. Flat branching habit, corky wings on stems; seeds orange. Good as a hedge. *Ht:* 8 ft; *Spd:* 8 ft+; *Fl:* 5–6; *Z:* Arct

E. europaeus Common spindle: Eur. Big bush; smooth soft lvs. Brilliant lf col, red frs and orange seeds in aut. 'Red Cascade' (AGM) rec. *Ht:* 12 ft+; *Spd:* 5 ft+; *Fl:* 5–6; *Z:* Arct

E. fortunei: E Asia. Sprawling sometimes climbing evergreen smotherer. Fls and seeds inconspic except in *E. f. virgatus*, seeds orange. Good varieg cvs 'Silver Queen'; 'Emerald n' Gold'. *Ht:* 30 in; *Spd:* 4 ft; *Z:* Arct

E. japonicus: Japan. Glossy evergreen. Best cv 'Duc d'Anjou'; the varieg 'Aureus' may revert. *Ht:* 6 ft; *Spd:* 5 ft; *Fl:* 6; *Z:* PF

E. planipes*: Japan. Splendid, decid. Lvs pointed, red-purple in aut, seeds red. Often offered as *E. sachalinensis*. *Ht:* 10 ft; *Spd:* 5 ft+; *Fl:* 6; *Z:* Arct

E. yedoensis: Japan. Name debatable but not its aut beauty, pink frs, red seeds, pink lvs. *Ht:* 10 ft; *Spd:* 5 ft; *Fl:* 6; *Z:* Arct

Exochorda

Pearl bush

E. racemosa (=grandiflora): China. Almond-like milky-white fls on a pendulous bush. Lvs oval, sea-green. Will tolerate some lime but *E. korolkowii* (AM) v happy on chalk. *Ht:* 12 ft; *Spd:* 8 ft; *Fl:* 5; *Z:* Arct

Fatsia

Fatsia

F. japonica

F. (=Aralia) japonica*: Japan. Lustrous, jungly, deep-lobed lvs to 15 in wide on green stks. Fls off-white, ball-shaped, several to a 1½ in head. Lvs of 'Variegata' irregularly tipped green. Smaller-lvd × *Fatshedera lizei* probably hyb with common ivy. *Ht, Spd:* to 15 ft; *Fl:* 10–11; *Z:* PF

Feijoa

Feijoa

F. sellowiana: S Amer. V pretty; small grey-green oval lvs, white felted below. Fls aromatic, ptls white, crimson at base, large boss of crimson stamens. Egg-shaped frs in warmth. *Ht, Spd:* 10 ft; *Fl:* 6; *Z:* NF

Fig

F. pumila

F. carica Common fig: Med, W Asia. Decid shrub/small tree. Lvs bold, 3–5 lobed, odd evocative smell. Restrict rts, keep soil poor. Reliable hardy cvs inc: 'Brown Turkey'; 'White Marseilles'. *Ht:* 15 ft; *Spd:* 20 ft; *Fl:* 7; *Z:* PF

F. pumila: China, Japan. Evergreen climber, bristling with aerial rts. *Ht:* 10 ft; *Spd:* 6 ft+; *Z:* SF

Forsythia

Forsythia

F. × *intermedia*

F.* × *intermedia: gdn origin. Easy and loud in fl: a sheet of striking yellow. 'Spectabilis' (AM) golden yellow twisted ptls. *Ht, Spd:* 8 ft; *Fl:* 3–4; *Z:* Arct

F. suspensa: China. More vig; try 'Beatrix Farrand'; *F.s. atrocaulis* (both AM). *Ht, Spd:* 10 ft; *Fl:* 3–4; *Z:* Arct

Fothergilla

Fothergilla

F. gardenii: SE USA. Small shrub, fiery aut col. Long oval lvs on crooked stems. Fls short, white, frag bottle-brushes. *F. major*★ and its clone *F. monticola* (AM) larger, better. *Ht, Spd:* 4 ft; *Fl:* 4–5; *Z:* Arct

Fuchsia

Fuchsia

South American natives ideal for bedding or conservatories for their long flowering season and ease of propagation (by cuttings). Fancy sorts are mainly hybrids of *F. fulgens*.

F. gdn hyb 'Mrs Popple'

F. gdn hyb 'Madame Cornelissen'

F. magellanica: S Amer. The hardiest sp. Woody bush to 6 ft, lvs thin, oval, toothed. Elegant single pendulous fls to 2 in with scarlet spls over purple ptls. There are cream-varieg and dwarf forms but best cv is 'Versicolor'★ (AM) wrongly called *F.m. variegata* with silvery grey-pink-tinted lvs and dripping with fls. 'Molinae' has dainty blush-pink to white fls and pale green lvs. *Spd:* 4 ft; *Fl:* 7–10; *Z:* PF

F. gdn hybs: Selections for sun and medium shade on most soils. Shrubby in mild gdns, herbaceous in cooler ones. Keep moist in smr. Best are 'Chillerton Beauty' (AM) blush-pink/violet; 'Mrs Popple' (AM) scarlet/purple, crimson anthers; 'Madame Cornelissen' (AM) semi-double, scarlet/white; 'Margaret' carmine/purple. *Ht:* to 5 ft; *Spd:* to 4 ft; *Fl:* 7–10; *Z:* PF

Garrya

Garrya

***G. elliptica**:** Cal, Oregon. Tough, rather dull lvs lighter below. Fls beautiful grey-green catkins to 9 in but to 15 in in cv 'James Roof'. Good wall-trained. Prop by cuttings. *Ht, Spd:* 10 ft; *Fl:* 1–2; *Z:* F

Gaultheria

Gaultheria

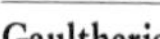

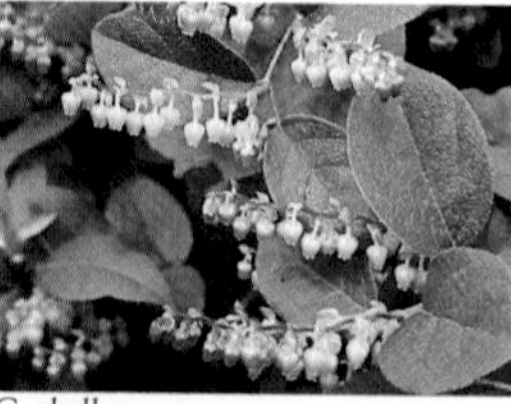

G. shallon

G. procumbens Creeping wintergreen: E N Amer. Suckering shrub. Fls globular/pitcher-shaped, pale pink or white; frs round, bright red amongst oval fol. *Ht:* 6 in; *Spd:* 3 ft; *Fl:* 7–8; *Z:* Arct

G. shallon: W N Amer. Rampant, stoloniferous, lvs leathery. Fls bell-shaped, pinkish-white. Can be a pest in damp, acid soil. *Ht:* 6 ft; *Spd:* 6 ft+; *Fl:* 5–6; *Z:* Arct

Genista

Broom

Pea-flowered brooms, related to *Cytisus*, very varied in habit, but almost always yellow-flowered. They are excellent for dry, limy soil, needing no food.

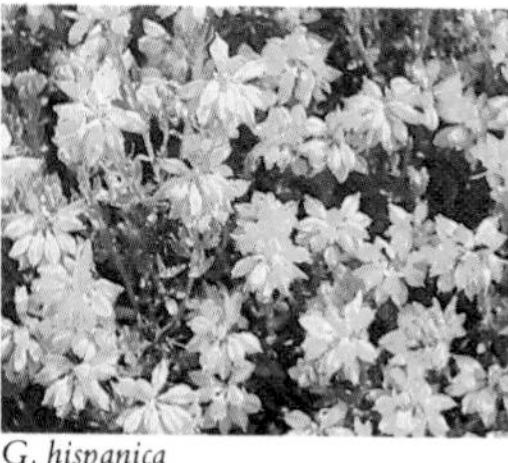

G. hispanica

G. aetnensis (=Spartium aetnense)* Mt Etna broom: Sicily. Rapidly makes small tree with near-lflss pendulous branchlets dripping with yellow fls. *Ht:* 18 ft; *Spd:* 10 ft+; *Fl:* 7–8; *Z:* PF

G. hispanica* Spanish gorse: SW Eur. Dense, prickly; makes pouffe of rich green growth studded with yellow fls. Prop by seed, cuttings. *Ht, Spd:* 4 ft; *Fl:* 5–6; *Z:* PF

Grevillea

Grevillea

G. rosmarinifolia

G. rosmarinifolia: Aust. Rosemary-like small shrub; lvs dark green needles, young shoots downy. Soft red fls in terminal bunches each narrow, tubular to 1 in, curved at ends. *Ht, Spd:* 4 ft; *Fl:* 5–6; *Z:* SF

G. sulphurea: Aust. Sim to above but lvs pale green, fls pale yellow with split, curled back ptl tube and protruding stigma. *Ht, Spd:* 4 ft; *Fl:* 5–6; *Z:* SF

Griselinia

Griselinia

G. (=Pukateria) littoralis: NZ. Tall, bushy, lvs glossy, spoon-shaped. Makes good hedge in mild areas esp nr sea. Fls inconspic. Young growth frost-tender. Prop by cuttings. *Ht:* 20 ft; *Spd:* 15 ft; *Z:* SF

Halesia

Snowdrop tree, Silver bells

H. carolina: SE USA. Decid small tree/big shrub beautiful in May when dripping with ½ in white bell-fls. Frs like small ribbed pears. *H. monticola* bigger esp in 'Vestita'★and perhaps better. *Ht:* 20 ft; *Spd:* 25 ft+; *Z:* Arct

Halimium

Halimium

H. ocymoides: SW Eur. Grey-green lvs; sol rich yellow fls, each ptl blotched chocolate at base. Hyb × *Halimiocistus* 'Ingwersenii' with white fls in May–July also good but smaller. *Ht, Spd:* to 3 ft; *Fl:* 6; *Z:* F

Hamamelis

Witch-hazel

H. × intermedia ("japollis"): gdn origin. Oval, hazel-like lvs col beautifully in aut. Fls to 1¼ in wide made up of strap-shaped ptls which are often wrinkled and have a slight fragrance. Best cvs 'Jelena' (AM) coppery-orange fls; 'Ruby Glow' coppery-red fls. Prop by layers, grafting. *Ht, Spd:* 5 ft; *Fl:* 12–3; *Z:* Arct

***H. mollis*★** Chinese witch-hazel: China. Sim to above but wider ptls with persisting coppery-red spls, penetrating sweet frag. Both will take some lime given enough humus and moisture. 'Pallida'★ (AM) pale sulphur fls, more ptls, highly rec. *Ht:* 8 ft; *Spd:* 6 ft; *Fl:* 12–3; *Z:* Arct

H. × intermedia

H. mollis

Hebe (=Veronica)

Hebe

Neat evergreens with small leaves in orderly ranks. Mostly tough and adaptable except in hard frost. Tiny flowers in spikes.

H. albicans: NZ. Hardy, glaucous lvs; fls 2 in compact white spikes. *Ht:* 18 in; *Spd:* 2 ft; *Fl:* 8–9; *Z:* F

H. brachysiphon: NZ. Tidy dome of dense fol, remarkably hardy. White fls, brown anthers. *H. rakaiensis* smaller, bright green. *Ht, Spd:* 5 ft; *Fl:* 7–9; *Z:* F/PF

H. gdn hybs: V many good cvs inc: 'Autumn Glory', 'Carl Teschner' violet, dwarf; 'Great Orme' pink; 'Midsummer Beauty' lavender blue for months on end. *Ht, Spd:* to 3 ft; *Fl:* 7–10; *Z:* SF

H. salicifolia Willow-leaved hebe: NZ. Wide willow-lvs. Fls white or pale lilac in tapering racemes. *H. s. variegata* less hardy. *Ht:* 4 ft; *Spd:* 5 ft; *Fl:* 7–9; *Z:* SF

H. speciosa: NZ. Thicker fls. Rec: 'Gauntletii' pink; 'La Seduisante' crimson; 'Veitchii' purple. *Ht, Spd:* 5 ft; *Fl:* 8–10; *Z:* NF

H. brachysiphon

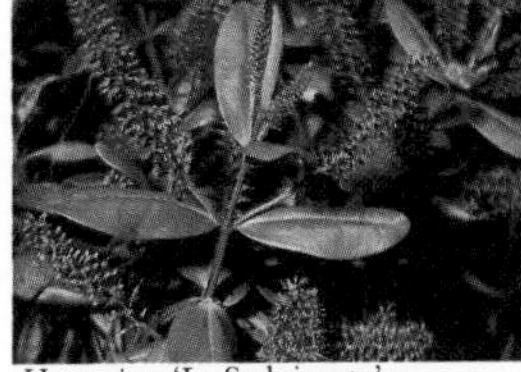

H. speciosa 'La Seduisante'

Helianthemum   

Sun rose

H. gdn hyb 'Wisley Pink'

***H. gdn hybs**:** Med (sp). Low, spreading shrubs producing profuse fresh crop of 1 in fls daily. Must have full sun. Rec sorts inc: 'Ben Ledi' rose-red, dark green lvs; 'Henfield Brilliant' orange-red, grey lvs; 'Wisley Pink' pale pink, orange anthers, grey lvs; 'Wisley Primrose' primrose yellow, grey lvs; 'Mrs C.W. Earle' double red. Prop by cuttings. *Ht:* 1 ft; *Spd:* 20 in; *Fl:* 5–7; *Z:* PF

Helichrysum    

Everlasting flower, Straw flower

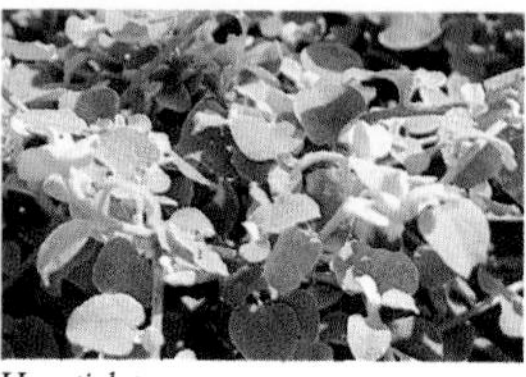
H. petiolatum

H. lanatum: S Africa. Sub-shrub; lvs long, narrow ever-grey. Flat heads small lemon-yellow fls. *Ht, Spd:* 18 in; *Fl:* 7; *Z:* F
***H. petiolatum**:** S Africa. Tender. Lvs oval, woolly grey. Long brs form dome shape. *H. p. aureum* has soft yellow flannel-lvs; *H. p. variegatum* silver and deep green fol. *Ht:* 15 in; *Spd:* 30 in; *Z:* NF

Hibiscus   

Hibiscus

Rich, expensive-looking late-summer feature with flowers in decadent colours. Late in leaf, rather slow-growing, will withstand hard pruning to shape.

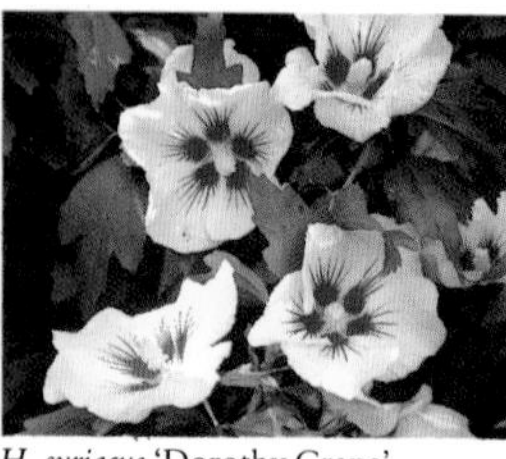
H. syriacus 'Dorothy Crane'

H. syriacus: Syria. Uprt late-flowering shrubby mallow with oval lvs and shuttlecock-shaped fls to 3 in wide. Best cvs 'Blue Bird,* (AM) strong blue, deeper eye; 'Hamabo' (AM) blush pink/crimson; 'Woodbridge' rich pink/carmine; 'Duc de Brabant' is a purplish-red double, 'Jeanne d'Arc' white semi-double. *H. sinosyriacus* sim, less hardy. *Ht:* 8 ft; *Spd:* 4 ft; *Fl:* 8–10; *Z:* PF/Arct

Hippophae  

Hippophae

H. rhamnoides* Sea buckthorn: Eur–E Asia. Spiny bush, grey-green lvs silvery below. Fls inconspic but with both sexes present amber berries load branches in aut. Resists sea. *Ht:* 10 ft; *Spd:* 6 ft; *Fl:* 4; *Z:* Arct

Hoheria    

Hoheria

***H. glabrata**:** NZ. Tall evergreen with soft serrated lvs and translucent white, cherry-like frag fls $1\frac{1}{2}$ in diam. Taller *H. lyallii** fls in June; semi-evergreen *H. sexstylosa* to 20 ft bears smaller more profuse fls in July–Aug. Prop by seed, cuttings. *Ht:* 15 ft; *Spd:* 10 ft; *Fl:* 6–7; *Z:* F

Hydrangea

Hydrangea

Most garden sorts are varieties of *H. macrophylla*; divided into mop-headed Hortensias and flat-headed Lacecaps, which have open sterile florets around a mass of smaller fertile ones.

***H. aspera*★:** E Asia. Magnificent shrub. Lvs softly bristly; pink-mauve inner florets, pale blue outer ones. *H. villosa* v sim. *Ht, Spd:* 8 ft; *Fl:* 6–8; *Z:* PF

H. gdn hybs: Vig, bushy. Best Hortensias inc 'Altona' (AM) rosy-pink; 'Madame Emile Mouillière' (AM) white, blue eye; 'Générale Vicomtesse de Vibraye' (AM) pure blue. Best Lacecaps inc: 'Blue Wave' (AM); 'Sea Foam' blue edged white; 'Veitchii' white in shade, pink in sun. Blue fls turn pink on akaline soil. *Ht, Spd:* to 6 ft; *Fl:* 7–9; *Z:* PF

H. paniculata: China, Japan. Uprt with lilac-like 8 in white fl plumes. 'Vera' is excellent. *Ht, Spd:* 6 ft; *Fl:* 6–7; *Z:* Arct

H. serrata: Japan, Korea. At most attractive in 'Grayswood' (AM) white turning pink-tinged then red. Also 'Bluebird' (AM) and 'Preziosa' (AM) pink, then red. *Ht, Spd:* 5 ft; *Fl:* 7; *Z:* PF/Arct

H. quercifolia Oak-leaved hydrangea: N Amer. Vig, spreading, grown for its splendid lobed lvs to 8 in with rich aut col. *Ht:* 4 ft; *Spd:* 6 ft; *Fl:* 6–9; *Z:* PF

H. aspera

H. 'Générale Vicomtesse de Vibraye'

H. quercifolia

Hypericum

St John's wort

Adaptable long-flowering shrubs and ground cover with buttercup-like shining yellow flowers. Useful but easily overused.

H. androsaemum Tutsan: Eur, N Africa. Neat bush; fls small, frs berries. *Ht, Spd:* 3 ft; *Fl:* 6–9; *Z:* PF

H. calycinum Rose of Sharon: Eur, Asia Minor. Semi-evergreen, vig ground cover. Fls to 4 in wide, central boss of anthers. *Ht:* 1 ft; *Spd:* 2 ft+; *Fl:* 6–9; *Z:* PF

***H. 'Hidcote'*★:** gdn origin. Semi-evergreen. Fls to 3 in diam, orange anthers. *Ht:* 5 ft; *Spd:* 6 ft+; *Fl:* 6–10; *Z:* PF

H. forrestii: Asia. Fls saucer-shaped, rust-col frs persist in aut with crimson fol. *Ht:* 5 ft; *Spd:* 4 ft; *Fl:* 7–10; *Z:* PF

H. × inodorum: Canary Is. Best in cv 'Elstead' with long red-orange frs and sev fls in flat head. *Ht, Spd:* 3 ft; *Fl:* 6–9; *Z:* PF

H. × moseranum: gdn origin. Dwarf; fls 2½ in wide, ptls overlapping. Prop all by cuttings. *Ht:* 18 in; *Spd:* 2½ ft; *Fl:* 7–10; *Z:* PF

H. calycinum

H. × moseranum 'Tricolor'

Holly

England's native holly is shiny-leaved and cheerful in berry but slightly tender. N America's is hardy but dull-leaved. Asia provides many other leaf forms of a most valuable, varied shrub.

I. aquifolium 'Silver Queen'

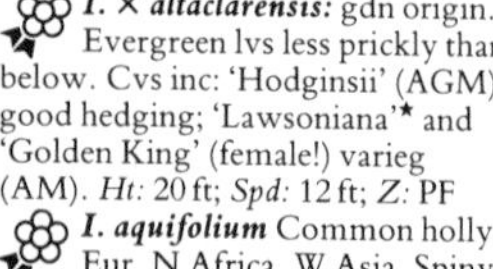

I. × altaclarensis: gdn origin. Evergreen lvs less prickly than below. Cvs inc: 'Hodginsii' (AGM) good hedging; 'Lawsoniana'* and 'Golden King' (female!) varieg (AM). *Ht:* 20 ft; *Spd:* 12 ft; *Z:* PF

I. aquifolium Common holly: Eur, N Africa, W Asia. Spiny sparkling-lvd dense bushy evergreen. Dozens of good cvs, many varieg, inc: 'Argentea Marginata' (AM) broad lvs, silver-edged, frs freely; 'J.C. van Tol' pyramidal, lvs almost spineless, frs freely; 'Madame Briot' lvs edged and mottled gold. *Ht:* 30 ft; *Spd:* 10 ft; *Z:* PF

I. cornuta Horned holly: China, Korea. Dense bushy evergreen; lvs almost rectangular, spines at top and corners. Frs big, red, sparse. *Ht, Spd:* 8 ft; *Z:* PF

I. crenata: Japan, Korea. Slow-growing. Lvs small, narrow, evergreen. Use 'Mariesii' in rock gdn. *Ht:* 8 ft; *Spd:* 3 ft; *Z:* PF

I. pernyi: China. Lvs triangular, spiny, paler green. Berries red in 2s or 3s. *Ht:* 10 ft; *Spd:* 6 ft+; *Z:* PF

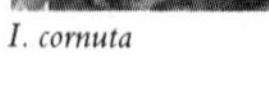

I. cornuta

Indigofera   

Indigofera

I. heterantha (=gerardiana): Him. Fine-textured bushy shrub, late coming into growth. Lvs vetch-like, fls pea-like, bright purplish-pink in 5 in spikes. Frs long, thin pods. *Ht:* to 4 ft; *Spd:* 4 ft+; *Fl:* 6–10; *Z:* PF

Itea   

Itea

I. ilicifolia

I. ilicifolia: China. Evergreen holly-like shrub. Lvs glossy, dark green. Fls catkin-like, greenish-white, lightly frag to 1 ft long in late smr. Prop by cuttings. *Ht:* to 12 ft; *Spd:* 5 ft+; *Fl:* 8; *Z:* PF

Jasminum    

Jasmine

J. humile Italian jasmine: SE Eur, China–Him. Bushy dark-green-lvd; yellow flared tubular fls; glossy black round frs. Cv 'Revolutum' better and more frag. Prop by cuttings. *Ht:* 6 ft; *Spd:* 5 ft; *Fl:* 6–7; *Z:* PF

Juniperus

Juniper

The genus of conifers providing the most shrubs (apart from dwarfs) widely varied in habit, texture and colour, easy to grow and therefore of great interest. Two leaf forms, juvenile (spiky) and adult (scale-like) may appear on the same branch.

J. chinensis Chinese juniper: E Asia. Bushy, often pyramidal, aromatic. Innumerable cvs, eg 'Kaizuka' bright bottle-green, gesticulating branches. Smaller hyb *J.* × *c.* 'Pfitzerana (AGM) sturdy, spreading; golden-lvd 'Pfitzerana Aurea' and glaucous *J.* × *c.* 'Hetzii' all first class. *Ht:* to 40ft; *Spd:* 8 ft+; *Z:* Arct

J. conferta* Shore juniper: Japan. Prostrate, lvs large, prickly, pale green. *Ht:* 8 in; *Spd:* 4 ft; *Z:* Arct

J. communis Common juniper: N Hem. Narrow columnar sorts inc 'Compressa' dwarf, spire-like, 1 ft; 'Hibernica'* uprt, 12 ft; 'Hornibrookii' prostrate, 4 in. *Z:* Arct

J. horizontalis Creeping juniper: N Amer. Pop blue-green, prostrate. 'Bar Harbour' is glaucous. *Ht:* 8 in; *Spd:* 4 ft; *Z:* Arct

J. squamata 'Meyeri': China. Lurid steel-blue forward-pointing lvs, long brs. *Ht:* 15 ft; *Spd:* 7 ft; *Z:* Arct

J. chinensis

J. squamata 'Meyeri'

Kalmia

Kalmia

A close relation of the rhododendron with small but stylish pink/white flowers and good glossy foliage. Among the hardiest of all broadleaved evergreens.

K. angustifolia Sheep's laurel: E N Amer. Narrow lvs; rosy-red saucer-shaped fls up-facing in round heads 2 in wide. 'Rubra' has redder fls. *Ht, Spd:* 3 ft; *Fl:* 6; *Z:* Arct

K. latifolia* Calico bush: E N Amer. More common. Fls like upturned Victorian lampshades in larger groups white to pink, deeper col in bud and along pleats. *Ht, Spd:* 6 ft; *Fl:* 6; *Z:* Arct

K. latifolia

Kerria

Jew's mallow

K. japonica: China, Japan. Uprt, bamboo-like shrub with bright green stems and light green lvs hry on underside. Fls orange-yellow to 1½ in diam. More elegant than commoner form 'Pleniflora' (Bachelor's buttons, AM). Dwarf 'Variegata' (='Picta') creamy-white varieg lvs but is inclined to revert to type. Prop by veg means. *Ht:* 6 ft; *Spd:* 3 ft+; *Fl:* 4–5; *Z:* Arct

K. japonica

Kolkwitzia  

Kolkwitzia

K. amabilis

K. amabilis* Beauty bush: China. Stems stiff but soon arch over to form dense bush. Lvs small, pointed, matt green. Fls foxglove-like, 2½ in, pale pink with yellow throat and freely produced. Alas no scent. 'Pink Cloud' (AGM) is clear pink. Prop by cuttings, suckers. *Ht:* 6 ft+; *Spd:* 8 ft+; *Fl:* 5–6; *Z:* Arct

Laurus   

Bay laurel, Sweet bay, Royal bay

L. nobilis* Bay: Med. Shiny-lvd wide pyramidal bush, can be trained to mop-head or conical shape. Lvs narrow oval, used for flavouring. Fls inconspic, frs round, black. *Ht:* 18 ft; *Spd:* 5 ft+; *Fl:* 4; *Z:* PF

Lavandula   

Lavender

L. angustifolius 'Munstead'

L. angustifolius (=officinalis)*: Med. Grown as a bush or clipped as a hedge. Narrow 2 in grey flat lvs, fls in 2½ in spikes on long stems. Cvs inc 'Alba' white 'Hidcote' (AM) purple; 'Munstead' (AM) lavender-blue; 'Twickel Purple' deep blue/purple, spreading; 'Vera' wider lvs, fls lavender-blue. *Ht, Spd:* 3 ft; *Fl:* 6–7; *Z:* Arct

Lavatera   

Mallow

L. olbia Tree mallow: Med. Usually planted in form 'Rosea'* which has rosy-pink mallow fls 4 in wide over a long period and 3–5 lobed softly hry lvs. Sp is pink/purplish. *Ht:* 6 ft; *Spd:* 5 ft; *Fl:* 6–10; *Z:* F

Leptospermum   

Leptospermum

L. scoparium

L. scoparium Manuka: Aust, NZ. Liberal clothing of tiny oval pointed lvs. Fls ¾ in wide, 5 white ptls, followed by woody, persistent seed capsules. Cvs inc 'Nichollsii' (AM) crimson ptls, darker centre, lvs bronze-purple; 'Red Damask' (AM) deep double red. Prop by seed (sp), cuttings. *Ht:* 15 ft; *Spd:* 10 ft; *Fl:* 5–6; *Z:* SF

Lespedeza (=Desmodium)   

Lespedeza

L. thunbergii: China, Japan. Woody plant that dies down annually. Long, lax stems, pale green, silky lvs. Fls pea-like, rosy purple in loose poker-like heads. Prop by div. *Ht:* to 8 ft; *Spd:* 5 ft; *Fl:* 9–10; *Z:* Arct

Leucothoe

Leucothoe

L. (=Andromeda) fontanesiana: SE USA. Suckering; ideal ground cover. Fls pitcher-shaped, white in dense spikes on stem undersides. 'Rainbow' has lvs splashed cream. *Ht:* 5 ft; *Spd:* 4 ft; *Fl:* 5; *Z:* Arct

Leycesteria

Leycesteria

L. formosa: Him. Bright eau de nil green hollow stems useful in wtr; lvs heart-shaped, fls pale pink, becoming white, alternating with pale crimson bracts. Frs round, reddish-purple. Seeds itself. *L. crocothyrsos* (AM) rarer and less hardy has golden-yellow fls, green bracts. *Ht, Spd:* 6 ft; *Fl:* 6–9; *Z:* PF

L. formosa

Ligustrum

Privet

L. japonicum Japanese privet: E Asia. Bushy evergreen, lvs deep green. Fls white, small in 6 in pyramidal heads with heavy scent. *Ht, Spd:* 10 ft; *Fl:* 7–9; *Z:* PF

L. lucidum*: China. May make a small tree. Lvs glossy to 4 in, fl heads to 8 in. Frs like small grapes. Varieg cvs inc 'Excelsum Superbum'* and 'Tricolor'. *Ht:* 18 ft; *Spd:* 10 ft; *Fl:* 8–9; *Z:* PF

L. ovalifolium Oval leaf privet: Japan. Ubiquitous hedging, nasty smell. 'Aureum' gold varieg. *Ht, Spd:* 10 ft; *Fl:* 7; *Z:* Arct

L. ovalifolium 'Aureum'

Lonicera

Honeysuckle

L. nitida: China. Fast-growing densely bushy; lvs tiny, oval, evergreen, often used for hedging; inconspic, tubular ¼ in frag fls. Berries (if any) purple. Cv 'Baggesen's Gold'* yellow-lvd. *Ht:* 6 ft; *Spd:* 5 ft+; *Fl:* 5; *Z:* PF

L. pileata: China. For full or part shade. Semi-evergreen, densely twiggy, excellent ground cover. Fls tiny, frag, yellowish-white, frs round, violet, translucent. *Ht:* 3 ft; *Spd:* 4 ft; *Fl:* 5; *Z:* Arct

L. × purpusii*: gdn origin. Twiggy, round bush. Lvs broadly oval; fls on bare wood in wtr creamy-white, honeysuckle-like to ¾ in sweetly and intensely scented. *Ht, Spd:* 6 ft; *Fl:* 12–2; *Z:* Arct

L. tatarica Tartarian honeysuckle: USSR. Narrower lvs and pink fls, red berries. Cvs 'Hack's Red' and 'Arnold Red' have red fls. *Ht, Spd:* 12 ft; *Fl:* 5–6; *Z:* Arct

L. nitida 'Baggessen's Gold'

L. tatarica

Lupinus

Lupin

L. arboreus

L. arboreus Tree lupin: Cal. Bushy evergreen with typically lupin-like lvs and creamy-white or yellow fls. Short-lived but v attractive and useful esp by the sea. Seeds freely. Hybs with pink or mauve fls sometimes seen by roadsides and are worth taking cuttings from. *Ht:* 6 ft+; *Spd:* 5 ft; *Fl:* 6–7; *Z:* F

Magnolia

Magnolia

A genus including the finest of all flowering trees. Those chosen here are the most popular and adaptable smaller ones, of superlative beauty in their tulip-textured flowers and great quality in leaf and even in bud, twig and branch.

M. stellata

***M. × soulangiana*★:** gdn origin. Best basic sp. Fls on bare brs, 6 in ptls white, purple backs, reflexed. Best (AGM) cvs: 'Alba Superba'; 'Brozzonii' and 'Lennei' purple and white. *Ht, Spd:* 15 ft; *Fl:* 4–5; *Z:* Arct

***M. stellata*★:** Japan. Fls before lvs; many (to 18) strap-shaped ptls turn pink with age. Best (AM) cvs 'Rosea' pink buds, paler in ptl; 'Rubra' deeper col. *Ht:* 10 ft; *Spd:* 15 ft; *Fl:* 3–4; *Z:* Arct

Mahonia

Mahonia

Like a larger-leaved evergreen *Berberis* without the vicious prickles. All yellow-flowered, starting in the depths of winter.

M. aquifolium

M. japonica

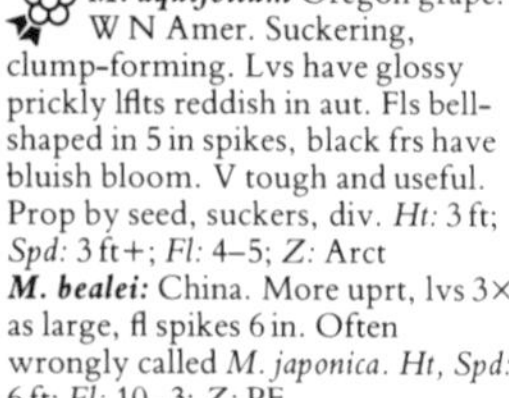

M. aquifolium Oregon grape: W N Amer. Suckering, clump-forming. Lvs have glossy prickly lflts reddish in aut. Fls bell-shaped in 5 in spikes, black frs have bluish bloom. V tough and useful. Prop by seed, suckers, div. *Ht:* 3 ft; *Spd:* 3 ft+; *Fl:* 4–5; *Z:* Arct

M. bealei: China. More uprt, lvs 3× as large, fl spikes 6 in. Often wrongly called *M. japonica*. *Ht, Spd:* 6 ft; *Fl:* 10–3; *Z:* PF

***M. japonica*★:** origin unknown. Sprawling, lvs darker green. Fls larger, frag. *Ht:* 6 ft; *Spd:* 8 ft+; *Fl:* 11–3; *Z:* PF

***M. × media 'Charity'*★:** gdn origin. Superb uprt hyb; plumes of fl to 1 ft, frs violet, tinted grey. Prop by cuttings *Ht:* 10 ft; *Spd:* 8 ft+; *Fl:* 11–3; *Z:* PF

M. lomariifolia: China, Burma. The finest lvs; but may be so leggy it looks like a palm. *Ht:* to 12 ft; *Spd:* 5 ft; *Fl:* 11–1; *Z:* SF

Melianthus

M. major*: S Africa, India. Huge pale sea-green v decorative lvs divided into toothed lflts. Fls woolly plumes of soft crimson-red in July–Sept. Only hardy in a sheltered corner of a warm gdn. Prop by div, cuttings. *Ht, Spd:* 4 ft; *Z:* NF

M. major

Metrosideros

Metrosideros

M. lucida: NZ. Bottle-brush shrub/small tree. Lvs small, elliptic, pointed, burnished hue when young. Fls terminal, fluffy bright crimson stamens. Tolerates a little lime. *Ht, Spd:* 10 ft; *Fl:* 8; *Z:* NF

Michelia

Michelia

M. doltsopa (=excelsa): Him, China. Rounded bush related to magnolia. Lvs leathery, shimmering, paler below. Fls waxy white, heavily frag, may be tinged yellow in aut. *Ht:* 30 ft; *Spd:* 25 ft; *Fl:* 4; *Z:* F

Myrtus

Myrtle

M. communis* Common myrtle: S Eur–W Asia. Densely bushy; pointed lvs aromatic, esp when crushed. Rose-like white fls 1 in wide have delightful central boss of stamens. Frs purple-black berries. *M.c. tarentina* (Tarentum myrtle) less hardy, smaller lvs, yellowish-white berries. Prop by cuttings. *Ht, Spd:* 5 ft; *Fl:* 7–8; *Z:* SF/F

M. communis

Nandina

Chinese sacred bamboo

N. domestica*: China. Little uprt plant. Long lvs divided into thin lflts reddish when young, purple-tinted in aut. Fls creamy-white in pyramidal terminal plumes to 15 in wide followed, in warm gdns, by bright red berries. Universal in Japanese gdns. 'Nana Purpurea' dwarf, purplish lvs. *Ht:* 6 ft; *Spd:* 4 ft+; *Fl:* 6–7; *Z:* PF

N. domestica

Neillia

Neillia

N. thibetica (=longiracemosa): China. Tall bushy; dense uprt stems arch towards tips. Lvs small, oval, toothed. Fls rose-pink, tubular in terminal groups, long spls. *Ht:* to 6 ft; *Spd:* 4 ft; *Fl:* 5–6; *Z:* PF/Arct

Nerium

Nerium

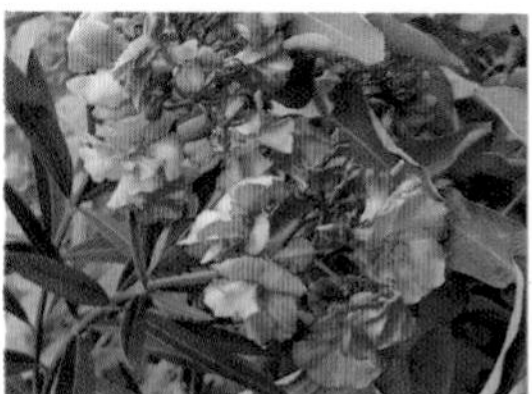

N. oleander

N. oleander Common oleander, Rose-bay: Med, Asia. Leathery-lvd shrub of Med streets and gdns. Fls open periwinkle-like to 1½ in diam, several in a head, are usually pink or white although yellow and double-flowered sorts are obtainable. Will take some lime. Good in tubs with protection in wtr. Prop by cuttings. *Ht:* 12 ft; *Spd:* 15 ft+; *Fl:* 6–10; *Z:* F

Olearia

Daisy bush

An entirely Australasian genus of evergreen shrubs, mainly easy and fast-growing in full sun but none hardy against extreme frost. Daisy-like flowers are mainly white or off-white.

O. × haastii

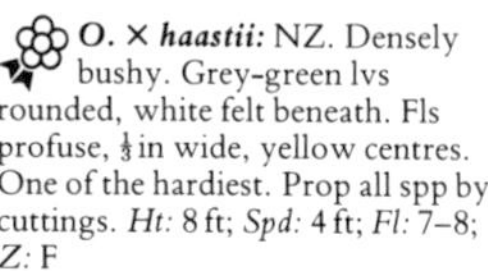

O. × haastii: NZ. Densely bushy. Grey-green lvs rounded, white felt beneath. Fls profuse, ⅓ in wide, yellow centres. One of the hardiest. Prop all spp by cuttings. *Ht:* 8 ft; *Spd:* 4 ft; *Fl:* 7–8; *Z:* F

O. macrodonta: NZ. Lvs larger, holly-like, leaden green, silver-white beneath. Fls tiny in round heads to 6 in diam. Extreme frost can kill. *Ht:* 10 ft; *Spd:* to 20 ft; *Fl:* 7; *Z:* F

O. phlogopappa: Aust. Branching, uprt, lvs and young stems felted. Fls in loose clusters sometimes blue or pink. *Ht:* 6 ft; *Spd:* 4 ft; *Fl:* 5; *Z:* SF

O. × scilloniensis: gdn origin. Grey-green lvs and white fls in profusion in May. *Ht:* to 8 ft; *Spd:* to 5 ft; *Z:* SF

O. stellulata: Aust. Larger lvs than *O. phlogopappa*, yellowish felt. 'Splendens' has larger fls. Selected forms blue or pink. *Ht:* 6 ft; *Spd:* 5 ft; *Fl:* 5; *Z:* SF

O. macrodonta

Osmanthus

Osmanthus

Relations of the olive: in appearance somewhere between olive and holly. Fragrant fillers rather than the focus of a garden.

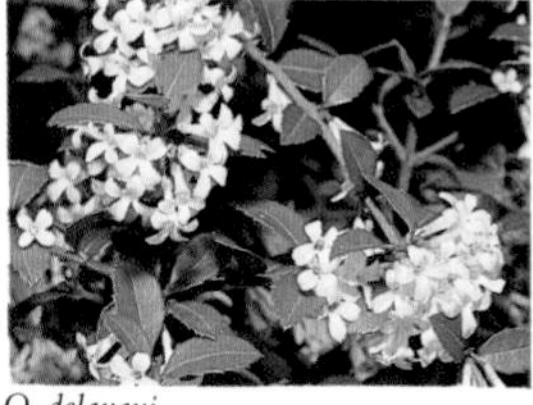

O. delavayi

O. (=Osmarea) × burkwoodii*: gdn origin. Dense, slow-growing with small, toothed oval lvs. White tubular ½ in fls richly frag. Prop by cuttings. *Ht:* to 10 ft; *Spd:* 6 ft; *Fl:* 4–5; *Z:* PF

O. (=Siphonosmanthus) delavayi*: China. Lvs smaller, more toothed and pointed. Fls sim to above earlier, more frag. *Ht, Spd:* 8 ft+; *Fl:* 4; *Z:* PF

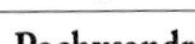

Pachysandra

P. terminalis: Japan. Creeping. Lvs diamond-shaped, pale green, toothed near tip. Fls 2 in terminal spikes, pale green or whitish, purple tinge. 'Variegata' white varieg lvs. *Ht:* 1 ft; *Spd:* 20 ft; *Fl:* 2–3; *Z:* Arct

Paeonia

Paeony

"Tree" paeonies are not greatly different from herbaceous ones in action, merely keeping woody stems, but their young growth can be nipped by spring frosts. Well worth growing.

P. delavayi: China. Fls 2 in wide, single, crimson-red, gold stamens. Frs big, dark seeds. *Ht:* 4 ft; *Spd:* 3 ft; *Fl:* 5; *Z:* PF

P. lutea ludlowii*: Tibet. Larger all over, striking lvs. Fls single, yellow, 2½ in diam. *Ht, Spd:* 6 ft; *Fl:* 5–6; *Z:* PF

P. suffruticosa* Mountain paeony: China, Tibet. Bushy sp of incomparable beauty. Fls to 1 ft wide, ptls white or palest pink, maroon blotch at base. Cvs inc fuller and double sorts from scarlet to wine coloured. Plant in cool spot to delay flowering until after frost. *Ht, Spd:* 6 ft; *Fl:* 5–6; *Z:* PF/Arct

P. suffruticosa cultivar

Parahebe

Parahebe

P. (=Veronica) catarractae: NZ. Shrublet; lvs coarsely toothed on wiry trailing stems. Fls speedwell-like in slim 8 in spires may have crimson/purple lines. Also pink/purple/blue forms. *Ht, Spd:* 1 ft; *Fl:* 8–9; *Z:* PF

Parrotia

Parrotia

P. (=Hamamelis) persica* Iron tree: Iran, Caucasus. Large bush with long branches often at 45°. Lvs green, cobnut-like, turning fiery red, orange, crimson and yellow in aut. Fls little tufts of red stamens on the bare branches in early spr. *Ht:* 20 ft; *Spd:* to 40 ft; *Fl:* 3; *Z:* Arct

P. persica

Pernettya

Pernettya

P. mucronata: S Amer. Suckering shrub, little leathery lvs. Fls white, bell-like, ¼ in long, frs white, pink or purple berries. Plant in gps with ♂ plant to ensure fruiting. Cvs inc 'Davis's Hybrids' (AGM), frs large; 'Bell's Seedling' (AGM), frs dark red; 'Pink Pearl' frs soft pink. *Ht:* 3 ft; *Spd:* 3 ft+; *Fl:* 5–6; *Z:* PF

P. mucronata

Philadelphus

Mock orange, "Syringa"

Easy, profligate with white flowers famous for their far-carrying scent. Otherwise a dull bush. Prune hard after flowering.

P. 'Belle Etoile'

P. 'Belle Etoile'*: gdn origin. White fls 2 in wide, soft crimson stain at ptl base. 'Beauclerk' (AM) pure white. Prop by cuttings. *Ht:* 6 ft; *Spd:* 8 ft; *Fl:* 6–7; *Z:* PF

P. coronarius (=pallidus): Eur, Asia Minor. Creamy-white fls. 'Aureus'* is one of best golden-lvd shrubs but less free in fl. *Ht, Spd:* 10 ft; *Fl:* 6–7; *Z:* Arct

P. microphyllus: W N Amer. Dwarf twiggy bush. Free-flowering, strongly frag. 'Manteau d'Hermine' cream, double. *Ht:* 3 ft; *Spd:* 4 ft; *Fl:* 6–7; *Z:* PF

Phillyrea

Phillyrea

P. latifolia*: SE Eur, Asia Minor. Lvs glittering, dark green ovals. Fls small, greenish-white, frag may be followed by black berries. *P. (=Osmanthus) decora* larger lvd. *Ht:* to 15 ft; *Spd:* 10 ft; *Fl:* 4–5; *Z:* PF

Phlomis

Phlomis

P. *fruticosa*

P. fruticosa: Med. Low, soft hry shrub of character for hot, dry places. Fls soft yellow, nettle-like in whorls to 1¼ in on spikes. *P. chrysophylla* sim but yellow-green lvs. Prop by seed, cuttings. *Ht:* 3 ft; *Spd:* 4 ft; *Fl:* 6–9; *Z:* F

Photinia

Photinia

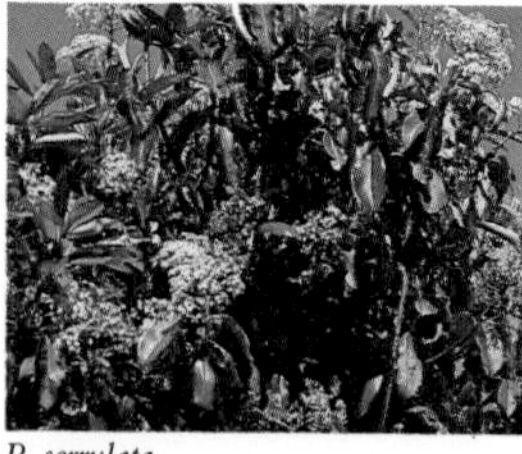

P. *serrulata*

P. × fraseri*: gdn origin. Young shoots coppery-red, lvs sim turning rich green. Replaces *Pieris* on chalk. Try 'Birmingham'; 'Red Robin'; 'Robusta' (AM, hardy). *Ht:* 6 ft; *Spd:* 8 ft; *Fl:* 4–5; *Z:* F

P. serrulata Chinese hawthorn: China. Often leggy. Worthy for early flush of red new lvs. Fls white, frs haw-like if present. *Ht:* 18 ft; *Spd:* 12 ft; *Fl:* 4–5; *Z:* F

Phygelius

Cape figwort

P. capensis: S Africa. Rapidly forms thicket in sheltered gdns. Fls like scarlet hunting horns to 1½ in, yellowish throats, singly or in 2s or 3s. 'Coccineus' deeper red. *Ht:* 10 ft; *Spd:* 18 ft; *Fl:* 7–10; *Z:* PF

Pieris

Of many virtues but demand acid soil and shelter from late frosts for their beautiful new growth. *P. formosa* hardier but less striking than *P. japonica*. Plant only selected forms.

P. formosa: Burma, China, Him. Bushy; lvs narrow. Young stems pale green, young fol bronze; fls closed white bells. Young lvs of *P.f. forrestii*★ (AM) brilliant red; of 'Wakehurst' bright red turning pale pink then green. *Ht, Spd:* 8 ft; *Fl:* 4–5; *Z:* PF

P. japonica: Japan. Lvs v shiny, tinted red-bronze when young. Cvs inc excellent 'Variegata' (AGM). *P.* × 'Forest Flame' an easier hyb of the 2 spp but less vivid than 'Wakehurst'. *Ht:* to 10 ft; *Spd:* 8 ft; *Fl:* 3–4; *Z:* Arct

P. formosa

Pittosporum

Pittosporum

P. eugenioides Tarata: NZ. Dark stems; wavy-edged lvs pale beneath. Fls yellowish bell-shaped, sweet frag. 'Variegatum' excellent. *Ht:* 20 ft; *Spd:* 8 ft; *Fl:* 4–5; *Z:* NF

P. tenuifolium: NZ. Paler lvs on black stems. Fls chocolate-purple, frs contain glistening black seeds. *Ht:* to 30 ft; *Spd:* 8 ft+; *Fl:* 4–5; *Z:* PF

P. tenuifolium

Polygala

Milkwort

P. chamaebuxus Bastard box. Dwarf creeping evergreen. Lvs box-like, fls white and yellow, pea-like; frs flat. *P.c. grandiflora* (='Purpurea', AM) magenta/yellow fls. *Ht, Spd:* 1 ft; *Fl:* 4–6; *Z:* PF

Potentilla

Cinquefoil

Among the longest-flowering shrubs, rarely covered in flowers but cheerful in summer and pleasantly twiggy in winter.

P. arbuscula: Him, China. Fls single, bright yellow, 1 in diam. *Ht, Spd:* 4 ft; *Fl:* 6–10; *Z:* Arct

P. 'Manchu': gdn origin. Dwarf shrub, white fls. *Ht:* 8 in; *Spd:* 30 in; *Fl:* 6–9; *Z:* Arct

P. fruticosa Shrubby cinqefoil: N Hem. Yellow fls. Cvs inc 'Abbotswood' white, 'Elizabeth' rich yellow; 'Longacre'★ pale yellow; 'Red Ace' brick red. *Ht:* 3 ft; *Spd:* 4 ft; *Fl:* 6–9; *Z:* Arct

P. × 'Vilmoriniana'★: gdn origin. Uprt hyb; lvs silvery-green, fls pale primrose yellow. *Ht:* 4 ft; *Spd:* 30 in; *Fl:* 6–10; *Z:* Arct

P. fruticosa

Prunus

The genus that includes cherries, plums, peaches and almonds also furnishes two important evergreen "laurels".

P. laurocerasus

P. mume

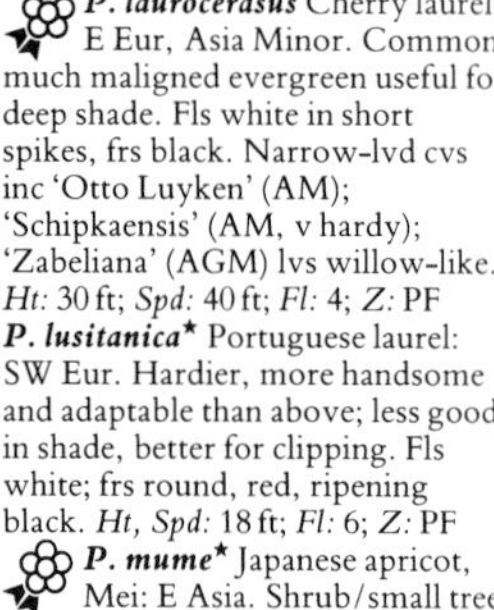

P. laurocerasus Cherry laurel: E Eur, Asia Minor. Common, much maligned evergreen useful for deep shade. Fls white in short spikes, frs black. Narrow-lvd cvs inc 'Otto Luyken' (AM); 'Schipkaensis' (AM, v hardy); 'Zabeliana' (AGM) lvs willow-like. *Ht:* 30 ft; *Spd:* 40 ft; *Fl:* 4; *Z:* PF

P. lusitanica* Portuguese laurel: SW Eur. Hardier, more handsome and adaptable than above; less good in shade, better for clipping. Fls white; frs round, red, ripening black. *Ht, Spd:* 18 ft; *Fl:* 6; *Z:* PF

P. mume* Japanese apricot, Mei: E Asia. Shrub/small tree. Young stems green, fls frag, single, pink. 'Beni-shi-dori' (AM) soft crimson double. *Ht:* to 18 ft; *Spd:* 6 ft+; *Fl:* 3; *Z:* PF

Punica

Pomegranate

P. granatum

P. granatum: Afghanistan, Iran. Tall; needs protection in cool zones. Dwarf 'Nana' hardier and more useful; easy in a well-drained spot. Lvs narrow, light green. Fls bright scarlet, tubular to 2 in, ruff at mouth. Edible fr ripens only in warmth. *Ht:* 12 ft; *Spd:* 8 ft; *Fl:* 6–9; *Z:* PF/F

Pyracantha

Pyracantha

P. atalantioides

P. atalantioides: China. Tall, vig, narrow lvs. Fls white in flat clusters 2 in wide, long-lasting red berries delicacies to birds. 'Aurea' (AM) yellow frs. *Ht:* 15 ft; *Spd:* 8 ft+; *Fl:* 5–6; *Z:* PF

P. coccinea Firethorn: S Eur, Asia Minor. Less vig, wider lvs. Frs red-orange. 'Lalandei' (AGM) more pop with larger lvs. *Ht, Spd:* 15 ft; *Fl:* 6; *Z:* PF

P. 'Watereri': gdn origin. More compact; lvs long thin; red frs. *Ht, Spd:* 10 ft; *Fl:* 5–6; *Z:* PF

Raphiolepis

Raphiolepis

R. × delacourii: gdn origin. Neat round bush, young growth pale green, hry, lvs dark green. Fls pale pink, 5 ptls. Shelter from severe frost. *R. indica* less hardy, paler fls. *Ht, Spd:* 5 ft; *Fl:* 1–10; *Z:* F

Buckthorn

R. alaternus: Med. Vig, densely glossy evergreen; lvs oval to 2 in. Fls tiny, yellowish green, frs red berries. 'Argenteovariegata'* greyish-green-lvd, irregular white edge. *Ht:* 8 ft; *Spd:* 6 ft; *Fl:* 4; *Z:* PF

Rhododendron

Rhododendron, Azalea

A thousand species right round the Northern Hemisphere make this the single most important shrubby genus. In gardening (but not botany) it divides into azaleas, thin branched, mainly deciduous shrubs, and rhododendrons which are generally evergreen with flowers often in a single raceme or spike. All prefer and most need acid soil. Being shallow-rooted they move well.

Decid Azaleas: gdn origin: Sev series of hybs in fl from early May to late June. Many are frag. Often fine aut col. *Z:* Arct
Ghent*: Tall, late-flowering. Try 'Daviesii' white, creamy-yellow throat, fls long, tubular, flared; 'Narcissiflorum' (AGM) light yellow, deeper throat, frag.
Mollis*: Usually to 6 ft, less twiggy, earlier, bigger fls in hotter cols (LF) 'Spek's Orange' (AGM) dark orange in bud opening to bright orange with greenish flare.
Knap Hill: Young growth may be bronze. 'Exbury' strain best. Plants reach 5–8 ft, eg 'Hotspur' (AM) glowing flame red, yellow flare in throat; 'Strawberry Ice' (AGM) flesh pink, deeper pink markings and yellow flare. Dense round truss of flowers.

Evergreen Azaleas: gdn origin. Hybs of Japanese spp. Cooler cols; less hardy. *Ht:* to 4 ft; *Spd:* to 6 ft; *Fl:* 4–5; *Z:* PF
Glenn Dale: USA. Medium size. Best is 'Elizabeth' old rose-pink.
Kurume: Japan. Densely bushy with layers of small lvs. Can reach 5 ft. Named sorts inc 'Blaauw's Pink' salmon pink fls one inside another; 'Hinamoyo' (=Hinomayo, AM) fierce magenta, needs careful placing.
Vuyk hybs: Holland. Large funnel-shaped fls on small bushes. Good clean cols, fl May–early June. Try 'Blue Danube' piercing violet-blue; 'Palestrina' fls white with pale green stripe; 'Vuyk's Scarlet' (AGM) brilliant light crimson.

R. augustinii*: China. One of the bluest sp (none is true blue) with fls 3–5 in a cluster, pale lavender to rich violet-blue. 'Electra' (AM) violet-blue, blotch of yellowish-green in throat. *Ht:* 8 ft; *Spd:* 6 ft; *Fl:* 4–5; *Z:* PF

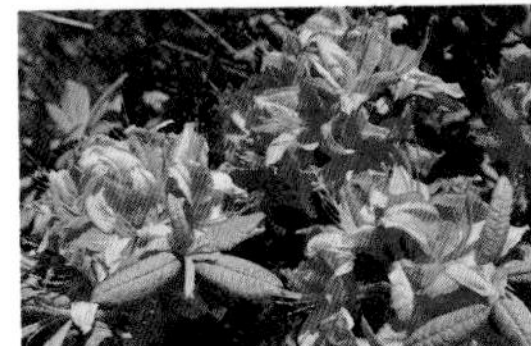

Azalea Knap Hill 'Hotspur Orange'

Azalea Knap Hill 'Persil'

Azalea Knap Hill 'Fireglow'

Azalea Kurume 'Blue Danube'

Rhododendron

R. × 'Praecox'

R. racemosum

R. williamsianum

R. hybrid 'Pink Pearl'

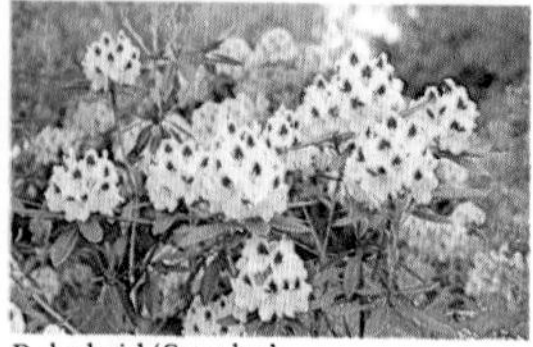

R. hybrid 'Sappho'

R. dauricum: Asia. Decid or semi-evergreen. Fls intense rosy purple. 'Midwinter' (AM) rec. *Ht:* 5 ft; *Spd:* 3 ft; *Fl:* 1–2; *Z:* PF

R. luteum (=Azalea pontica)* Common European azalea: Turkey. Vig, yellow flowered, wonderfully frag; often rich aut col. *Ht, Spd:* to 12 ft; *Fl:* 5; *Z:* PF

R. × 'Praecox': gdn origin. Early and worth planting in sheltered spot. Semi-evergreen, twiggy; fls wide open, funnel-shaped, light purple with pink tinge. *Ht:* 4 ft; *Spd:* 3 ft; *Fl:* 2–3; *Z:* PF

R. ponticum: SW Eur, Asia Minor. Much maligned vig sp. Lvs long, pointed, dark glossy green; fls mauve to rosy purple. Excellent as informal screen or for large clumps. There is a rare white varieg form. *Ht, Spd:* 15 ft; *Fl:* 5–6; *Z:* PF

R. racemosum: China. Slender shrub, stems reddish; fls small, clustered, pale or deep pink. *Ht:* 4 ft; *Spd:* 3 ft; *Fl:* 3–4; *Z:* Arct

R. (=Azalea) schlippenbachii*: Korea, China, USSR. Outstanding decid; lvs light green, oblong, pointed usually in whorls of 5, often purplish when young. Fls wide open, funnel-shaped, pale rosy pink soft brown spots on top 3 ptls, long stamens. Rich yellow/orange and crimson aut col. Protect from spr frost. *Ht:* to 10 ft; *Spd:* 6 ft+; *Fl:* 4–5; *Z:* Arct

R. williamsianum*: China. Hummock-forming evergreen; lvs nearly round, notched at base, glaucous beneath. Young growth bronze. Fls bell-like, 2½ in wide, rose-pink. *Ht, Spd:* 5 ft; *Fl:* 4; *Z:* PF

R. yakushimanum*: Japan. Very beautiful low dome-shaped bush. Lvs part-rolled, soft brown felt beneath. Buds striking deep pink opening to v pale pink. *Ht:* 3 ft; *Spd:* 4 ft; *Fl:* 5; *Z:* Arct

R. hybs: gdn origin. "Hardy hybs" combine best features of sev spp. Better and more easily available award-winning cvs inc: 'Britannia' rich crimson; 'Cunningham's White' v tough, dense; 'Cynthia' rich rose-pink; 'Elizabeth' dwarf, creeping, glowing dark red; 'Fastuosum Flore Pleno'* full-petalled to double, blue-mauve; 'Gomer Waterer'* white, warm mauve flush, yellowish eye; 'Lady Chamberlain' pendulous narrowly tubular orange-red pink-tinged fls; 'King George' v vig, big lvs, fls pale pink, turning white; 'Pink Pearl' pale pink; 'Sappho'* white, purple-black blotch in each fl. *Fl:* 5–6; *Z:* Arct

Rhus

Sumach

R. typhina Stag's horn sumach: E N Amer. Gaunt bush/small tree. Stout pithy stems, many slim lflts. Distinctive woolly crimson fr. Glorious aut col. 'Dissecta' (AM) smaller. *Ht, Spd:* 12 ft; *Fl:* 4–5; *Z:* Arct

Ribes

Currant

Fruit-bush relations grown for their dangling single or tassel-grouped flowers including some of the earliest spring blooms.

R. odoratum (=aureum) Buffalo, Clove or Golden currant: W N Amer. Open, uprt bush, shiny pale green deep-lobed small lvs. Fls frag, bright yellow in 2 in tassels; frs black. *Ht, Spd:* 6 ft; *Fl:* 4; *Z:* Arct

R. sanguineum Flowering currant: W N Amer. Erect, bushy, typical currant lvs and smell. Fls in 4 in tassels white, pink or crimson according to cv. Frs black. Rec (both AM) 'King Edward VII' less tall, fls rich crimson; 'Pulborough Scarlet' soft light red. *Ht, Spd:* 6 ft; *Fl:* 4; *Z:* Arct

R. speciosum*: Cal. Like a gooseberry with spiny stems. Fls bright red, pendulous, fuchsia-like to 1½ in. Good against a wall. *Ht, Spd:* 6 ft; *Fl:* 4–5; *Z:* PF

R. sanguineum

R. speciosum

Robinia

Rose or False acacia

R. hispida: SE USA. Awkward but beautiful suckering sprawler. Young stems bristly; pale, oval lflts. Fls rose-pink, pea-like, frs bristly pods to 2 in. Prop by seed. *Ht, Spd:* to 8 ft; *Fl:* 5–6; *Z:* Arct

Rubus

Rubus

R. cockburnianus*: China. Like an elegant blackberry, stems ghostly white. V effective in wtr. Fls inconspic, frs black. *Ht:* 8 ft; *Spd:* to 30 ft; *Z:* PF

R. tricolor: China. Vig, trailing semi-evergreen, stems bristly. Fls white, rose-like, frs red. *Ht:* 1 ft; *Spd:* 5 ft; *Fl:* 7; *Z:* Arct

R. 'Tridel': gdn origin. Stems soft grey-brown, flaking. Fls white, 2 in wide, golden stamens. Look for 'Benenden'. *Ht, Spd:* 8 ft; *Fl:* 5; *Z:* PF

R. 'Tridel'

Ruscus

Ruscus

R. aculeatus Butcher's broom: Eur–Iran. Sturdy, vig, savagely prickly. Lf-like stems have tiny greenish-white fls in centre. Frs glossy red berries if ♂ and ♀ plants are grown together. *Ht:* 3 ft; *Spd:* 18 in+; *Fl:* 3–4; *Z:* PF

Salix

Willow

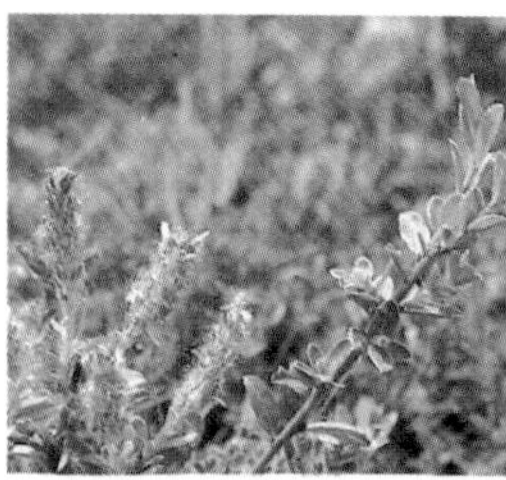

S. repens

S. hastata 'Wehrhahnii'*: gdn origin. Best small bushy pussy willow. V many 2 in soft catkins yellowing with pollen. *Ht, Spd:* 4 ft; *Fl:* 5; *Z:* Arct

S. eleagnos Hoary willow: Eur. Vig; lvs show white undersides in wind. *Ht, Spd:* 8 ft; *Z:* Arct

S. repens Creeping willow: Eur. V pretty but not dense ground cover. Lvs oval or spoon-shaped, young catkins silvery. *Ht:* 1 ft; *Spd:* 3 ft+; *Fl:* 4–5; *Z:* Arct

Salvia

Sage

S. microphylla

S. microphylla (=grahamii) Graham's sage: Mexico. Thin-stemmed small-lvd sub-shrub; needs warmth. Lvs oval, pointed, irregularly toothed in pairs. Fls slim, salvia-like to 2 in, bright red becoming bluish-purple with age. Young growth has purplish tinge. *Ht, Spd:* 4 ft; *Fl:* 6–10; *Z:* SF

Sambucus

Elder

S. nigra

S. nigra 'Aurea' Golden elder: Eur (sp). Bright yellow-lvd cv. White frag fls in flat heads; glistening black berries. Also varieg, lacy-lvd and purple-lvd cvs. *Ht, Spd:* 8 ft; *Fl:* 6; *Z:* Arct

S. racemosa 'Plumosa Aurea'* Red-berried elder: Eur (sp). Lvs deeply toothed. Fls white, frs bright red. Prune hard. *Ht:* 8 ft; *Spd:* 5 ft; *Fl:* 4–5; *Z:* Arct

Santolina

Lavender-cotton

Mediterranean dwarf daisy-bushes with aromatic very fine-textured evergreen foliage forming dense low hummocks. For sharp-drained soil.

S. chamaecyparissus

S. chamaecyparissus: S Eur. Grey-white dense fol composed of tiny lflts. Yellow fls in domed heads to ¾ in wide. *S.c. corsica** (='Nana', AGM) 2 ft tall is dense with shorter lvs and good for edging or dwarf hedges. *Ht, Spd:* 30 in; *Fl:* 7–8; *Z:* PF

S. virens (=viridis) Holy flax: S Eur. Shrublet to 2 ft forming low hummock. Lvs deep green. Fls pale yellow. Prop both spp by cuttings. *Spd:* 2 ft; *Fl:* 7; *Z:* PF

Sarcococca

S. humilis*: China. Dwarf slow-growing suckering shrub. Lvs narrowly oval, pointed, glossy. Tiny white fls in mid-wtr, in little bunches in lf axils are sweetly frag and followed by shiny black berries. Prop by div, cuttings. *Ht, Spd:* 18 in; *Fl:* 1–3; *Z:* Arct

S. humilis

Sassafras

S. albidum (=officinale): N Amer. Fascinating aromatic tree (but can be used as a large shrub) with variable lvs, sometimes with 1 lobe, sometimes more. Fls pale greenish-yellow usually borne before lvs are fully developed. Good aut col. Prop by seed. *Ht:* 30 ft; *Spd:* 10 ft; *Fl:* 5; *Z:* Arct

S. albidum

Senecio

S. monroi: NZ. Rounded evergreen. Lvs pewter-grey, oval, 1½ in long, white felt beneath; fls daisy-like in flat round heads to 6 in wide. The Dunedin hybs of *S. laxifolius (=greyi)*, notably 'Sunshine' are larger in all their parts reaching 4 ft to 8 ft and flower from July–Aug. Prop all sorts by cuttings. *Ht:* 30 in; *Spd:* 4 ft; *Fl:* 7; *Z:* F

Skimmia

Glossy evergreens grown chiefly for the pleasure of their sealing-wax-red berries nestling among rich green leaves: a non-berrying male plant is usually needed to achieve this.

S. japonica*: Japan. Dense round shrub, lvs narrowly oval, pointed, leathery, often yellowish-green. Frag fls white in pyramidal heads to 3 in. Berries waxy red, persistent. Cv 'Rubella'* (=*reevesiana* 'Rubella', AM) selected male clone with dull reddish stks and more compact form. Prop by cuttings. *Ht:* to 5 ft; *Spd:* 5 ft+; *Fl:* 4–5; *Z:* PF

S. reevesiana: China. Slow-growing and smaller, both sexes on same plant; has white fls and red frs. Will not tolerate chalk. *Ht:* 2 ft; *Spd:* 30 in; *Fl:* 5; *Z:* PF

S. japonica

Sorbaria

S. aitchisonii: C Asia. Quick-growing; young stems reddish. Lvs have linear and oval lflts. Fls white plumes to 18 in; seed heads red-brown. *S. arborea* (AM) less delicate. *Ht, Spd:* 9 ft; *Fl:* 7–8; *Z:* PF

Sparmannia     

Sparmannia

S. africana* African hemp: Africa. Fast-growing, tender; good indoors in tubs. Lvs huge maple-like, soft green. Fls white, red and yellow stamens Dec–April indoors. *Ht:* 8 ft; *Spd:* 6 ft; *Fl:* 5–6; *Z:* SF

Spartium   

Spanish broom

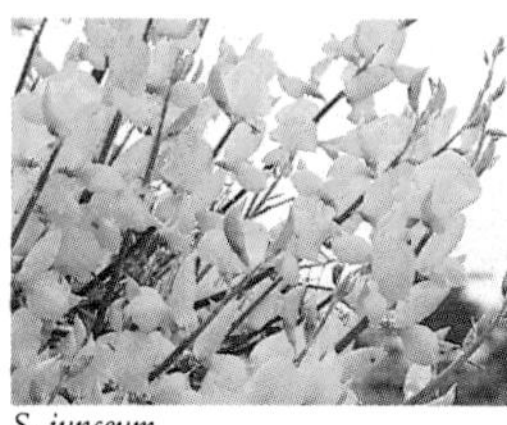

S. junceum

S. junceum: Med, Canary Is. Quick-growing, uprt. Stems rush-like, deep green with occasional tiny lvs. Fls pea-like, $\frac{3}{4}$ in wide, rich yellow, pleasantly frag. Seed pods black. Best if last year's wood pruned hard in March. Plant v small (before rts have coiled round inside fl pot). *Ht:* 10 ft; *Spd:* 5 ft; *Fl:* 7–9; *Z:* PF

Spiraea   

Spiraea

Twiggy relations of roses with myriads of very small flowers. Often gracefully arching but need intelligent pruning to look their best: cut away old wood on early-flowering sorts; shorten last year's growth in spring on later-flowering ones.

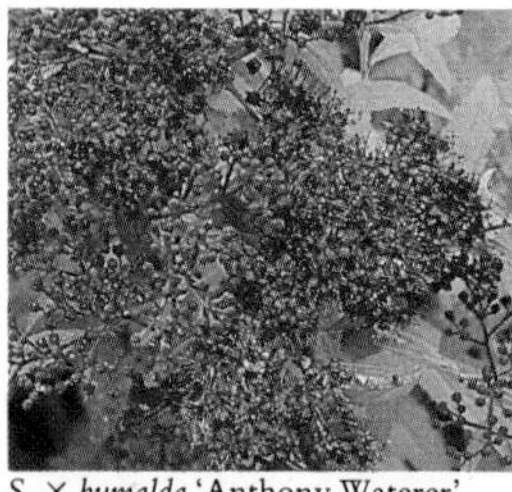

S. × *bumalda* 'Anthony Waterer'

S. × *vanhouttei*

S. × arguta Bridal wreath: gdn origin. Froth of tiny white fls on young brs. Lvs small, light green. Prop all spp by cuttings. *Ht, Spd:* 6 ft; *Fl:* 4–5; *Z:* Arct

S. × bumalda 'Anthony Waterer': gdn origin. Dense dwarf shrub. Lvs narrow, toothed, pointed, occasionally splashed cream with a little pink. Fls in flat round heads to 5 in wide, brilliant carmine fading to soft raspberry. *Ht, Spd:* 30 in; *Fl:* 6–9; *Z:* Arct

S. prunifolia: Japan. Arching bush; lvs often bright orange-yellow in aut. Fls individually displayed on last year's wood, neat, fully double white rosettes of ptls. *Ht:* 5 ft; *Spd:* 4 ft; *Fl:* 4–5; *Z:* Arct

S. thunbergii: China, Japan. Soft, twiggy. Lvs short, tapering. Fls white in clusters 1 in wide before lvs appear. V useful. *Ht, Spd:* to 5 ft; *Fl:* 3–4; *Z:* Arct

S. × vanhouttei: gdn origin. Tall uprt stems make thicket. Lvs glaucous beneath, toothed, spade or diamond-shaped. Fls white in clusters along stems. *Ht, Spd:* 6 ft; *Fl:* 6; *Z:* Arct

Stachyurus

 ***S. praecox**:** Japan. Wtr-flowering vase-shaped bush with stiff 4 in tassels of primrose-yellow fls. Buds formed in previous yr are catkin-like on lfless reddish branches. *Ht:* to 10 ft; *Spd:* 8 ft; *Fl:* 2–3; *Z:* PF, LF

Staphylea

Bladder-nut

S. colchica: Caucasus. Strong-growing, uprt. Lvs of 3–5 toothed lflts matt green above, shining beneath. White hyacinth-like fls have collar of greenish spls. V pretty but rare. *S. holocarpa* (AM) has trifoliate lvs and fls pink in bud opening white and inflated 2 in seed pods. Prop by cuttings. *Ht:* 10 ft; *Spd:* 6 ft; *Fl:* 5; *Z:* Arct

Stephanandra

Stephanandra

Quietly elegant shrubs not showy in flower but with pretty leaves, good autumn colour and unusual habit and stem colour.

S. incisa (=flexuosa): Japan, Korea. Twiggy shrub; lvs pale, triangular, rounded corners, deeply toothed. Fls tiny, whitish. 'Crispa' is also good ground cover. *Ht, Spd:* to 8 ft; *Fl:* 6; *Z:* Arct

S. tanakae: Japan. Graceful, uprt. Lvs 3× above. Fl sprays looser, more showy. Orange aut col; striking brown stems. *Ht, Spd:* 6 ft; *Fl:* 6–7; *Z:* Arct

S. tanakae

Stewartia (=Stuartia)

Stewartia

***S. malacodendron**:** SE USA. Distinguished shrub/small tree. Likes cool soil. Lvs softly downy on edges and undersides. Exquisite white fls, ptls just indented, 2 in wide; purple stamens, bluish anthers. Bark flakes in shades of blue and brown. *Ht:* 15 ft; *Spd:* 10 ft; *Fl:* 7–8; *Z:* PF

***S. pseudocamellia**:** Japan. Lvs not hry. Fls sim, white stamens, orange anthers. Good aut col. *Ht:* 18 ft; *Spd:* 10 ft; *Fl:* 7–8; *Z:* Arct

S. pseudocamellia

Stranvaesia

Stranvaesia

S. davidiana: China. Stems tall, uprt, rather sparsely lfy. Lvs long, narrow, rich shining green, pale when young and on underside, older lvs often redden in aut. Fls small, white, 5-petalled, in loose heads to 3 in wide followed by glistening crimson berries. Prop by cuttings. *Ht:* 16 ft; *Spd:* 6 ft; *Fl:* 6; *Z:* PF

S. davidiana

Styrax

Styrax

S. hemsleyana: China. Tall shrub/small tree. Lvs tapered at base. White fls like half-open stars on downy 6 in spikes, yellow anthers in prominent tuft. *S. obassia* taller, slower-growing, fl spikes terminal, drooping. Prop both by seed. *Ht:* 18 ft; *Spd:* 15 ft; *Fl:* 6; *Z:* PF

Sycopsis

Sycopsis

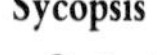

S. sinensis: China. Evergreen cousin of witch-hazel less fussy about soil. Fls have no ptls but tuft of yellow stamens and red-brown anthers cupped in dark brown bracts. *Ht:* 12 ft; *Spd:* 6 ft; *Fl:* 2–3; *Z:* Arct

Symphoricarpos

Snowberry

Obliging and original genus easy to grow and offering unique white (or pink) marble-like berries. Good ground cover.

S. albus 'Laevigatus'

S. albus: E N Amer. Invasive, suckering. Lvs oval; frs white. *Ht:* 4 ft; *Spd:* 16 ft; *Z:* Arct

S. × chenaultii: gdn origin. Cv 'Hancock' excellent ground cover; frs reddish, purple or pink. *Ht:* 18 in; *Spd:* 3 ft; *Fl:* 6–7; *Z:* Arct

S. × doorenbosii (=hybrida): gdn origin. Non-suckering, uprt. Try 'Magic Berry' frs rich pink; 'Mother of Pearl (AM) frs white; 'White Hedge' frs small. *Ht:* 5 ft; *Spd:* 4 ft; *Fl:* 6–7; *Z:* Arct

Syringa

Lilac

Fancy-flowered forms of lilac are splendid and richly scented in late May or early June but for the rest of the year there is scarcely a more tedious bush. Increase by cuttings.

S. microphylla

S. vulgaris 'Alba'

S. microphylla Small-leaved lilac: China. Dainty; buds deep rose-pink opening to lilac. With 'Superba'* fls over long period. *Ht:* 6 ft; *Spd:* 4 ft; *Fl:* 6, 9; *Z:* Arct

S. persica* Persian lilac: Iran–N China. More rounded, fls frag in plump bunches. 'Alba' white. *Ht, Spd:* 6 ft; *Fl:* 5; *Z:* Arct

S. × prestoniae: gdn origin. Vig; fls in drooping pointed 9 in plumes. Try 'Bellicent' (AGM) rose-pink; 'Fountain' soft pink; 'Isabella' purple. *Ht:* 13 ft; *Spd:* 10 ft; *Fl:* 5–6; *Z:* Arct

S. vulgaris Common lilac: Eur. Sp dull but gloriously frag; many good cvs inc: Singles: 'Maud Notcutt' (AM) white; 'Primrose'; 'Firmament' blue; 'Buffon' pink; 'Congo' deep red; 'Massena' purple. Doubles: 'Madame Lemoine' (AM) white; 'Michael Buchner' (AM) lilac-blue. *Ht, Spd:* 10 ft; *Fl:* 5–6; *Z:* Arct

Tamarix

Tamarisk

  ***T. pentandra (= hispida aestivalis):*** Eur. Feathery bush. Lvs tiny stem-hugging, young growth purple. Fls frag, tiny in 3 in plumes of pale pink. *Ht:* 12 ft; *Spd:* 8 ft; *Fl:* 8–9; *Z:* Arct

T. tetrandra: SE Eur, Asia. Sim but fls on previous yr's growth in spr when pale pink fls are uncommon, esp on alkaline soil. *Ht:* 12 ft; *Spd:* 8 ft; *Fl:* 5–6; *Z:* Arct

T. pentandra

Taxus

Yew

T. baccata* English yew: Eur, Asia. Dark green needle-lvs. Frs cup-shaped, fleshy, bright red, seeds v poisonous. Invaluable for hedges and topiary, excellent as a bush. 'Fastigiata' (Irish yew, AGM) columnar; 'Dovastoniana' (Westfelton yew, AGM) and its gold-lvd form have spreading brs. *Ht:* to 40 ft; *Spd:* 15 ft; *Z:* PF

T. baccata

Teucrium

Germander

T. fruticans: S Eur. Quick-growing, dense evergreen bush. Lvs white felted beneath, aromatic when bruised. Fls lobelia-like to ¾ in, pale blue with large lower lip. *Ht:* 5 ft; *Spd:* 4 ft+; *Fl:* 6–10; *Z:* SF

Tibouchina

Tibouchina

T. urvilliana (=semidecandra)*: Brazil. Frost tender but highly desirable conservatory plant. Fls single, saucer-shaped to 4 in wide with 5 overlapping glowing purple ptls with reddish tinge. Lvs oval, pointed, silky with 5 deep parallel veins. Prop by cuttings. *Ht:* 6 ft; *Spd:* 5 ft; *Fl:* 6–10; *Z:* NF

T. urvilliana

Ulex

Gorse

U. europaeus: Eur. This and *U. gallii* 2 most common spp, mainly fl in Mar–May and Aug–Sept resp but odd fls seen at any time. Spiny stems; yellow pea-like fls. 'Plenus' (AGM) double. *Ht, Spd:* 8 ft; *Z:* PF

Umbellularia

Californian bay or laurel

U. californica: Cal, Oregon. Large bush/small tree. Lvs tough, oval, tapering, giving off pungent "headachy" aroma when crushed. Fls greeny-yellow in clusters, ripe frs purple. *Ht, Spd:* 20 ft; *Fl:* 4; *Z:* PF

Vaccinium

The genus of blueberries, cranberries and whortleberries, sub-shrubs only at home in gardens of very acid nature.

V. vitis-idaea

V. arctostaphylos Caucasian whortleberry: Caucasus. Lvs red in aut. Fls closed bells in short sprays, white, purple tint. Frs edible. *Ht, Spd:* 6 ft; *Fl:* 6; *Z:* Arct

V. glauco-album*: Him. Evergreen lvs blue-white beneath. Fls pale pink bells; frs black, bluish bloom. *Ht, Spd:* 4 ft; *Fl:* 5–6; *Z:* Arct

V. vitis-idaea Cowberry, Mountain cranberry: N Temp mts. Creeping dwarf evergreen. Lvs tiny; fls pale pink or white, frs deep red. *Ht:* 6 in; *Spd:* 2 ft; *Fl:* 5–6; *Z:* Arct

Viburnum

Viburnum

One of the 3 or 4 most important genera of garden shrubs, offering white or pink flowers from mid-winter to summer, evergreens, striking shapes, sweet scent and rich autumn colours. Most are easy to grow and to propagate by cuttings.

V. carlesii

V. plicatum tomentosum

V. tinus

V. betulifolium*: China. Lvs diamond-shaped, fls small, white, 5 ptls in round flat heads 3 in wide; frs red, currant-like. *Ht:* 12 ft; *Spd:* 8 ft; *Fl:* 6; *Z:* Arct

V. × burkwoodii: gdn origin. Evergreen; buds pink, fls white, frag, in heads to 3½ in wide. *Ht:* 5 ft; *Spd:* 6 ft; *Fl:* 4–5; *Z:* Arct

V. carlesii: Korea. Rounded shrub. Fls heads dome-shaped, fls white, tubular, v frag. *V. × juddii* (AGM) v sim but taller, less hardy. *Ht, Spd:* 5 ft; *Fl:* 4–5; *Z:* Arct/PF

V. davidii: China. Lvs long, 3 parallel veins. Fls small, white in flat heads 3 in wide. Frs oval, turquoise if sev planted. *Ht:* 4 ft; *Spd:* 5 ft; *Fl:* 6; *Z:* PF

V. opulus Guelder rose: Eur. Decid, lvs maple-like. Fl heads hydrangea-like, frs red. *Ht:* 15 ft; *Spd:* 8 ft; *Fl:* 6–7; *Z:* Arct

V. plicatum Japanese snowball: Japan, China. Vig, uprt. Fl heads white balls to 3 in wide. *Ht:* 8 ft; *spd:* 10 ft; *Fl:* 5–6; *Z:* Arct

V. rhytidophyllum: China. Bold evergreen. Fls tiny, yellowish-white in heads 4 in wide. Frs red, profuse if sev planted. *Ht:* 8 ft; *Spd:* 12 ft; *Fl:* 5; *Z:* Arct

V. tinus Laurustinus: Eur. Bushy evergreen. Buds pink, fls tiny in flat heads to 4 in wide; frs dull blue ripening black. *Ht:* 15 ft; *Spd:* 10 ft; *Fl:* 12–4; *Z:* PF/F

Vinca

Periwinkle

V. major Greater periwinkle: Eur. Adventurous evergreen. Lvs heart-shaped; fls bright blue, 1 in diam. 'Variegata' white varieg; 'Maculata' gold varieg. *Ht:* 1 ft; *Spd:* 4 ft; *Fl:* 4–5(–9); *Z:* PF
V. minor Lesser periwinkle: Eur. Smaller, better ground cover. Cvs white, burgundy or pale blue fls, also varieg and double forms. *Ht:* 6 in; *Spd:* 3 ft; *Fl:* 4–5(–9); *Z:* Arct

V. major

Vitex

Vitex

V. agnus-castus Chaste tree: S Eur. Grey-green shrub; needs wall protection in cool zones. Lvs horsechestnut-like. Frag violet fls in slim branched spikes. 'Alba' white fld. *Ht, Spd:* 10 ft; *Fl:* 9–10; *Z:* PF

Weigela (=Diervilla)

Weigela

W. florida (=amabilis): China. Sp undistinguished with oblong soft green lvs, tubular pink or red fls, but try 'Foliis purpureis' smaller, purple lvs, pink fls; taller 'Variegata' (AM) fls pink, lvs edged creamy yellow; 'Abel Carrière' (AGM) fls rose-carmine, yellow throat; 'Bristol Ruby' deep pink. *Ht, Spd:* 6 ft; *Fl:* 5–6; *Z:* Arct

W. florida 'Bristol Ruby'

Yucca

Yucca

Spiky, attention-getting with a sub-tropical air. Rosettes of tapering leaves and spectacular spikes of flower.

Y. filamentosa*: SE USA. Suckering shrub. Thread-like filaments at lf edges. Plume of bell fls to 6 ft. 'Variegata' creamy-yellow varieg. *Y. flaccida* sim, taller, lvs wider; best cv 'Ivory'* (AM). *Ht, Spd:* 3 ft; *Fl:* 7–8; *Z:* Arct
Y. gloriosa* Adam's needle: SE USA. Woody palm-like trunks; lvs stiff sharp points; fls creamy-white. *Ht, Spd:* 4 ft; *Fl:* 7–9; *Z:* PF
Y. recurvifolia: SE USA. Lf ends curved back; fls as above. *Ht, Spd:* 4 ft; *Fl:* 7–9; *Z:* Arct

Y. filamentosa

Zenobia (=Andromeda)

Zenobia

Z. pulverulenta (=speciosa pulverulenta)*: SE USA. Enchantingly pretty; lvs oval, young fol glaucous, young stems whitish. Fls richly frag white bells. Frs like flattened balls. *Ht, Spd:* 6 ft; *Fl:* 6–7; *Z:* Arct

Index

For easy reference, where plants appear in more than one section of the book those sections are marked with a letter in brackets as follows: annuals (A); herbaceous perennials (P); alpines and rock garden plants (R); bog, waterside and pond plants (W); herbs (H); bulbs, corms and tubers (B); climbers (C); shrubs (S).